51.67:114

878

Cultural Relations Programs of the U.S. Department of State

Historical Studies: Number 3

Bureau of Educational and Cultural Affairs
U.S. Department of State
Washington, D.C.

German Political Subdivisions
Zones of Occupation and States
1951

SOURCE: "Report on Germany", Oct. 1 - Dec. 31, 1951, Office of the U.S. High Commissioner for Germany

Cultural Relations as an Instrument of U.S. Foreign Policy

The Educational Exchange Program
Between the United States and Germany
1945–1954

by
Henry J. Kellermann

LIBRARY OF CONGRESS CATALOG CARD NUMBER: 78-600002

DEPARTMENT OF STATE PUBLICATION 8931
International Information and Cultural Series 114
Released March 1978

For sale by the Superintendent of Documents, U.S. Government Printing Office
Washington, D.C. 20402
Stock Number 044-000-01688-5

Foreword

This volume is the third in the monograph series on specific aspects of the international educational and cultural exchange program of the U.S. Department of State as they have developed since the inception of the program in 1938. The series is published by the Bureau of Educational and Cultural Affairs (CU) for the purpose of providing a wider knowledge of the history of the Department-sponsored person-to-person program, designed to foster mutual understanding between the people of the United States and other peoples of the world. At the same time, as this volume shows, the Department-sponsored program has been dependent from the outset on a solid and enthusiastic partnership with a large body of private organizations, and citizens too numerous to count, here and abroad.

In planning this series, three scholars and educators long associated with the program have provided advice and guidance: Ben M. Cherrington, first chief of the Department's cultural relations program, and for many years a recognized leader in the field of international educational and cultural relations; John Hope Franklin, Professor of American History at the University of Chicago; and Frank Freidel, Professor of American History at Harvard University.

The first volume in the series, *America's Cultural Experiment in China, 1942–1949* by Wilma Fairbank, was published in June 1976. The second, written by the director of the CU History Office, J. Manuel Espinosa, entitled *Inter-American Beginnings of U.S. Cultural Diplomacy, 1936–1948*, appeared in February of 1977.

This monograph reviews the history of the reestablishment of educational and cultural relations between the United States and Germany after World War II. At its peak period it was the largest single U.S. Government-sponsored program with another country either before or since that time. Initiated, as it was, in the wake of the bloodiest conflict in history, moreover, the program was a gesture seldom equaled in international cultural rapprochement and diplomacy. The record of this part of U.S. relations with postwar Germany, as here written, places in perspective a neglected aspect of the basis of our present close friendly relations with the Federal Republic of Germany.

Though these studies are being published under the sponsorship of the Department of State, they do not in any sense embody official U.S. Government views or policy. The author of each monograph is responsible for the facts and their interpretation as well as for the opinions expressed.

WILLIAM K. HITCHCOCK
*Acting Assistant Secretary for
Educational and Cultural Affairs*
U.S. Department of State

Preface

This is not the first account of cultural and educational exchanges between the United States and Germany in the decade following World War II and it is unlikely that it will be the last. Previous writings have dealt in whole or in part with the background, organization, content, and some of the results of the program. (See Henry P. Pilgert, *The Exchange of Persons Program in Western Germany* (Historical Division, Office of the U.S. High Commissioner for Germany, 1951); Howard Wright Johnston, *United States Public Affairs Activities in Germany, 1945–1955*, doctoral dissertation, Columbia University, 1956 (Ann Arbor, Michigan: University Microfilms, 1974); Harold Zink, *The United States in Germany, 1944–1955* (Princeton, New Jersey: D. Van Nostrand Company, Inc., 1957); Lucius D. Clay, *Decision in Germany* (Garden City, New York, 1950).)

The approach chosen in this study differs from previous ones in that, having been intimately involved in developing the policies which shaped the character and growth of the program, the author has presented the story from the point of view of the policy maker. From its uncertain beginnings under the Office of Military Government U.S. (OMGUS) to its climax under the Office of the U.S. High Commissioner for Germany (HICOG), this exchange of persons program, as will be shown, was an instrument of U.S. policy, deriving its impetus and content from the objectives which U.S. policy pursued in Germany. After completion of the punitive period, these objectives were physical and political reconstruction and reeducation; and, with changing conditions, reorientation; and, finally, binational cooperation and partnership.

I have tried, therefore, to highlight those features which distinguished the U.S.-German exchange program of this period from others operated by the U.S. Government then and later, and which, in effect, made it a venture *sui generis*. Its uniqueness must be understood as the result of circumstances unprecedented in human history. Policy makers and administrators of cultural exchanges may therefore find it difficult to use the German experience as a model for other programs. Yet, while history may not repeat itself, there are certain lessons, both positive and negative, to be learned from the German example. The innovations it introduced, its very size, and last but not least, its impact over the years have had an effect beyond its immediate historical and geographical scope. In fact, as will be shown, many of its features, including the wide and generous participation of the American people, have proved their continued relevance and validity. There is, then, some ground for hope that a more extensive reconstruction of the genesis and development of the program will not only be of interest to students of the history of the period, but may also stimulate future policy makers and program planners and operators in the field of educational and cultural relations.

A word about the sources used: To a large extent they consisted of official documents of the Office of Military Government U.S. (OMGUS), the Office of the U.S. High Commissioner for Germany (HICOG), the Department of State, and the War Department (later the Department of the Army). Most of them were found in the files of the Foreign Affairs Document and Reference Center of the Department of State; at the Washington National Records Center, Suitland, Maryland; in the files of the Bureau of Educational and Cultural Affairs; in the National Archives; and in published reports, collections, studies, and biographies. Regrettably, the governmental files proved to be incomplete as a number of critical documents have been destroyed. The documents that could be located contained essentially records of policy and procedures, tables of organization, budgets, opinion surveys, and official reports. They included only to a limited extent samples of personal accounts submitted by German and American participants in the program reflecting on their experience and on the results of their efforts.

I had, therefore, to rely to a degree on personal recollections. Due to my association from 1945 to 1949 with the division in the Department of State responsible for the formulation of policy and plans for cultural affairs with Germany, and later, during the first years of HICOG, as Director of the Office of German Public Affairs in the Department, I was able to restore parts of the missing record from memory. I offer my apologies for the gaps which I could not fill. In particular, there is a scarcity of data documenting the long-range effect of the exchange program in terms of basic institutional changes. This kind of evidence has never been traced and assembled in a systematic fashion. Early studies of attitudinal changes were made in abundance and are cited in the last chapter to verify partial and often highly personal accounts of program effectiveness, but they do not necessarily permit firm or final conclusions with regard to the permanence of these changes and their impact upon contemporary German society. Whether such effects can be established beyond reasonable doubt 25 years after the event may be questionable. They could and perhaps should be the subject of a special study.

I am therefore grateful to the many persons, both in the United States and in Germany, who at one time or another were associated with OMGUS, HICOG, the Department of State, and private organizations affiliated with the exchange program, whom I consulted in the course of the study and who helped me fill the gaps in my memory and in the official files (see Acknowledgments).

HENRY J. KELLERMANN

Washington, D.C.,
December, 1977.

Contents

	Page
Map of Germany	ii
Foreword	v
Preface	vii
Acknowledgments	xiii
Terms and Abbreviations	xv
INTRODUCTION	3

THE BEGINNING

Chapter I.	The OMGUS Exchange Program: 1945–1949	17
Chapter II.	Administration of the OMGUS Program	55

THE CLIMAX

Chapter III.	Transition from OMGUS to HICOG: Reeducation to Reorientation	75
Chapter IV.	The HICOG Exchange Program: 1949–1953	95
Chapter V.	Administration of the HICOG Program	133

RETURN TO NORMALCY

Chapter VI.	Revision of Policy—From Unilateralism to Bilateralism	153
Chapter VII.	The Fulbright Program	173

THE IMPACT

Chapter VIII.	Measuring the Results of the Program	209
EPILOGUE		253
Appendixes		261
Index		277

Acknowledgments

I am particularly indebted for advice and assistance to Dr. Herman B Wells, President Emeritus of Indiana University and former Educational and Cultural Adviser to General Lucius D. Clay; Shepard Stone, former Director of the Office of Public Affairs (HICOG); Dr. James Morgan Read, former Chief of the Division of Education and Cultural Relations (HICOG); Mrs. Mildred ("Pat") Allen, a former officer of the Department of State and HICOG; Peter Frankel, Indiana University; Dr. Ulrich Littman, Executive Director of the United States Educational Commission in Germany, more popularly known as the Fulbright Commission; Dr. Heinz L. Krekeler, first postwar Ambassador of the Federal Republic of Germany; Dr. Niels Hansen, Minister (a former participant in the exchange program), and Dr. Jurgen Kalkbrenner, former Cultural Counselor of the Embassy of the Federal Republic of Germany; Professor Dr. Hellmut Becker, Director of the Max Planck Institute for Educational Research, Wilhelmshaven; Richard Straus, former associate and Director, Office of Western European and Canadian Programs (CU); Dr. Henry B. Ollendorff, Secretary General, Council of International Programs for Youth Leaders and Social Workers, Cleveland; Dr. Harold E. Snyder, former Director, Commission on the Occupied Areas, American Council on Education; Ralph H. Vogel, Director, Operations Staff, Board of Foreign Scholarships, which administers academic exchanges under the Fulbright-Hays Act; Dean B. Mahin, formerly with the Governmental Affairs Institute and now with the Institute of International Education, Washington, D.C.; Vaughn DeLong, former Officer-in-Charge of Cultural Affairs, Office of German Public Affairs, Department of State; Dr. Thomas P. Holland, Case-Western Reserve University, Cleveland; and Frau Eva Ackermann-Stroetzel, American Embassy, Bonn.

For reviewing and editing the manuscript for publication, I wish to thank Vaughn DeLong, Richard Straus, Ralph Vogel, and Elwood Williams, formerly of the Office of Central European Affairs, Department of State, who read sections of the manuscript and offered helpful suggestions.

Special tribute is due to J. Manuel Espinosa and James A. Donovan, jr. of the CU History Office who guided the author through the intricacies of the research and gave valuable technical suggestions for the preparation of the manuscript, and to Helen Shaffer who furnished expert typing skills.

I also wish to acknowledge the help I received from Anne Katherine Pond of the Publishing and Reproduction Division for technical editing; and from Wilmer P. Sparrow and Jessie M. Williams at the Foreign Affairs Document and Reference Center of the Department of State, and officers of the National Archives and of the Washington National Records Center, Suitland, Maryland, for their assistance in locating documents.

Terms and Abbreviations

The superior figures in the text refer to Notes at the end of each chapter or section. The following is a guide to abbreviations and documentary sources used in the Notes and Appendixes.

ACE.................. American Council on Education, Washington, D.C.

CAD.................. Civil Affairs Division, U.S. War Department.

CIER................. Commission on International Educational Reconstruction. Organized in June 1946 with funds from the Carnegie Corporation in response to a recommendation from UNRRA, q.v., the Preparatory Commission for UNESCO, and the Department of State. Designated by the U.S. National Commission for UNESCO as the official agency to conduct its post-World War II reconstruction appeal.

COA.................. Commission on the Occupied Areas, American Council on Education. Established in 1948 to promote cultural and educational affairs in the occupied countries. Terminated in 1951.

CU/BFS............... Files of the Secretariat of the Board of Foreign Scholarships, U.S. Department of State, Washington, D.C.

CU/H................. History Files, Bureau of Educational and Cultural Affairs, U.S. Department of State.

DIVO–INSTITUT....... Deutsche Institut fuer Volksumfragen; Marktforschung, Meinungsforschung, Sozialforschung. Research Institute, Frankfurt am Main, Germany.

GARIOA	Government and Relief in Occupied Areas, Department of the Army.
GOAG	Government in Occupied Area of Germany, Department of State. The funds annually appropriated by the U.S. Congress to meet the obligations of the U.S. Government in connection with the government, occupation, and control of occupied areas of Germany, were referred to as the GOAG budget.
HICOG	Office of the High Commissioner (U.S.), Germany.
JCS	Joint Chiefs of Staff, U.S.
NA	National Archives, National Archives Building, Washington, D.C.
O/FADRC	Foreign Affairs Document and Reference Center, U.S. Department of State, Washington, D.C.
OMGUS	Office of Military Government (U.S.), Germany.
OPA	Office of Public Affairs, HICOG.
RG 59	Record Group 59, General Records of the U.S. Department of State, NA and WNRC.
RG 107	Record Group 107, Records of the Office of the Secretary of War, WNRC.
RG 165	Record Group 165, Records of the War Department, General and Special Staff, WNRC.
RG 260	Record Group 260, Records of United States Occupation Headquarters, WNRC.
RG 306	Records of the U.S. Information Agency, WNRC.
RG 319	Records of the Army Staff, WNRC.
RG 331	Records of Allied Operational and Occupation Headquarters, WNRC.
RG 353	Record Group 353, Interdepartmental Committee on Scientific and Cultural Cooperation, NA.
SWNCC	State-War-Navy Coordinating Committee, 1944–1947.

TERMS AND ABBREVIATIONS   xvii

UNRRA............... United Nations Relief and Rehabilitation Administration.
USEC/G............... United States Educational Commission in the Federal Republic of Germany, the binational body in Germany responsible for the overseas administration of academic exchanges with the United States under the Fulbright Act (now Fulbright-Hays Act).
WNRC................ General Archives Division, Washington National Records Center, Suitland, Maryland.

Introduction

Introduction

German-American cultural relations began much earlier than the start of the first official educational and cultural exchange activities between the United States and Germany under governmental auspices. Educational interchange had its real beginnings, under private auspices, in the early part of the 19th century, when American scholars visited Germany and other countries of western Europe to meet with their European colleagues in fields of common interest and to pursue research in local libraries and archives. German scholars were invited to visit American universities for a variety of purposes. Yet to attribute these early initiatives to the presence of millions of Germans who had come to the United States over the years and to the sentimental attachment of a German-American minority to their former homeland would be a mistake. It was, rather, growing respect on the part of American intellectuals for German science and scholarship that stimulated these first contacts and that also prompted American universities to emulate German standards in the buildup of their graduate schools.

It would be an even greater mistake, however, to assume that the exchange program which began after the conclusion of World War II merely continued where relationships established during the 19th and the first part of the 20th century had left off. The break between the United States intellectual community and Germany in the thirties was radical and complete. With few exceptions the postwar effort to restore the broken ties started from point zero.

Nor would it be correct to regard the post-World War II exchange program with Germany, at least in its initial stage, as a chapter of the worldwide effort carried on under governmental auspices. Its purpose, scope, and structure in the late forties and early fifties defied any simple comparison. In the case of the policy pursued by the United States in occupied Germany, it was conceived and designed more sharply than any other program as an instrument of foreign policy. Moreover, with the United States exercising, jointly with the other three occupying powers, supreme governmental authority, the program itself was intended as, and indeed was used as, a branch of the executive arm with appropriate force and reach to assure compliance with official U.S. policy on all levels. It was an integral part of the total military, political, and economic operation. It is worth remembering, then, that although the exchange program with Germany was eventually absorbed by the worldwide cultural exchange program of the Department of State, based on the principle of reciprocity, the German program started out as a unilateral American-initiated, American-funded, and American-directed implement of United States policy serving primarily United States interests, first under the aegis of the Office of U.S. Military Government (OMGUS) and subsequently of the Office of the U.S. High Commissioner (HICOG).

Because it was a program without precedent and presumably without expectation of recurrence, other standards normally used to evaluate exchange programs are not applicable. The immediate benefits all appear to have accrued to the Germans who in the late forties and early fifties were brought from conditions of extreme austerity and political confinement into an environment of economic and social abundance, and who were permitted to reap the benefits of full and unhindered exposure to conditions of freedom and to contacts denied them during the period of Nazi repression, terror, and war. Americans, on the other hand, who were sent to Germany by their government during the occupation period were less likely to profit in similar fashion or degree. Their reward was mainly the kind of intellectual or personal satisfaction that comes from participation in a highly challenging and, historically speaking, truly unique mission.

Yet to view the OMGUS and HICOG exchange programs strictly in terms of immediate, short-term advantages, means to overlook the ultimate benefits of a program with long-term objectives. The exchange experience, after all, was no more than a means to an end; its purpose was to help assist Germans in creating a new society modeled on western democratic concepts. At the same time, both German and American participants contributed to the success of a venture that in the last analysis was expected to be of far-reaching benefit to their countries. It is, then, the political and social benefits rather than the personal gains that will have to serve as the principal yardsticks in measuring the accomplishments of the program.

The Worldwide Program

The importance of official exchanges has never been defined solely in terms of personal benefits. Policy makers have preferred, as a rule, to use national interest as the basic rationale and only more recently, notably after World War II, have come to justify cultural exchange in terms which transcend the frame of national

INTRODUCTION

interest by adding broader considerations, such as international cooperation and peace.

The first government-sponsored exchange program was probably instituted by the French in the latter part of the past century. Its announced objective was "to spread the French language and to increase French commercial influence." Prior to and during World War II, Nazi Germany turned cultural exchanges into a propaganda device and a stratagem to prepare, support, and exploit military aggression. The U.S. Government responded to the challenge at the Pan American Conference for the Maintenance of Peace held in Buenos Aires in 1936. It proposed to the other American Republics a Convention for the Promotion of Inter-American Cultural Relations which provided for the exchange of university professors and students under joint governmental sponsorship. This was the first official U.S. initiative in the field of cultural exchange. The Convention was eventually ratified by 17 Latin American countries.

Triggered by extraneous political developments, the character of U.S.-sponsored exchange programs, though basically and avowedly a cooperative educational and cultural enterprise, thus assumed certain political overtones. It was to accomplish "the purpose of encouraging and strengthening cultural relations and intellectual cooperation between the United States and other countries." Also, the exchange of cultural assets was to serve the purpose of promoting the growth, intensification and consolidation of inter-American relations, and the projection and improvement of the American image abroad. This U.S. initiative, which began on a very modest scale, set the stage for the larger government-wide programs that followed.[1]

A Division of Cultural Relations was established in the Department of State in 1938 to initiate the U.S. Government's new venture in cultural relations. The first director of the Division, Ben M. Cherrington, summarized the principles governing the Department's international educational and cultural exchange program when he wrote:

> "Two fundamental principles were established at the outset to guide the developing program: first, cultural relations activities of our country would be reciprocal, there must be no imposition of one people's culture upon another; second, the exchange of cultural interests should involve the participation of people and institutions concerned with those interests in the respective countries, that is, the program should stem from the established centers of culture." [2]

It was also emphasized from the beginning that the program was essentially long-range, and nonpolitical in purpose. Its basic goal was to promote mutual understanding. This was the philosophy and purpose of the program as established and pronounced by the Department of State in the thirties, and even during the war years, by President Franklin D. Roosevelt, Secretary of State Cordell Hull, and other high government officials.

Meanwhile, in the early forties, as the United States girded for war against Axis aggression, the U.S. Government mounted an extensive propaganda program in support of Allied aims, principally through two generously funded wartime agencies, the Office of War Information and the Office of the Coordinator of Inter-American Affairs. The single goal of these agencies was to help win the war, and the modest efforts of the Department's Division of Cultural Relations were enlisted to contribute to that goal.

In the postwar years, from 1945–1949, the OMGUS period in Germany, the role of cultural and educational programs in international relations, along with information programs, including an overseas broadcasting service, was gaining in favor, stature, and support from the Congress and the American people. With the dismantling of the Office of War Information and the information program of the Coordinator's Office, their activities were reconstituted as an information program in the Department of State in 1945, under the direction of the Assistant Secretary for Public Affairs who also had under his direction the Department's educational and cultural exchange program. With the cold war warming up in the late forties, the educational and cultural exchange program was overshadowed by the much larger information program.

The passage, after much Congressional debate, of the Smith-Mundt Act in January 1948 (Public Law 402, 80th Congress, the Information and Educational Exchange Act of 1948) provided authorization for the first time for a worldwide peacetime program of informational and educational exchange. It established two offices under the Assistant Secretary for Public Affairs, an Office of International Information and an Office of Educational Exchange. The Act defined the purpose of the Office of Information as "to disseminate abroad information about the United States, its people, and the policies promulgated by the Congress, the President, the Secretary of State and other responsible officials of Government having to do with matters affecting foreign affairs." It defined the purpose of the Office of Educational Exchange "to cooperate with other nations in the interchange of persons, knowledge, and skills; the rendering of technical and other services; the interchange of developments in the field of education, the arts and sciences." It included authorization for the expenditure of hard American currencies for these purposes, thus contrasting with the earlier Fulbright Act of 1946 (Public Law

584, 79th Congress). PL 584 authorized academic exchanges under binational agreements which in the beginning were financed only by foreign currencies paid to the U.S. Government for the purchase of war surplus materials that remained in the various signatory countries after the war.

One of the provisions of the Smith-Mundt Act created two advisory commissions, the Advisory Commission on Information and the Advisory Commission on Educational Exchange. The latter was created to advise the Department of State on all aspects of the conduct of its worldwide educational and cultural exchange program. The Advisory Commission on Educational Exchange met for the first time on September 10–12, 1948. One report of this first meeting noted that among its deliberations the Commission reviewed "policies to be recommended for handling . . . this country's responsibility for orientation through reeducation in Germany."[3] Another mentioned briefly that the Commission "reviewed certain key problems which will be subjects for more intensive study at subsequent sessions. Typical of these are such questions as this country's responsibility for reeducation in Germany . . ."[4]

The Chairman of the Advisory Commission on Educational Exchange, B. Harvie Branscomb, Chancellor of Vanderbilt University, proposed to free the rationale for educational exchange as defined in the Act from consideration of narrow political or national interest when he stressed, in a statement to the Commission, the need for the broadest possible role for educational and cultural relations among nations in the pursuit of a world of neighbors living in peace. Chairman Branscomb said:

"We do have a stake in the preservation of a world order in which countries can live at peace . . . But so do the other democratically minded people . . . It will be by cooperation among those nations and peoples who believe that the spiritual heritages of the race are worth preserving, that the present difficulties will be overcome and the problems of our times resolved . . . The program of educational and cultural exchange—not cultural penetration rests then on a simple and familiar principle. Neighbors who are to cooperate need to become acquainted. In the modern world all nations are neighbors, and all need to cooperate . . ."

Chairman Branscomb continued:

"There is . . . a second reason for the program of educational and cultural exchange. It is the basic fact that such a program of exchange is the natural expression of the democratic principles on which and for which we stand. The cultural achievements of the civilized world have been brought about by such cooperation . . . We shall continue, in cooperation with other peoples, to build the good life which flows across national boundary lines . . ."[5]

The pursuit of international understanding and cooperation no doubt was meant to, and indeed did, reflect the prevailing mood in the postwar period. It was a highly idealistic premise, but the Smith-Mundt Act and the guidance of the Advisory Commission turned theory into practice. The Act assigned to cultural exchanges the role of helping to build the foundation of an enduring peace and a more stable world order. Furthermore, by casting the government itself in the role of sponsor, it was clearly suggested that greater encouragement of private initiative as the major government task was required, and this called for strong government leadership. Cultural relations had to become a permanent, securely funded function of the government.

As our national experience with exchanges matured and as more sophisticated programs evolved with increasing numbers of individual countries in all parts of the world, greater allowance was made for political, social, and cultural differences in fashioning individual exchange programs with them. Beyond this, World War II and postwar reconstruction proved to be major catalysts in clarifying the direction, scope, and variety of exchange programs. Some programs, notably in the occupied countries (Germany, Austria, and Japan), acquired a political and pragmatic quality never before attained in cultural exchanges. To engage in such programs became in fact a recognized policy of the U.S. Government in foreign affairs. Such was the case in Germany. But it must be added that the Advisory Commission fully recognized that relations with Germany and the other occupied countries were *sui generis*, requiring a temporary special relationship. Moreover, while educational and cultural activities and, with them, exchange programs were acknowledged to constitute "an essential part of America's total international effort" and "an aspect of American foreign policy," administrators of the program remained wary of attempts to become too closely allied with specific political objectives.[6] "If we were to make the mistake," a later U.S. Advisory Commission said, "of supposing that the primary purpose of the exchange program is to serve narrowly political ends, the effectiveness of the whole program would be seriously undermined. It is not that kind of program, and in imagining it to be so we would defeat our own ends . . ."[7]

Actually the conflict between purists and pragmatists was never fully resolved. Political considerations continued to motivate and often to shape policies governing the U.S. exchange program. Fundamentally humanitarian and avowedly "nonpolitical," the educational and cultural relations program sponsored by the Department of State was established because international communication and understanding through cooperative person-to-person relations were considered to be a necessary aspect of foreign relations. Mutual understanding through this means was considered to be an important part of the larger foreign policy goal of international peace. Thus the exchange program was from the beginning a part of the international political scene. As we have seen, it was an international political crisis that awakened the U.S. Government to give active attention to the cultivation of a better understanding and appreciation of the cultural and intellectual contributions of our neighbors to the south, and vice versa. The cold war was to introduce another political element by drawing the exchange program into the orbit of the "Campaign of Truth" mounted against the violent anti-U.S. propaganda campaign of the Soviet Union in the late forties and the fifties. In many ways these shifting currents reflected domestic political and hence Congressional interest in enlisting educational and cultural programs in the service of political goals as the world power structure turned sharply to a balance of goals and interests between the two great powers, the United States and the Soviet Union.

It should also be noted that during the years under review both the volume and quality of the programs improved with the growing awareness of the Congress of the political potential of exchanges on the international scene. The recognition of such programs as a part of foreign policy and thus deserving of official support had occurred earlier in other countries than in the United States, each for its own reasons. For the United States, this recognition came about only gradually. The Buenos Aires Convention of 1936, which sparked the initiation of the Latin American program, noted above, waited several years for meager funding. Supplementary legislation on behalf of educational and cultural exchanges, passed in 1939,[8] eventually produced the modest Congressional appropriations of $29,240 in 1939 and $75,000 in 1940. With the threat of and finally the outbreak of World War II the amount was boosted to $508,620 in 1941, jumped to $844,390 in 1942, and passed the million-dollar mark in 1943 ($1,685,000). After that, the total amount quadrupled reaching a temporary peak in 1947 of $6,040,064.[9] These figures included money from the President's emergency fund for China, the Near East, and Africa. Furthermore, the exchanges thus financed by the Congress and the President included substantial cultural activities that were not only person-to-person exchanges but which also included libraries, books, films, and other types of educational cooperation.

Thereafter, the Fulbright Act and the Smith-Mundt Act made possible the extension of the exchange program to a significant supportive factor of U.S. foreign relations around the globe. Yet it was the post-World War II German exchange program that boosted the total program to unprecedented levels and established an alltime maximum for a single country, with creative ideas for all American government-sponsored educational and cultural relation programs here and abroad, as will be indicated later in this study. Indeed, the U.S.-German exchange program experience, in its essence and quality, spurred at least two other governments to emulate it (Austria and Japan), though on a somewhat lesser scale.

The German Program

The German exchange program, especially under Military Government (OMGUS) and even more pronouncedly under the U.S. High Commissioner (HICOG), had a series of features which made it exceptional and indeed unprecedented in its rationale, the variety of its innovative features, the sophistication of its targets and project-oriented approach, the extent of public and private support, and above all, its sheer size. In each of its peak years of 1951 and 1952, under HICOG, it provided for more than 3,000 participants—Germans, other Europeans, and Americans. All told, under OMGUS and HICOG, a total of 14,000 persons moved between the United States and Germany and an additional 2,228 persons moved between Germany and other European countries under the program from 1948 to 1956.[10]

A program of this nature could be neither explained nor justified under the terms of then existing worldwide policies and legislation. Additional authorization was needed. It had to be found in the mandate of the Military Government and the High Commissioner to help reconstruct Germany on a democratic basis and thus to achieve a reorientation of the German people toward a stable peace and a democratic system supported by the consensus of the governed. The whole apparatus of military and civilian control was placed at the service of these objectives. All elements of OMGUS and later of HICOG attuned their operation to the specific requirements of U.S. policy for Germany, but key responsibility for directing and supervising the reorientation effort was delegated to the Public Affairs Office of HICOG which thus became in effect the focal point of U.S. reorientation policy. Within the public affairs program itself it was the exchange of persons which provided the long arm for implementation of the reorientation policy. Initiated and operated by what was then the highest authority in Germany, acceptance was assured.

Here was a case without precedent. For the first time in modern history a victor used the vast range of his cultural resources and the potential of his citizens in a common and contributing effort to assist the vanquished in rebuilding his national institutions and his relations with the entire world. Indeed, the reeducation or reorientation program must have appeared as a wholly inconsistent and unorthodox undertaking to a people who remembered the reparations of the "dictate of Versailles" and could therefore rightfully expect far more severe retribution. To many Americans, even when allowing for the accommodation of certain political objectives in U.S. exchange policy, the use of educational and cultural exchanges as an instrument of occupation policy serving the political, economic, social, cultural, and even military aspects of U.S. policy, and performing a highly interventionist function in the internal affairs of another country, may have meant to flout the established and pronounced principles of U.S. cultural exchanges.

In fact, the seeming contradiction between the worldwide purpose of U.S. exchanges and the German exchange program can only be fully understood if it is recognized that OMGUS, and to a lesser degree HICOG, acted as quasi-governments in Germany with all the trappings of national authority—a situation that was extraordinary and not likely to recur.

Nearly from the very beginning, American public opinion was divided on the question of treatment of Germany, with some arguing for harsh and long punishment and others for early rehabilitation. Reorientation was by and large accepted as the correct policy to achieve democratic reforms, but even here critics deplored the "undemocratic" nature implicit in any kind of "occupation policy." At the bottom of such criticisms was the discomfort, even impatience, of the American people with finding themselves in a position of quasi-authoritarian power, and their propensity for rapid change and effective short cuts. With a cooperative and friendly German population evidently eager for change, a policy of protracted regimentation seemed uncalled for and counterproductive. Another factor that was ever-present in those years was the skepticism of the American people toward the corrigibility of a people whose government had twice caused a world war and the second time around adopted and mercilessly carried out the unparalleled atrocities of the Nazi regime. Finally, the program came under fire from those who insisted that it demonstrated an American posture of paternalism toward the vanquished.

As the record will show, the exchange program underwent almost constant adjustments. The latter were necessary, because policies kept changing. Policies, in turn, had to be readjusted to developments, inside and outside of Germany, which forced the course and the pace of Allied decisions within ten years from total control and tutelage to nearly complete restoration of sovereignty. In corresponding stages the exchange program grew from a modest unilateral venture, wholly controlled by the U.S. Government or that of other

Allies, to a full-fledged binational effort based on equality and reciprocity.

A number of factors contributed to these radical and rapid changes. The "miracle" of German recovery, no doubt, demanded recognition and reward. Acquiescence had turned into cooperation which permitted substitution of voluntary contribution in place of mandatory controls. Political, social, and educational reforms were producing viable institutions which deserved encouragement and support (through cultural exchanges along with similar technical exchanges under the Marshall Plan). Extraneous developments accelerated the process. The breakdown of the quadripartite alliance and of its control apparatus, the blockade of Berlin, and the cold war opened the door for West German alliance with the West far ahead of any timetable envisaged in 1945. There was a growing recognition that among the many measures adopted by the United States and the other Allied authorities in Germany, from punitive to reconstructive, the exchange program ranked among the most positive and least controversial of all public affairs programs. Moreover, being, by definition, a bilateral rather than a multilateral effort the program was intended to and eventually so organized as to involve German nationals progressively in the implementation of U.S. policy aiming toward democratic reform. A major turning point in this direction was the transfer of the administration of the exchange program activities from the Department of the Army to the Department of State in 1949, and of its operation from OMGUS to HICOG.

As participation of German authorities and citizens was gradually increased in the control and conduct of the program, and as their role of mere beneficiaries gradually changed to that of participants, the exchange program helped turn the reorientation program itself into a binational undertaking. This fact as much as any other must be credited for the success of the program, especially as reinforced by the introduction of the binationally administered Fulbright program in Germany in 1952. It also explains why the exchange program outlived most other features of the reorientation effort, and makes understandable the great popularity which the program enjoyed from its inception to the present, why it gained continuously in prestige, and why it attracted an ever-increasing German financial contribution.

The rationale of the program as part of the postwar reconstruction effort also explains its vast size. Looking back, perhaps nothing but a massive effort engaging nearly all strata of German society could have achieved the political and social changes needed for democratic reform.

INTRODUCTION

The momentum generated by the Allied or more specifically the U.S. program of democratic reconstruction assured the success of this effort and permitted the step-by-step elimination of controls and steady progression toward partnership on equal terms. As the reorientation program changed its character and methods over the years, gradually losing its earlier didactic approach, so, as one of its principal features, did the program for educational and cultural exchange. Toward the end of the period under discussion the exchange program between the United States and Germany had become fully assimilated into the worldwide educational and cultural program of the U.S. Government.

Notes

INTRODUCTION

1. See J. Manuel Espinosa, *Inter-American Beginnings of U.S. Cultural Diplomacy, 1936–1948*, Dept. of State, publ. 8854 (Washington, D.C.: U.S. Government Printing Office, 1976). The United States was a latecomer in establishing an official program in international cultural relations. For a comparative study of the beginnings of such programs, see Ruth E. McMurry and Muna Lee, *The Cultural Approach* (Chapel Hill: The Univ. of North Carolina Press, 1947).
2. Ben M. Cherrington, "Ten Years After," *Association of American Colleges Bulletin*, XXIV (Dec. 1948), p. 2.
3. "International Educational Exchange. United States Advisory Commission and the Program of the Department of State." First meeting of the U.S. Advisory Commission on Educational Exchange, Sept. 10–12, 1948, Dept. of State (Washington, D.C.: U.S. Government Printing Office, 1948), p. 2.
4. *The Record*, Dept. of State, IV (Nov.–Dec. 1948), p. 9.
5. "International Educational Exchange . . .," *op. cit.*, pp. 3–4.
6. See *A Beacon of Hope*, Report of the U.S. Advisory Commission on International Educational and Cultural Affairs (Washington, D.C.: U.S. Government Printing Office, 1963), pp. 13–14.
7. *Ibid.*, p. 28.
8. Public Law 63, 76th Cong., May 3, 1939; Public Law 355, 76th Cong., Aug 9, 1939.
9. In the aggregate the U.S. Government expended an estimated $22,918,314 between 1940 and 1947 for exchanges with all countries. Fourteenth Semi-annual Report on Educational Exchange Activities, U.S. Advisory Commission on Educational Exchange, 84th Cong., 1st sess., House Doc. no. 219, (Washington, D.C.: U.S. Government Printing Office, 1955), p. 12.
10. The total estimated number of exchanges with Germany from 1949–1970 is 18,558, nearly one-fourth the size of the program for Western Europe (69,786) and nearly one-eighth of the worldwide program (137,018),

exceeding by one-third those with France and the United Kingdom and by two-thirds those with Japan—the three countries which led all the others in size. (Statistics from the annual Congressional budget hearings of the Department of State for the years indicated, published by the U.S. Government Printing Office.)

The Beginning

CHAPTER I

The OMGUS Exchange Program: 1945-1949

Policy in Transition

Following the defeat of the German armed forces in 1945 and the end of National Socialism, Germany became an occupied country, consisting of four zones, each controlled by one of the four victorious powers—France, the Soviet Union, the United Kingdom, and the United States. Each zone was headed by a Supreme Commander subject to the instructions of his government, all four cooperating through the Allied Control Council, and issuing joint and separate (for each zone) directives.

The years 1945 and 1946 were the punitive period. The principal Nazi leaders were brought to trial. Nazi activists and militarists were rooted from public life. Fraternization between occupiers and occupied was forbidden. Military Government was installed to exercise supreme legislative, executive, and judicial authority. The Potsdam Conference of July 17 to August 2, 1945 [1] defined the purposes of the occupation as "disarmament, demilitarization" and the destruction of all remnants of Nazism.[2] But it left the door open to "the eventual peaceful cooperation in international life by Germany."

To the authors of the policy, the last objective may have seemed a distant prospect. There was certainly no agreed plan of the Allies as to how this ideal objective should be pursued nor when it might be attained. It was, as the record shows, the inability of the Allies to achieve a modicum of agreement on this objective that led eventually to the breakdown of quadripartite policy and of the control mechanism. Previously, the Berlin Declaration of June 5, 1945,[3] i.e., the Declaration Regarding Defeat of Germany and Assumption of Supreme Authority by Allied Powers, issued by the four occupying powers (France, the Soviet Union, the United Kingdom, and the United States) had authorized Allied representatives "to impose on Germany . . . political, administrative, economic, financial, military,

17

and other requirements arising from the complete defeat of Germany."[4]

The first directive issued to the Commander-in-Chief of the U.S. Forces of Occupation in April 1945 by the Joint Chiefs of Staff (JCS 1067) (1.b.)[5] had contained no promise of redemption. In terms as harsh as appeared appropriate to the occasion, JCS 1067 declared defeat, not liberation, the reason for the occupation. It stipulated as the principal Allied objective "to prevent Germany from ever becoming a threat to the peace of the world," and it prescribed a system of rigid political, economic, and other, including educational, controls to be exercised by the Control Council as the supreme organ of control over Germany, in support of this objective.[6] Addressed to General Eisenhower as the U.S. Commander-in-Chief, the directive was to guide him in governing the part of Germany occupied by U.S. forces. At the same time, he was directed to urge the adoption of the policies set by JCS 1067 upon the Control Council for enforcement throughout all of Germany.

JCS 1067 was a stern reminder to Germans that they had lost the war, had surrendered unconditionally, and had to bear the consequences. It declared as the objective of Military Government that "it should be brought home to the Germans that Germany's ruthless warfare and the fanatical Nazi resistance have destroyed the German economy and made chaos and suffering inevitable and that the Germans cannot escape responsibility for what they have brought upon themselves."[7] Denazification and demilitarization and the prosecution of Nazi criminals were keystones of U.S. policy incorporated in JCS 1067. Disarmament implied not only military but industrial disarmament as well. Agricultural output, on the other hand, was to be maximized. Living standards were to be kept to a level required to prevent starvation, widespread disease, or such civil unrest as would endanger the occupying forces. Germans were made responsible for providing for themselves. The Directive did not contain any demands for reparations pending final agreement of the Allied powers, which was never reached.

Latter-day critics have characterized JCS 1067 as "a heavy millstone around the neck of the American Military Government," showing the United States as a "short-sighted country motivated largely by revenge, and with little appreciation of the fundamental problems of an occupation."[8] Their criticism was warranted by hindsight only. JCS 1067 was soon overtaken by subsequent developments, notably the deterioration of quadripartite relations which necessitated a gradual revision of policy, at least on the part of France, the United Kingdom, and the United States.

On September 6, 1946, Secretary of State James F. Byrnes delivered an address in Stuttgart, Germany,[9] which marked a turning point in U.S. and Western Allied relations and policy toward Germany. Referring specifically to the reconstruction stipulation of the Potsdam Agreement "to start building a political democracy from the ground up", Secretary Byrnes asserted that it "never was the intention of the American Government to deny to the German people the right to manage their own internal affairs" and, furthermore, that "the purpose of the occupation did not contemplate a prolonged foreign directorship of Germany's peacetime economy." Byrnes proposed, then and there, that there should be "economic unification of Germany" and that "the German people throughout Germany, under proper safeguards, should now be given the primary responsibility for the running of their own affairs." "All that the Allied governments can and should do," Byrnes said, is "to lay down the rules under which Germany can govern itself." This involved, according to Byrnes, among other things, clarification of the essential terms to the peace settlement and the early establishment of a provisional German government which, in turn, would prepare a draft of a federal constitution for Germany. Byrnes concluded:

"The American people want to return the government to the German people. The American people want the German people to win their way back to an honorable place among the free and peace-loving nations of the world."

One of the first steps taken, still in 1946, in conformance with the Byrnes proposal, was the decision to transfer legislative, executive, and judicial powers to the Laender (States) within the U.S. Zone by March 1, 1947.[10] Also, before the end of the year, the German Economic Council was established, which prepared the economic fusion of the American and British Zones, confirmed by the military governments of the two zones on May 29, 1947. But it was only after the failure of the third Foreign Ministers Conference in Moscow (March–April 1947) that the trend toward German self-government gained real momentum.[11]

The time had come for a second phase in German-U.S. relations. General Clay, then Deputy Military Governor, later Military Governor, himself favored a change. In a message to the War Department of September 16, 1946, he suggested "that a revision of JCS 1067 into a new policy statement is desirable and that this statement should be positive in character." He further suggested that Secretary Byrnes' Stuttgart speech be taken "as a basis for a positive political stand."[12] A directive to the Commander-in-Chief of the U.S. Forces of Occupation (JCS 1779), issued on July 15, 1947,[13] and superseding JCS 1067, initiated this new phase. While it still maintained disarmament, demilitarization, and denazification as objectives of U.S. policy, it now placed major emphasis on the physical, political, and cultural reconstruction of Germany as part of and prerequisite to European recovery. In pursuit of this objective, the task of the U.S. Commander-in-Chief was declared to be that,

> "of helping to lay the economic and educational bases of a sound German democracy, of encouraging *bona fide* democratic efforts and of prohibiting those activities which would jeopardize genuinely democratic developments."

In fact, the severe restrictions of JCS 1067 had already been relaxed as regards the German economy, first because of the impact of large quantities of foodstuffs to stem the threat of nationwide famine, followed by a "Level of Industry Plan" and a subsequent "Revised Plan for Level of Industry in the U.S.-U.K. Zones of Germany" in August 1947. The latter confirmed the new U.S. policy of promoting economic growth by doubling the production of steel, raising industrial production generally to 75 percent of prewar levels, and removing many restrictions on German exports.[14] The issuance of JCS 1779 coincided with the coming into force of the Marshall Plan of which West Germany eventually became a full beneficiary.

Actually, JCS Directive 1779 merely reaffirmed and made operative the earlier "Long-Range Policy Statement for German Reeducation" of June 5, 1946, which had been drafted by a group of American educators under the chairmanship of Archibald MacLeish, then Assistant Secretary of State for Public and Cultural Relations, in May 1945. It was released on August 21, 1946, by the State-War-Navy Coordinating Committee (SWNCC) as Policy Statement 269/5.[15] The statement placed reeducation squarely within the framework of the total reconstruction effort. It declared that,

> "the reeducation of the German People can be effective only as it is an integral part of a comprehensive program for their rehabilitation. The cultural and moral reeducation of the nation must, therefore, be related to policies calculated to restore the stability of a peaceful German economy and to hold out hope for the ultimate recovery of national unity and self-respect."

After having devoted much of its effort in the initial phase of control to the elimination of National Socialist and militaristic doctrine, U.S. Military Government was now directed to complement its policies and programs by initiating "a program for the reconstruction of German cultural life." Moreover, SWNCC 269/5 postulated that, "the reconstruction of the cultural life of Germany must in large measure be the work of the Germans themselves," and, furthermore, that "the Nazi heritage of Germany's spiritual isolation must be overcome by restoring as rapidly as possible those cultural contacts which will foster the assimilation of the German people into the society of peaceful nations." SWNCC 269/5 had laid the groundwork for the elevation of reeducation to a priority aim of U.S. policy intimately related and, in a sense, prerequisite to political and economic recovery.

JCS 1779 now followed through and instructed the U.S. Commander-in-Chief that "the reeducation of the German people is an integral part of policies intended to help develop a democratic form of government and to restore a stable and peaceful economy." To that end, the Commander-in-Chief was directed "to encourage and assist in the development of educational methods, institutions, programs and materials designed to further the creation of democratic attitudes and practices through education." [16] Finally, as a means of encouraging German participation in the work of cultural reconstruction and of overcoming spiritual isolation, JCS 1779 opened the doors to the restoration of international contacts. It told the Commander-in-Chief "to permit and assist the travel into and out of Germany of persons useful for this program within the availability of your facilities." This was not yet the authorization of a full-fledged exchange program, but a first barrier had been removed.

JCS 1779 had been preceded a few weeks earlier by an Allied Control Council Directive which called for fundamental reform of the entire system of formal education. Allied Control Council Directive 54, issued on June 25, 1947, spelled out the ten "Basic Principles for Democratization of Education in Germany." [17] It demanded equal educational opportunity for all: free tuition, textbooks and other scholastic materials and maintenance grants for the needy; compulsory full-time school attendance for all between the ages of 6 and 15; a comprehensive educational system eliminating the so-called "two-track system"; emphasis on civic responsibility in education; promotion of international understanding; provision for educational and vocational guidance; health supervision and health education; teacher training at the university level; and full participation of the public in educational reform, organization and administration.

The Directive was followed in October 1947 by a second one setting forth five "Basic Principles for Adult Education." Reeducation had become one of the few policies that had quadripartite endorsement although the meaning of many of the terms was quite different as between the Western powers and the USSR.

Reeducation has been a concept never entirely free of controversy. To be sure, it was denounced by unreconstructed German nationalists and conservatives who were infuriated by the intrusion of outsiders into the classrooms of the nation and who questioned the competence of the latter to sit in judgment over the moral and social codes of German society. But even more moderate elements were offended by the imposition of reforms that went beyond denazification and attacked time-honored standards and institutions on the assumption that the vanquished was subject to total rehabilitation by the victor.[18]

There can be no doubt that reeducation had certain moral, even moralistic, overtones. Social scientist Hans Speier, himself one of the architects of American postwar policy for Germany, contended and not without justification, that "American policy toward Germany was initially conceived in military and moral terms rather than as a political issue." Being moral, U.S. policy at times sounded almost chiliastic, for instance, when it proclaimed its intention to prevent Germany from "ever" again becoming a threat to peace. The expectation to turn around a whole people—from "evil to good," from Nazism to democracy—moreover, may have impressed and, in fact, did impress many critics as somewhat naive or at least unrealistic. Yet, as Speier rightly emphasized,[19] there was an element of strong realism in U.S. and Allied policy. Reeducation was never conceived as an end in itself—to remake German man—but as an in-depth defense of U.S. national self-interest. Reeducation was to provide long-range protection against a recurrence of aggression by building a psychological foundation on which political and economic reform could rest with hope of survival—the assumption being that neither reform would be of much avail nor long duration if each was not grounded in basic changes in values, attitudes, and institutions. Again, this proposition may have sounded presumptuous to some and unrealistic to others. Subsequent developments have shown that they were neither. Those who did the planning in 1946 were in dead earnest about it. Their principal spokesman, Archibald MacLeish, insisted that reeducation had to be the governing principle of all policies toward Germany, including those governing political and economic reconstruction. He did not fully succeed. Reeducation did not emerge as the supreme goal of Allied or even U.S. policy. But SWNCC 269/5 made it at least an "integral" all-pervasive part of rehabilitation directly related to political and economic reform.

Private Initiative

The elevation of reeducation to priority rank was not the result of government initiative alone. The U.S. educational community can take major credit for having played a decisive role in the development and execution of U.S. policy. It took its cue from a school of thought which emphasized a positive long-range approach to the problems of postwar reconstruction—a concept which actually antedated the end of hostilities. As early as 1944, an "Interdivisional Committee on Germany" of the Department of State had warned that:

"in the long run . . . a purely negative program can result only in chaotic educational procedures. The elimination from the schools of the ultranationalism and militarism and related doctrines . . . can be accomplished only by supplanting the perverted concept of the Hitler regime by a constructive set of beliefs and objectives based on the best elements of the German tradition and offering the German people hope for the future.

"The problem . . .," the recommendation concluded, "consequently is (1) to decide what kind of teaching in Germany would be most conducive to world security, and (2) to determine what means should be employed to foster that teaching." [20]

In August 1946, the educational community, jointly with Military Government, took the initiative by sending to Germany, upon OMGUS invitation, a Mission of 11 prominent members, under the chairmanship of George F. Zook, President of the American Council on Education.[21] The Mission traveled through the U.S. Zone for a month studying conditions and developing recommendations for a report which was filed with General Clay, the Department of State, and the War Department. It returned from its visit profoundly impressed with the urgent need for prompt and systematic assistance on all levels of education and convinced of the grave responsibility of the U.S. Government to respond to this need.

"The reeducation of the German people," the report of the Mission stated, "is an undertaking of the greatest magnitude, which can be accomplished only if, on the one hand, Germans draw upon their own residual resources and, on the other, are given adequate direction and aid by those who have, by the exigencies of history, achieved control over German life."

The Mission, shocked not only by the chaotic conditions caused by wartime destruction and the total corruption of standards by the Nazi regime, but also by the undemocratic structure of the traditional German school system, which predated the Nazi period, proposed a thorough reform of all aspects of education. But it felt strongly that this task had to be performed by Germans themselves. The members of the Mission found some Germans eager to establish cultural contacts with the United States and called the attention of Military Government to what they considered "a unique opportunity to influence the fundamental reorientation of the national educational program in the direction of democratic goals and procedures." They pointed out, however, that in order to discharge this long-term obligation, "the combined resources of the U.S. Government, of voluntary agencies, and of private individuals must be utilized and coordinated." Here was indeed the first preliminary sketch of things to come. The Mission spelled out some of the details. It endorsed the incipient OMGUS program of sending American experts to Germany for direct personal contact and discussion with their German colleagues. It mapped out some of the areas needing urgent attention, such as classroom management, student government, curriculum building, teaching of social studies, training of teachers and youth leaders, and universities in general.

But the Mission took a significant step beyond the scope of OMGUS policies. It recommended that OMGUS' expert program be supplemented by the provision of funds for bringing carefully selected German students to the United States for a period of training. "This is essential," the report said, "to enable those Germans showing promise of leadership to study in the United States and to receive the benefit of our experience for the training of their youth, the rewriting of their school books, and the preparation of cultural material for adult education." The Mission even recommended extension of the provisions of the Fulbright Act to Germany to include German students, teachers, and intellectual leaders, "as soon as conditions permit,"—a recommendation which proved to be premature by 6 years.

The Mission was aware of the fact that the resources available to Military Government for carrying out its program were at best modest. It concluded with commendable insight that the staff of the Education and Religious Affairs Branch "should be double its present size if a thorough job is to be done." Yet, with curious inconsistency it failed to carry its proposal to its logical conclusion. Instead of urging OMGUS or, for that matter, the U.S. Government to assume full financial responsibility for a more adequate program and staff support, it simply suggested that the budget "should remain at least [sic] its present size." Moreover, it relieved OMGUS of much of its burden by calling on the U.S. private sector to come to the aid of its government. "The official program of the U.S. Government," the Mission said, "is only one of many sources of education that must be tapped . . ." Private individuals and organizations, such as churches, trade unions, youth organizations, and professional societies were suggested as the logical elements to open cultural channels between the United States and Germany, thus constituting "a supplement to the governmental program." Official authorities, the Mission proposed, were to assume a new kind of responsibility, namely, to act as a "service agency" of private individuals and organizations, with appropriate administrative adjustments being made in the United States and in the field. Only cooperative action by government and the private sector, the Mission concluded, would insure a full measure of American influence.

This would have been sound advice had it been conceived and interpreted as opening an avenue of enlisting auxiliary aid. But in effect, it provided OMGUS with a convenient rationale to avoid any significant changes in the program and to take on the kind of responsibility that the authorities ought to have exercised. The Mission had performed a valuable, in many ways truly pioneering job, but the caution it observed in not demanding drastic changes in the organization, scope, and budget of the program enabled OMGUS to proceed more or less on its previous scale, and delayed the emergence of an effective program by nearly 3 years.

On the other hand, the Mission's call for a contributory role of the private sector produced remarkable results. Given the more limited resources available to the private sector, it did not achieve the breakthrough of scale that was needed. But it succeeded in moving education into the proper focus and in clarifying the long-term nature of the U.S. commitment in Germany. It endorsed and expanded the pattern of all U.S. Government educational and cultural programs and of government-private partnership as a vital instrument to carry out the overall objectives of U.S. policy. And it helped build up a broad base of organized citizen support which was not only a windfall for OMGUS, but which continued to prove enormously useful when the Department of State and HICOG assumed responsibility for a program then substantially planned, conducted, and financed by the Government.

The reaction of OMGUS to the report was strongly affirmative in language, but weak in action. General Clay's comment to the War Department was to the effect that provisions had been made for the recruitment of American personnel in educational fields; that the services of 40 experts would be obtained before mid-1947; that coordination of educational aid and exchanges was heartily supported and that an agency should be set up in the United States parallel to a central agency in the U.S. Zone to bring about such coordination; that "no recommendation would be more supported than the recommendation that German students, teachers and school officials should spend a period of training in the United States," and that permission had already been granted a number of German theological students to pursue their studies in Switzerland and Italy. All this, OMGUS said, could be done "as soon as foreign exchange has been established for Germany." [22] There was no further word on how this exchange could be "established," certainly no suggestion that government funds should be used or procured. There was, in fact, no immediate follow-up.

The winter of 1946–1947 was a time of extreme austerity with food and coal in very scarce supply. Europe was in the grip of a severe cold wave. General Clay had made clear that reeducation of the German people to a liberal philosophy of life and government was an objective of his policy,[23] but he did not believe that democracy could be either taught or learned on empty stomachs. Quite consistently, he refused for some time to spend his funds on paper and newsprint for textbooks and newspapers. Between education and the necessities of life, named as the prerequisites to the growth of democracy, Clay, understandably, assigned priority to the latter. "We realize," he wrote in a letter of May 1, 1947, to the Secretary of State, "that there is no limit to the funds which could be expended for reorientation in Germany. However, we believe that with the appropriations which have been made in the amount of $1,025,433 and with the continuation of the services enumerated above furnished by the War Department during the past year, we will give our reorientation program a status proportionate and comparable with our overall program."[24]

Clay was reluctant to ask more money of Congress for a number of other reasons. He had reached rather early the conclusion that responsibility for the punitive as well as the positive aspects of rehabilitation had to be turned back to the Germans. Moreover, he was critical of the visiting expert program and even more so of proposals to extend the program to U.S. specialists and to students. As regards the former, he considered the short visits of American and European experts a failure and preferred the alternative of having them serve as members of his staff, at least on a semipermanent basis. As for students, Clay hesitated to accept the Education Mission's proposal of having them go to the United States and of underwriting the expense out of OMGUS funds. In his letter to Major General Daniel Noce, Chief of the Civil Affairs Division of the War Department, Clay expressed the "hope to see German students ... visit the United States," but suggested that such travel would have to be financed from private sources.[25]

As a result of his letter, only four major categories of German citizens were given permission to travel to the United States, namely, (1) displaced persons and persecutees (by Presidential Directive of December 22, 1946); (2) theological students (upon endorsement by General Clay); (3) clergymen and educators traveling on visitors' visas to attend conferences and the like (upon clearance by the European Command); and (4) scientists traveling in the interest of War Department research (upon clearance by the War Department and the Department of State).[26]

Washington Intervention

Eventually it was Washington rather than OMGUS that responded affirmatively to the recommendation of the Education Mission. Under direct reference to the Long-Range Policy Statement on German Reeducation (SWNCC 269/5), which had declared that "the reconstruction of the cultural life must be in large measure the work of the Germans themselves," and in accordance with the policy established by that SWNCC directive that Germany's spiritual isolation had to be overcome by a restoration of cultural contacts, the State-War-Navy Coordinating Committee, on March 31, 1947, issued its Directive 269/8 which announced the decision of the U.S. Government "to permit and encourage the revival of visits of Germans to the United States . . . and of persons from the United States to Germany." [27]

The new policy, which was given wide media coverage, contained a number of innovative features. It defined the categories of persons eligible for participation in exchange visits between the United States and Germany—namely, leaders in formal and extracurricular education; leaders in religious activities; leaders in informational and related fields of activity, such as press, radio, and films; leaders in civic and welfare organizations, youth and other social organizations; leaders in occupational and professional organizations; leaders in art, letters, music, and the stage; students from recognized educational institutions, and trainees; and persons of outstanding promise who were about to enter upon or who were in the early years of their active careers in the above fields.

Next, the policy established the criteria of selection of candidates, such as: concern with educational, religious, scientific, informational or cultural affairs and interest in the reorientation of the German people toward peace and democracy; willingness to further through their trips the work of Military Government in the reeducation of the German people; proficiency in the language of the country to which they were going; intent not to use the trip for commercial purposes; a satisfactory record as regards past and present political activities and affiliations to meet established security requirements; preference to be given to persons who had demonstrated their opposition to Nazism and their belief in democratic principles; and, finally, a written statement affirming their understanding that they were required to return to Germany upon the expiration of their permission to visit the United States (or another country).

Furthermore, the policy established criteria of sponsorship in that the trip of each individual had to be recommended or sponsored by a recognized American nongovernmental organization or institution or by an agency or institution of the U.S. Government.

With respect to candidacy, the eligibility of each person and of his sponsor, the length of his stay, and the program of his visit had to be approved by OMGUS in Germany, the War Department in Washington, and, finally, before the issuance of passport and visa, by the Department of State—approval depending in turn on the completion of a thorough security check giving no cause for reasonable doubt that the above criteria had been met.

Except for the explicit criteria relating to reeducation and reorientation of the German people, many of these criteria were not so different from those already in use for foreign students, professors, scholars, and leaders who had been coming here during the previous 6 to 7 years from Latin America. They, too, were to be chosen with great care as regards influence among significant social groups at home, academic qualifications, and ability to speak and understand fluent English.

As regards money, the program was to be financed from private and public funds in the United States and, whenever possible, from German public and private sources, subject in the case of private sponsorship to the approval of the War Department and the Department of State. As a practical matter, the number of travel permissions was made contingent upon the availability of suitable placement facilities and financial resources of each traveler. The study of American students in German educational institutions of higher learning was deferred until conditions at German universities appeared sufficiently stabilized. Directive 269/8 of the State-War-Navy Coordinating Committee constituted marked progress toward the attainment of the comprehensive U.S. objectives. It provided a tool for reeducation that left no longer the whole onus nor the exclusive responsibility with U.S. authorities. For the first time, in this Directive, Germans were assigned a participatory and supportive role, though still largely as beneficiaries and only to a very limited degree as cosponsors.

Although announced in press releases and widely welcomed amongst persons concerned as a "cooperative venture of the United States Government and private institutions and organizations interested in furthering democratic reeducation and reconstruction in Germany," [28] SWNCC 269/8 hardly got off to a flying start. The policy itself had cautioned that participation would depend on the availability of funds. Such funds were, in fact, provided for U.S. experts and specialists; but for Germans, sources for financial assistance to defray the cost of transportation, study, and daily living depended, as heretofore, on the generous, albeit limited voluntary contributions from the private sector. Appropriations by Congress were neither allotted nor, indeed, yet requested.

Considering the stringency of conditions for approval of each German who was to travel, the difficulty of finding private sponsors and, even more so, the paucity of money for implementation, it was small wonder that the program started with a mere trickle of 81 persons traveling on government funds during fiscal year 1947 (i.e., July 1, 1946–June 30, 1947). Most of these (50) were specialists going to Germany. The rest consisted of German leaders going to European countries (21) or to the United States (8) and of European specialists to Germany (2).[29] No students or trainees traveled on U.S. Government money, although according to War Department estimates, 50 German students attended a variety of American institutions under private auspices. Among the first students permitted to visit the United States was Benigna Goerdeler, daughter of the former Lord Mayor of Leipzig who had been executed by the Nazis for participation in the 1944 plot against Hitler. She had been invited by Briarcliff College.

Aside from its modest volume, it was the composition of the sample that made the program in the early years less than satisfactory. Since participation depended largely on private contributions, the program included primarily those Germans who either had relatives and friends in the United States or were members of politically untainted organizations with affiliates in the United States. Since most secular organizations had either been destroyed or corrupted by the Nazi regime, the churches emerged as logical and qualified sponsors of exchanges. Indeed, during the first years of any kind of "exchanges," religious organizations and colleges assumed major responsibility for sponsoring, stimulating, facilitating, and financing the travel of individuals and groups.[30]

The preponderance of persons meeting OMGUS and State Department criteria for travel because of personal relationships and/or religious affiliation left out large numbers of qualified candidates. More seriously, as long as the program remained truncated and unbalanced, it could not possibly be expected to perform its assigned function as a vehicle and supplement of educational reform. Indeed, the latter itself was now running into trouble, weakening the rationale for educational exchange. The attempts of Military Government to revamp the German educational system on all levels began to meet with increasing resistance on the part of members of the educational bureaucracy and educational traditionalists in certain Laender (States).

In accordance with the proposals of the Education Mission of 1946, U.S. policy called for fundamental changes in the philosophy and structure of German education, including the elimination of the so-called "two-track" system. This system separated children after the fourth grade with a mere 10 to 20 percent moving on to secondary school and more than 80 percent staying behind in elementary and vocational schools and thousands dropping out before graduation from even these low-level institutions. The "selection out" process favored in effect and largely by intent the sons and daughters of the upper middle class who upon graduation from the secondary schools were entitled to enter the universities and technical academies and thereafter the ranks of the higher civil service, the professions, and academia.[31]

German conservatives rose to the defense of the system which they believed had produced, and they hoped, insured, the resurgence of a professional elite and, with it, the return of the standards of excellence that, in the past, had established Germany's international reputation in science, technology, and the professions. They argued that there was no need for studying, and even less for imitating foreign models. Near the end of 1947 resistance reached a crescendo, nearing outright sabotage in the form of deliberate foot-dragging by Land authorities, and rumor-mongering, distortion of and active opposition to U.S. intentions on legalistic and plainly political grounds by recalcitrant elements. In a report summarizing the situation in the U.S. Zone of Occupation in 1948, the author reported that military directives proposing ten principles of educational reform had not been implemented and that general agitation was fast approaching a point where not just the policies but the authority of Military Government was called into question.[32]

What had brought such a situation about, considering the generally benign attitude of the military toward the former enemy? For one thing, external resistance and perhaps an overcautious attitude on the part of Military Government combined to delay a vigorous, broad and imaginative educational exchange program. Observers found the OMGUS program lacking in substance and focus, middle-brow in its approach, aiming at an amorphous mass audience or low level functionaries instead of concentrating on the potential leadership, still harping on negative and restrictive measures rather than promoting positive reconstructive objectives, and lagging behind that of our Western Allies. The caliber of the OMGUS staff was questioned, especially by German authorities and educators who began to challenge the credentials of their American tutors. Some of the criticism was justified. In contrast to the British, and especially the French authorities, who at a very early stage began to cultivate the more sophisticated elements in German society and who flattered them by sending outstanding members of their own intellectual elite to Germany, American military authorities exhibited for a while a curious indifference towards catering to the tastes of the intelligentsia. Except for certain cultural areas, namely, theater and music, in which under the direction of Eric T. Clarke, formerly Secretary of the Metropolitan Opera Association, and other highly competent experts in the field of music such as Benno Frank and John Evarts, who were successful in restoring intercultural contacts by the display of artistic capabilities of high quality, there was no sign of any significant or systematic effort of the U.S. Military Government to recreate relations between the intellectual leadership of both countries.

Many of the arguments leveled by German and American critics, especially against the caliber of U.S. personnel and against the validity of U.S. policies, were neither fair nor correct nor indeed substantiated by the response of their own compatriots. There were many extremely able officers in the ranks of OMGUS whom HICOG later was glad to accept and assign to key positions. It should also be recorded that, notwithstanding mounting resistance to educational reform, there were notable exceptions. School reform in Berlin, Bremen, and Hamburg was progressing substantially along the lines of U.S. proposals for a "one-track" system. Furthermore, democratic elements within the German educational community welcomed Allied policies throughout Germany and endorsed wholeheartedly the purpose of Control Council Directive 54 of June 25, 1947 which had set forth the "Basic Principles for Education in Germany." The U.S. program, in particular, had found a loyal constituency among German teachers which continued into the fifties. It was not U.S. policy so much as the implementation of U.S. policy that caused growing concern in Germany and in the United States.

Thus the time seemed to have come for Washington to intervene directly and to draw General Clay's attention to the simple fact that the objectives of SWNCC 269/8 were not being achieved and that, to the extent to which the policy was implemented, it appeared to operate chiefly for the benefit of the fortunate few who had family, friends, or other personal connections in the United States. Some Pentagon officials, alarmed about the lack of progress actively argued for a "retention of controls . . . over the mechanism of education," and advised the General to that effect.[33] The time had passed for restrictions of this sort.

The Department of State chose a different approach. In an internal briefing paper [34] the author suggested that any prospect of realizing the purpose of SWNCC 269/8 depended on full compliance of interchange programs with the objectives of this directive, that such coordination, in turn, was possible only if the Government determined the use of funds for such programs and if the Department of State, the Department of the Army, and OMGUS assumed exclusive or chief responsibility for the selection of persons and projects. Such funds, moreover, would have to be provided by Congress. Any alternative, such as the exclusive use of private funds, would be possible but less likely and doubtless less effective. A systematic effort by the Departments of State and the Army was required to enlist the active interest of U.S. private individuals and organizations in the support of this policy. But an appeal of this kind could be successful only if the private sponsor were convinced that its money and facilities would be used in such a manner as to guarantee a maximum effect of a long-range and well-defined program and of procedures which would insure an effective selection of projects and persons over a specified period of time. At the same time the sponsor had to be granted, for reasons of fairness and expediency, a reasonable measure of responsibility in the recommendations and, if feasible, in the formulation of individual projects. Flexibility of conditions governing priority, type and length of programs, availability of accommodations, and travel facilities would give the Government some, but hardly adequate, leverage for decision, and still provide an effective inducement to the individual sponsor.

General Clay should, therefore, the author noted, be asked whether he would agree to request, or to support a request for, Congressional appropriations for purposes of cultural interchanges, over and above current requests for the program of visiting experts. Furthermore, the Department of State should ascertain whether General Clay would be prepared to extend existing time limits of 3 months for visits of American experts and use of facilities, if such limits would prove to constitute a serious handicap to the effective accomplishment of the mission or endanger the purpose or result of the project. Finally, the briefing paper pointed out that General Clay should be willing to assure private sponsors that their interests regarding purpose, type and length of project, accommodations and travel facilities would be considered. An appendix to the memorandum proposed that OMGUS be queried specifically regarding the number of persons going in each direction under the exchange program, facilities for travel and accommodations, types of trainee programs, establishment of priority areas, length of projects, organization in the field, e.g., coordination and administration under OMGUS and German auspices, selection of candidates, types of private sponsorship desired, coordination with British and French occupation authorities and with other countries, and the like.

The Wells Mission

The event which finally broke the impasse and provided the needed momentum for educational reform and, with it, for the educational exchange program, was the appointment by **OMGUS of Dr.**

Herman B Wells, President of Indiana University, as Educational and Cultural Adviser to Military Government. Wells' mission, as described by General Clay to Major General Daniel Noce of the Civil Affairs Division of the Department of the Army, was to "participate in formulating internal policy under our broad policy directives . . . with particular attention to work on information control and education branches." General Clay added: "I do not need to stress to you the importance of the assignment." [35]

In briefing sessions with Dr. Wells prior to his departure for Germany, Department of State officers emphasized the points made by the earlier survey mission, stressing in particular the need for elevating the status of educational and cultural activities to a level on a par with other OMGUS functions and for integrating the reorientation effort which had now become the paramount civil function of OMGUS, with all other OMGUS activities rather than choosing a parochial and compartmentalized approach separating educational, religious, and informational programs. Military Government should furthermore be urged to avoid doctrinaire overtones, and, in dealing with Germans, to place maximum reliance upon identifying, encouraging, and supporting sound leadership and democratic initiatives in all phases of German life.[36]

Messages from Washington to OMGUS expressed satisfaction with the choice of Dr. Wells and underscored the importance of his mission by restating the need for a vigorous reorientation program, making the point that such a program should provide the means of free expression now in scarce supply, such as book paper and newsprint.

In November 1947, Dr. Wells went to work. Taking much encouragement from his discussions in Washington he set out to reorganize the educational and cultural activities. Within the organizational structure of OMGUS, the education program was raised from branch to division level. Its scope was enlarged to include the fields of community activities, women's activities, youth, health, and welfare. The concept of reeducation was no longer to be confined to technical reform of the institutions of formal education but was to include cultural exchange in the widest sense.[37] Although budget cutbacks had been ordered across the board, Dr. Wells managed not only to protect the new Division of Education and Cultural Relations from any retrenchment, but actually to increase its responsibilities.[38]

The exchange program was Dr. Wells' special concern. Largely due to his efforts, a number of changes were effected which changed the character and scope of the program. Dr. Wells was convinced that cultural and educational exchange was indispensable to the achievement of the objectives of educational reform. "For more than a decade," he summarized, "Germans were barred by the Nazi dictatorship from the thought and culture of the rest of the world. Today they are unaware of many of the advances that have been made in such fields as education, social science, medicine, art, and literature. It is not enough to say that success in reeducation will be *aided* by the importation of new ideas and methods through the exchange of textual matter, teachers, students, and leading personalities in the professions; it should rather be said that success is *not possible* without this exchange . . . In conclusion . . . Cultural Exchange is one of the keystones in the reeducation program. . ." [39]

In making his proposals Dr. Wells foresaw a truly two-way program although, for the time being, the emphasis was on Germans going to the United States. The selection of persons who might qualify extended across all sectors of cultural, professional, and civic life, with preference given to those concerned with educational, religious, scientific, informational, and cultural affairs, such as students, teachers, religious leaders, and young administrators in education and religion.[40] While his public appeal was addressed to private institutions for support, especially in the form of scholarships, Dr. Wells was personally convinced that without funding from public sources, the program would never achieve the impact needed to promote and sustain an effective reorientation effort. Yet he found General Clay still reluctant to request funds from Congress.

Moreover, Clay had other misgivings. He was concerned that German students would be harassed on American campuses—an apprehension which later proved to be wholly unwarranted. Eventually he gave Wells the green light, telling him that if he thought that he could get the money out of Congress, to go ahead and launch the program.[41]

Dr. Wells' efforts resulted in an almost immediate increase in funds and exchanges. Whereas in 1947 the total of exchanges sponsored by the Government was 81, it rose in 1948 to 354. Of these, 232 were Germans going to the United States, and 14 to other European countries. The balance were Americans (82) or Europeans (26) traveling to Germany. Significantly, the largest single group were German students (214) visiting the United States (see Appendix I).

Quite aside from raising the level and scale of exchanges, the major effect of the Wells mission was the emergence of an exchange program elevated in level of responsibility and with an identity of its own. Coordination with other programs of OMGUS provided breadth and sharper focus. Finally, Dr. Wells' interest in augmenting sources of support, both public and private, not only widened the base but insured continuity of the exchange program.[42]

The Wells mission ushered in the final phase of the OMGUS exchange program and, in some respects, laid the ground for the climactic developments under the U.S. High Commissioner. The grand design which determined the framework for all OMGUS activities during 1948–49 was drawn by General Clay himself in a speech which he delivered on October 13, 1948 at Berchtesgaden, Bavaria, to the staff of the Division of Education and Cultural Relations. He assigned to what then became known as the "reorientation" program, the long-range responsibility for assuring that the German (industrial) potential not be used again for aggression but for the common good; and he singled out the exchange program as the one phase of the OMGUS effort that, if properly conducted, could produce the needed changes in the German mind.

In a similar vein, Dr. Alonzo Grace, former Commissioner of Education in Connecticut, who after Dr. Wells' departure had been made Director of the Division of Education and Cultural Relations, described the objective of the cultural exchange program "to restore an intellectual, social, and cultural life based on the principles of freedom and social justice, humanity, and the recognition of the dignity of the individual." In a foreword to the draft of a handbook summarizing his philosophy on cultural exchanges, Dr. Grace accepted General Clay's thesis as the basic rationale for the exchange program. "Because the mentality of a people and the principles upon which its society is based," Dr. Grace wrote, "are fundamental factors in determining the economic and political course of that people, the success of the objectives [of the cultural exchange program] is vital to the security of the world." [43]

The joint efforts of Dr. Wells, SWNCC, and the Department of State had borne fruit. Reorientation and, implicitly, educational and cultural exchanges had become policy priorities on a par with and, in a wider sense, prerequisites to political and economic rehabilitation. The exchange program itself, in turn, had come to be recognized as an integral part of the reorientation effort. Summarizing the new trend, the cumulative report of OMGUS, covering the period from May 1, 1948 to April 30, 1949, defined the aim of OMGUS' cultural affairs activities as "the moral and spiritual reorientation of the German people through international exchange of persons and materials [and] the development of cultural relations between Germany and foreign countries." [44] Underlying the new trend was a growing recognition that with the accelerated pace toward the restoration of self-government, controls had to be relaxed and eventually abandoned altogether. In addition, alternatives had to be found to continue the task of democratic reform by persuasion and indirection, rather than by fiat and indoctrination, and by drawing increasingly on German's cultural resources and on German initiative. Cultural and educational exchanges which afforded Germans an opportunity for participation on a gradually rising level of responsibility, offered a most appropriate and logical instrument of continuing the reorientation policy by these means.

The Structure of the Program—Categories and Procedures

Soon after the release of SWNCC 269/8, the Secretary of War submitted to the Secretary of State for approval a standard operating procedure which was to govern the basic plans for the 1948 exchange program.[45] This procedure, which in line with SWNCC 269/8 was to regulate the exchange of persons between Germany and the United States (and Austria and the United States), made a distinction between two types of persons involved, namely, "United States visitors to occupied areas" and "foreign nationals to the United States." The first consisted of two groups, "experts and specialists (going to Germany) financed by the War Department," and so-called "volunteer projects," i.e., persons sponsored by private institutions and organizations. The second group included "experts and specialists from occupied areas" and "students from occupied areas" going to the United States.

On August 12, 1947 the State-War-Navy Coordinating Committee, in an amendment to SWNCC 269/8 (SWNCC 269/11), added two further categories to the above by permitting the "visits of Germans to countries other than the United States and of persons from countries other than the United States to Germany."[46] Procedures for travel and selection governing the aforementioned categories were the same for the new ones. In fact, the amendment merely confirmed a practice already in effect regarding interchanging persons between Germany and other European countries. Eventually, these categories were supplemented by the addition of trainees and teenagers going to the United States.

German Leaders and Specialists to the United States

The type of persons falling within this category had been identified in SWNCC 269/8, October 24, 1946, as had been the criteria of selection, conditions of approval, chains of authority, and processing procedures. The standard operating procedure issued in May 1947 refined and elaborated the rules laid down in the SWNCC policy. Criteria of eligibility were defined in considerable detail. General qualifications as set forth insisted on the consideration of such factors as personality and adaptability, English speaking and reading facility, untainted political background, education and professional attainment, and "probable ability to derive benefits from the sojourn in the United States which in turn would enable individuals to contribute to the program of democratic reorientation in their native country upon their return."[47] Security requirements were especially strict. Aside from the obviously necessary biographical data, statements had to be supplied covering political affiliations and organization memberships, both past and present; community contacts; denazification record, if any; and criminal record, if any. Moreover, the absence of any derogatory information had to be confirmed by officers of the G-2* Center in Berlin and by the office of the U.S. Political Adviser, also in Berlin.

Subsequent procedures issued in 1949,[48] relaxed some of the earlier requirements, stipulating that no rigid standards were to be applied with respect to education and experience except that candidates had to be well qualified in their particular fields. Command of the English language now became a matter of guaranteeing preference, other qualifications being equal. Age likewise was no longer made a firm criterion, though younger candidates were to receive preferential treatment provided they were mature enough to benefit from their visit. Personal qualifications, however, were spelled out with greater care with emphasis being placed on vitality, enthusiasm, and ability to pass on exchange experiences to others upon their return. To insure impact on the German community, evidence of "leadership," "progressiveness," and "initiative" was declared desirable. So was a reasonable expectation that the candidate would and could continue his previous employment in his field of specialization. But as far as the political requirements were concerned, OMGUS maintained throughout the rigid standards set forth in its earlier procedures. Excluded from eligibility were, reasonably enough, persons who had been convicted of a felony by an Allied Court or by another competent criminal court recognized by the Occupation Authorities; persons who were members of any organization designated as criminal by the International Military Tribunal (i.e., the Nazi Party, SS (Schutzstaffel [the Elite Guard]), SA (Sturmabteilung [the Brown Shirts]) ; persons who were classified by a denazification tribunal as Major Offenders, Offenders, Lesser Offenders, or Followers; persons who were members of the Communist Party or any of its affiliates; and persons who by their conduct or actions had demonstrated their opposition to democratic practices and principles.

Sponsors in the United States were selected from established and reputable organizations and institutions throughout the country.

---
*U.S. Military Intelligence.

Their credentials were checked mainly for "financial liability and responsibility" and they were asked to submit specific statements describing the program or course of study offered and the length of time involved, and to disclose their source of funds. Precautions of this nature were intended not merely to bar unqualified institutions and substandard programs, but equally to protect the integrity of the program as well as the interests of the Germans coming here.

As one example, the program procedures stipulated that in the case of professors invited to teach at American institutions the subject fields had to be such "as to contribute to the reorientation program" and also that "the actual teaching load could not exceed 50 percent of the normal teaching schedule." Most universities and colleges complied punctiliously with these requirements, but there were a few instances in which sponsors tried to exploit the visitor and the program by supplementing their own staff "on the cheap," using the services of a visiting professor in excess of the permissible 50 percent. The author, who at that time was responsible for passing on cases on behalf of the Department of State, denied or withheld approval pending clarification in several such instances. On similar grounds the author refused approval of applications from an industrial firm which proposed to send some of its employees to its branch in Germany for training purposes, claiming that the provisions of the exchange program applied.

Procedures governing the selection of candidates were quite specific, in fact, exacting. Considering the bureaucratic machinery needed to achieve a measure of coordination among the various authorities involved, a certain amount of red tape was to be expected. Selection of candidates was a multistaged process. Selection boards were established throughout the occupied zone which included "representatives of (German) democratic elements." Their function was to sort out suitable candidates and nominate them to the Theater Commander. The latter had the final responsibility for approval and also for the obligatory security check.

Names of approved candidates with supporting documentation were then forwarded to the Civil Affairs Division (CAD) of the War Department (and subsequently to the Department of the Army) in Washington. The Reorientation Branch of CAD would accept the Theater Commander's recommendations and submit them to the Department of State for policy check and security clearance on the basis of information supplied by the Theater Commander. Upon approval by the Department of State, the Reorientation Branch would notify the Theater Commander who in turn would certify to the appropriate consulate that the visit of the applicant in question was in the national interest.

Consular officers in Germany thereupon would issue nonimmigrant visas under Section 3(2) of the Immigration Act of 1924 if they found that the applicant met the requirements of the law. The process was completed with the Theater Commander's issuance of travel orders, as a rule limited to the use of military carriers, and giving CAD advance notice of the departure date. Responsibility for admission of the visitor to the United States rested with the Department of Justice (Immigration and Naturalization Service) which also kept track of him during his stay and saw to it that his departure occurred on the day his "permit to stay" expired. Arrangements of programs of study and of all related administrative functions involved were handled by the International Exchange of Persons Division of the Department of State with the use of funds transmitted to the Department of State for such purposes by the Reorientation Branch of CAD.

In the case of projects originating with private U.S. sponsors, procedures were somewhat simpler. Here all offers of placement had to be addressed to CAD with appropriate information on the sponsor's qualifications and nature and length of the project, as noted. The Reorientation Branch of CAD would forward the proposal to the Department of State for a decision on the eligibility of the sponsor and the desirability of the project. The Department would then send its decision to the Reorientation Branch of OMGUS. All costs would be charged to the sponsor who would pay for transportation and grant a per diem of $12; however, if room and board were provided by the sponsor, per diem would be lowered correspondingly.

The strictness of these requirements had to be understood in view of the highly sensitive nature of the program. Only 3 years after the end of hostilities, visits of Germans at U.S. taxpayers' expense, some feared, could evoke misgivings and even protests from domestic critics who contended that the experiment was premature and invited unnecessary risks. Most of these fears proved unwarranted. On the contrary, the program quickly gained surprising approbation, especially in the Congress, where year after year appropriations were granted in the requested amount during the OMGUS years. Such criticism as was occasionally heard came from rather unexpected quarters and was directed against the harshness of conditions which, it was claimed, excluded the participation of "nominal" young Nazi party members, thus "prevent[ing] educational reconstruction of the very group of young students and faculty [members] who are in a position to influence most widely the rebuilding of democratic ideas and methods in Germany." [49]

Partly as a result of the stringency of conditions of approval, partly for lack of funds, the leader-specialist programs had a somewhat inconspicuous start. The number of travelers to the United States in 1947 on Government funds was no more than 8. There were 18 in 1948 (see Appendix I). But those were not the only German leaders to come to this country. American churches, colleges, and nongovernmental organizations, such as Moral Rearmament, were among the first to sponsor visits of prominent Germans. Their choices were often haphazard and not always happy ones. Some, in fact, were highly controversial, such as that of former naval officer Pastor Martin Niemoeller, an anti-Nazi to be sure, but also an unreconstructed nationalist who used much of his time in the United States defending the cause of German nationalism. The Department of State had actually warned that it would be unfortunate to inaugurate the program with such dubious candidates as Niemoeller.

The first visitor under governmental auspices was a woman, Mrs. Strecker, an employee of OMGUS, who in 1946 attended a convention of the International Assembly of Women. Although at that time the new policy on exchange of persons had not yet been formally announced, the Department expedited approval of Mrs. Strecker's visit at the urgent request of General Clay. The project was obviously suited to further the objectives of reorientation, inasmuch as the Assembly was to discuss means of achieving a more active role of women in a democratic and internationally cooperative society, a key item on OMGUS' priority list.[50]

From its modest start, the number of leaders and specialists coming here soon soared to major heights to become eventually the largest single group of visitors, growing from 79 in 1947–1948 to 557 in 1949 (see Appendix III). In January 1949 alone, 189 German experts departed for the United States for visits ranging from 30–120 days. Most of them were sponsored by these Divisions: Education and Cultural Relations (137); Civil Administration (37); Legal (9); and Food and Agriculture (6). There were considerable variations in the number of visitors chosen from the different Laender (states), not always proportional to the size of the population. Bavaria led with 70, followed by Hesse with 42, Wuerttemberg-Baden with 32, Berlin Sector with 30, and Bremen with 15.[51]

In time the German leader-specialist exchange became not only the largest but, as regards impact on the German populace, the most significant and effective program. The secret of its success lay in the careful and calculated selection of the best participants, but, perhaps even more so, in its project-oriented nature. OMGUS started the so-called "project approach" which reached its peak under HICOG (see Chapter IV). Leaders and specialists were sent in small groups that were either professionally homogeneous or interested in studying problems of common concern. Teams of teachers, government administrators on all levels,[52] lawyers, journalists,[53] public health officials,[54] city planners, and eventually the first group of women leaders, visited the United States; the last, under the sponsorship of the Carrie Chapman Catt Memorial Fund of the League of Women Voters, came to study "practical techniques for enlarging the woman's sphere in government and politics." [55]

The caliber of these groups enhanced the value of the project idea, giving it sharper focus and greater effectiveness. Whether such group projects also intensified the long-range impact of the total program is more difficult to gauge, although there was evidence to that effect in cases where teams stayed together and took joint action upon their return to Germany.

German Students (and Trainees) in the United States

The directive SWNCC 269/8 had also granted permission to students from recognized educational institutions and trainees to travel to the United States. The objective of these programs was "to give a maximum number of young Germans on the secondary school, undergraduate, and graduate level the chance to study at an institution in a democratic country and, at the same time, to receive a first hand demonstration of democracy at work and to participate in community living." [56] Procedures developed by the War Department to determine eligibility of candidates, sponsors, and projects were, by and large, the same as those established for leaders and specialists with only a few added provisions to meet the special needs of students.

In the case of students financed from U.S. Government funds, the Reorientation Branch of the Civil Affairs Division, War Department, formulated the program which was then submitted to the Theater Commander for approval. Lists of opportunities for placement in American institutions would likewise be transmitted to the Theater Commander with requests for nominations.

For the administration of the program and for funds for regular graduate and undergraduate students (e.g., grants from private donors) and for placement, the War Department employed the services of the Institute of International Education (IIE), a private organization in New York with which the Department of State had had contracts for years. Names of student candidates nominated and security-checked by the Theater Commander were forwarded through channels (e.g., Reorientation Branch, CAD) to IIE for placement. IIE, after placement had been secured, would notify the Reorientation Branch to that effect and, through it, the Theater Commander. In the case of private sponsorship in the United States, all offers had to be addressed to CAD along with information including name of institution and organization, source of funds, nature of the course or training offered, extent of financial liability to be assumed by the sponsor, and type of individual desired. If the arrangements offered were acceptable all around, the Reorientation Branch would submit the program to the Department of State for approval. Subsequent to the approval by the War Department and the Department of State, the offer would be referred to the Theater Commander for acceptance. For the protection of students receiving fellowships, it was stipulated that teaching duties be limited to German language teaching but not for more than 10 hours per week. Compensation, if any, was to be given in the form of tuition grants and maintenance, but not in cash.[57]

Transportation to the United States was provided by official carriers (Army transport ships) on a space-available basis with a charge to the students (but reimbursed by OMGUS) for meals while *en route*. Sponsors could be asked to guarantee transportation for the return trip if no government transportation was available at the time the student's visa expired.[58] Visas for study were granted for one year but could be extended if the sponsor guaranteed the continued support of the student and if the government agencies concerned were in agreement that such an extension would be of value to the reorientation program.[59]

The standard operating procedure for student exchange issued on October 28, 1948 by the Cultural Branch of the Education and Cultural Relations Divisions of OMGUS [60] describes in considerable detail the application, review, and selection process as administered by the Land (State) Office or, in the case of applications from other zones of occupation, by the Cultural Exchange Office, and by the Land Student Exchange Committees. The latter were appointed in all Laender by the Interchange of Persons Officer (later called the Land Cultural Affairs Officer). These committees were composed of educational and civic leaders, representatives of cultural activities outside of formal education, and labor union members, all of whom, however, served in an individual capacity and not as delegates of their organizations. The Committees themselves acted only in an advisory capacity by reviewing applications and making recommendations.

Offers of scholarships received from IIE were few and hence were distributed on a quota basis, i.e., 5 for Bavaria, 3 for Wuerttemberg-Baden, 3 for Hesse, and 1 each for Berlin and Bremen. Land Cultural Affairs officers would fill their quotas with two nominations—a first and second choice for each opening.

The screening process itself was most carefully devised, with maximum attention paid to the background of the candidate. University students were interviewed by university presidents (Rektors), young teachers by the heads of teacher training institutes, youth leaders by members of Land or Kreis (County) youth committees.

Interviews covered security and were conducted on the basis of references supplied by school authorities, teachers, civic leaders, and religious personages who would attest to the candidate's scholarship, leadership potential, character, capacity to work, and ability to profit from studying abroad.[61] Health was also a prime consideration.

The reluctance of U.S. Military Government to use available, or request additional, public funds for student exchange and a corresponding apathy by Congress were chiefly responsible for the late start of the student program.[62] There is no record listing any significant student exchange by numbers under governmental sponsorship in 1947. HICOG charts (see Appendix III)[63] show student exchanges in 1947–1948 totaling 219. Nearly all of these, according to available information, went to the United States in 1948. Indeed, 1948 appears to have been the turning point. In 1949, there was a slight increase to 239, including 81 trainees and the first 65 teenagers. But the big jump was to come a year later under the aegis of the U.S. High Commissioner.

American Specialists to Germany

Visits of private American citizens to Germany preceded SWNCC 269/8. Military Government called in experts rather early in the occupation, mostly as consultants to assist its staff in critical areas, such as education on all levels, libraries, public welfare, social services, women's affairs, legal matters, religious and church work, and youth activities. For instance, Professor Herta Kraus of Haverford College was called in to aid in the rehabilitation of social work teaching and practices; Dr. Bernice Leary of the Milwaukee Public Schools to assist in the preparation of children's books; and Dr. Burr Phillips, professor of history at the University of Wisconsin, to aid in school textbook writing. Upon completion of their assignments, these experts submitted reports, normally containing specific recommendations to the Theater Commander. Some of the reports were highly critical of public attitudes and professional practices, deploring not so much the perpetuation of Nazi doctrines as a relapse into traditional patterns of education with overemphasis on specialization and little regard for the social sciences and the liberal arts. Many reports contained a wealth of positive, often very technical recommendations, some of which had great practical value to OMGUS officials and were seized upon eagerly for application to current programs.

Procedures developed to regulate the visits of American experts and to implement SWNCC 269/8 were understandably far less complex than those applied to Germans going to the United States. SWNCC 269/8 contained only a brief reference to the effect that the U.S. Government should "encourage" such visits, whether under governmental or private auspices.

The procedures distinguished between "experts and specialists financed by the War Department" and so-called "volunteer projects," i.e., those sponsored by private institutions and organizations. In the former case, all that was required was a request from the Theater Commander to the Reorientation Branch of CAD identifying the expert by name or by indication of qualifications and the assignment to be performed. The Reorientation Branch after approval of the request would forward it to the Personnel and Training Branch of CAD for recruiting and processing.

In the case of private U.S. sponsorship, the project had to be submitted likewise to the Reorientation Branch of CAD by the responsible institution or organization with full information on the kind of responsibility to be assumed by the sponsor, the sources of funds to be used, the name of the person to be sent, and a description of the type of service to be performed with indication of the length of time needed for completion. Once the project was approved by the Reorientation Branch, it was forwarded to the Department of State for a decision on the political and financial responsibility of the sponsor, on the individual to be sent, and on the desirability of the project. Upon approval by both the War and State Departments, the project would be sent by the Reorientation Branch of CAD to the Theater Commander for acceptance or rejection. In case of acceptance, the latter would furnish transportation, accommodations, rations and other facilities as needed to maintain the experts while in the area and to help them achieve the purpose of their visit. The Reorientation Branch, upon approval by the Theater Commander, would refer the project to the Personnel and Training Branch of CAD for processing, which, in turn, would arrange with the Intelligence Division for a security investigation. Upon completion of the investigation, the prospective expert going to Germany would be officially invited to participate in the program.

The number of this group was always substantial but gained measurably in scope after it had been given recognition and encouragement in official policy. In 1947 a total of 50 experts went to Germany. In 1948 the number had increased to 82. In 1949 it nearly doubled to 157 (see Appendix I). As the numbers grew, so did the quality of participants, and soon included leading representatives of academe and of the professions, including persons like Professor Sigmund Neumann of Wesleyan University who examined the status and progress of the social sciences at German universities; Mrs. Chase Going Woodhouse, who studied the situation of German women and recommended, among other things, a renewal of international contacts, especially between German women leaders and women's organizations in other countries; Alice Hanson Cook, a specialist in German labor affairs, who investigated workers' education programs; and Dr. William Constable, curator of the Boston Museum of Fine Arts, who made a survey of German museums and developed a three-point program for the revival of that form of artistic life.

Nevertheless, to judge from the report of the 1949 Survey Mission the experts appear to have been rather uneven in performance. While some did excellent work with German groups, others either went with no clear conception of their task, or departed too early, or devoted their time to self-serving study projects without benefit to their German clients or to the reorientation program as a whole. The failure seems to have been due to faulty selection, inadequate briefing, and inadequate supervision.[64]

A feature of the program which evoked unqualified acclaim and introduced an effective stimulant into U.S.-German cultural relations was the appearance of the American performing artist on the scene. Under procedures established in May 1948 American artists were given special treatment. Indeed, the standard operating procedure stipulated that they were to visit Germany "to give performances for the reorientation of the German people," and incidentally also for the benefit of Allied personnel. In fact, they were "cultural ambassadors" who projected a fresh image of American art. In the beginning, the artist program was limited to a small number, not exceeding 25, and to a total period of 6 months. They had to be of "front-rank" quality and, to satisfy these requirements, were selected by a special advisory committee established by the Civil Affairs Division of the War Department.

The artists exchange was in the truest meaning of the word a voluntary program. The participants were expected to donate their services. Expenses which they incurred, e.g., travel costs, were to be covered by private sources. A sum of $10,000 was collected and placed in a revolving fund. The artists were to be considered as "Category I personnel", i.e., persons entitled to appropriate accommodations, billeting, mess privileges, and the like. On the other hand, performances for German audiences were not free but were arranged "in accordance with standard commercial procedures."

Overall responsibility for the administration of this program was assumed directly by European Command Headquarters and by OMGUS headquarters. OMGUS delegated certain responsibilities to subordinate offices. The Information Control Division was charged, *inter alia*, with selecting artists and arranging their transportation, scheduling their appearances in the allied zones of occupation, preparing publicity, and providing escort officers with dollar instruments. The Land directors and the director of the Berlin Sector were given the job of selecting and supervising the German agencies which would then make the necessary arrangements for performances, including local publicity, and for collecting the proceeds which were to be sent to the Information Control Division of OMGUS.[65]

The arts program was a success. During 1948 outstanding musicians, actors, and writers visited Germany upon the invitation of Military Government. Not all of them were U.S. citizens, but many of them were. Among the most notable were conductors Leonard Bernstein and Otto Klemperer, concert violinist Patricia Travers, harpsichordist Ralph Kirkpatrick, composer and ballad singer Tom Scott, and author Thornton Wilder.

In retrospect, it must be recorded that the visits of U.S. citizens to Germany little resembled those of Germans going to the United States and hardly made the program a two-way affair, but such was not their purpose. Few Americans went to Germany under OMGUS to study for their personal benefit. Most of them went, as before, to assist Military Government and to lend their expertise for the achievement of specific reconstruction objectives. In terms of direct or personal benefits derived, there was no equivalence between the purposes pursued or experiences gained by German and American visitors.

Yet, Dr. Wells himself was persuaded of the importance of the program and would have preferred to see it substantially increased. In a letter to the author in which he commented on the future of the exchange program, he said: "I believe it is important that cultural exchanges continue on a two-way basis. In fact, I consider it essential that more Americans go to Germany in the future than have been going in the past." [66] His reasons were twofold: first of all, he felt that their stays being of short duration, the program for American experts needed to be supplemented by a broader effort permitting them to create a fuller understanding of the United States and its institutions, thus bringing the two countries and their peoples closer together; second, he believed that thorough personal observation of conditions in Germany would make American visitors better and more authentic interpreters of Germany, thereby sustaining interest and concern of the American public about the problem of postwar relations with Germany. Dr. Wells thereby foresaw a return to more "normal" programs based on reciprocity and serving the traditional purpose of projecting the American image as a prerequisite to better mutual understanding. It was not, however, until the advent of the Fulbright program in 1952 that this concept was more fully realized.

American Students in Germany

SWNCC 269/8 had placed a temporary embargo on the visits of American students going to Germany "until conditions at German educational institutions appear sufficiently stabilized." As a result, visits of American students to Germany during the occupation never reached proportions that added up to a full-fledged program. It was not until the conclusion of the Fulbright Agreement that student exchanges in the real meaning of the term came into existence. The reasons were obvious. Because of physical destruction of the university buildings, depletion of faculty staffs by war and the denazification process, scarcity of objective study materials and in some cases any materials, plus general uncertainty regarding their functions within the educational system, German universities, to no one's surprise, did not attract foreign students in the early postwar period. Universities, moreover, were overcrowded by German students seeking to start or resume their academic careers delayed or interrupted by the war. Thus, the Civil Affairs Division of the War Department discouraged American and other foreign applicants, pointing out that German institutions could not even take care of their own.

Nevertheless, in the spring and summer of 1948 a number of universities, such as Marburg, Munich, Heidelberg, and the Technical Academy of Darmstadt began to organize special courses for foreign students, ranging from 3 to 6 weeks. The "International Holiday Courses" arranged by the Universities of Marburg, Munich, and Heidelberg jointly with the U.S. Military Government provided for the enrollment of 100 foreign and 200 German students each.[67] The faculties were international, including Italian, Swiss, Swedish, French, British, and American professors, as well as some Germans with untainted political records. No tuition costs were charged. Students studied and lived in dormitories and student houses. Courses were offered in political science, economics, sociology, comparative religion, and other subjects. But while the major emphasis was obviously on the social sciences, the ultimate purpose of the course was "to foster international understanding." All lectures, workshops, discussions, and field trips were therefore organized around the central theme: "Man in Today's World." In addition, two International Youth Conferences were held in 1948 at Munich, where 800 foreign students met with 2,000 German students to study current problems.[68]

In April of 1948, Military Government revised its policy by granting permission to foreign students to study at German universities, up to a total of one percent of the total student enrollment, and in August 1948 by approving German universities for study under the G.I. Bill of Rights. Each Land university office was held responsible for not letting the quota be exceeded. American students had to obtain formal admission from the university they planned to attend as well as a certificate of permission from local authorities to reside in or near the university town. Proof of both and a recommendation from the university officer had to be submitted to the

Education Branch of the Education and Cultural Relations Division at OMGUS headquarters. After all conditions had been met satisfactorily, the students would then be entitled to German ration cards subject to presentation of further proof to the Food and Agriculture Land Office of Military Government that dollar instruments had been exchanged in sufficient amounts to defray expenses for food, rent, tuition, and other fees for the duration of the authorized stay.[69]

German Leaders and Specialists to Other European Countries

SWNCC 269/11 of August 12, 1947, which authorized exchanges between Germany and other European countries, did not introduce a new program but merely sanctioned a practice that had been in operation for some time. Criteria of selection and approval governing exchanges with the United States were declared applicable to the exchange program with Western Europe. The program achieved some momentum in 1949 and again in 1951–1952, though for reasons rather different from those prevailing in earlier years, but it never quite equaled in scale or importance German-American exchanges. A total of 21 German leaders were sent in 1947 and a mere trickle of 14 in 1948.[70]

OMGUS did not discourage the idea of sending Germans to other European countries *per se*. But it did not favor the use of dollars, because it was convinced that "the limited amount available for cultural exchange could be more appropriately used," and with better prospects of Congressional approval, for financing the visits of Germans to the United States. It was thought, furthermore, that American funding of such programs might stunt or altogether stifle the growth of European interest in German reorientation, thus prematurely closing potential third sources of support.[71] As an alternative OMGUS proposed, therefore, the use of foreign exchange revenues derived from tourism and from "compassionate" travels up to an amount of $50,000 to finance German representation at international and other conferences held in European countries, such as those sponsored by the World Health Organization or the International Union of Local Authorities.[72] In fact, other countries showed themselves quite receptive to the OMGUS proposal, notably the United Kingdom, which, under the Education Branch of its Control Commission, began to arrange exchange visits of various kinds of persons. While most of these projects did not materialize until 1950, Great Britain had accepted in 1948–1949 a sizable number of German nationals, including nine economists, to attend a 2-week conference at Oxford; 38 to work on educational projects; and 40 to help with harvesting. Switzerland employed no less than 220 in harvesting.

European Specialists (Consultants) to Germany

Like most American experts who went to Germany in the early days of the occupation, European specialists were part-time employees of OMGUS and assisted their American colleagues and German clients in working toward democratic reform. The Standard Operating Procedure of September 29, 1948 indeed states explicitly that "the European Consultant Program can be considered as the European counterpart of the U.S. Expert Consultant Program." [73]

Procedures for project approval and administration were largely similar to those applied to American experts and consultants. Projects had to be submitted to the Special Projects Section of the Cultural Affairs Branch, Education and Cultural Relations Division, Nuremberg, Germany. Information had to be supplied on the purpose of the project; the office or individual supervising the project; place of operation and an explanation of the way in which consultant services would be used; dates, duration, and location of the project; evidence of cooperation by a responsible German agency or institution; endorsement by the OMGUS counterpart, i.e., the division or office supervising the project; and the name, address, and nationality of the person desired. Upon receipt of all required data, the Cultural Affairs Branch would procure invitational travel orders and the supervisor of the project would furnish briefing and background data to the consultant. Responsibility for the administration of the project rested with the competent initiating division or office acting through the project supervisor. The rate of payment for each person was to be not more than $35 per day.[74] Subsequent procedures [75] were sharpened and updated by adapting them to certain internal organizational changes. Approval of the project became the responsibility of the Inter-Divisional Reorientation Committee (IRC). A detailed account of the qualifications of the consultant and a resume of the job requirements were requested. Later, the payment rate was raised to $40 per day. A memo of July 26, 1949 [76] requested each OMGUS division to set up its own projects and present them to IRC for approval. Upon approval, the sponsoring division or office would, in cooperation with its Land office, select the consultant.

The program had a modest and somewhat uncertain beginning. Official records list a total of 2 participants for 1947 and 26 in 1948. The figure for 1949 was 119 (see Appendix I) on the basis of a budget request of $168,240, of which $60,000 was earmarked for the Education and Cultural Relations Division, $64,800 for the Civil Administration Division, $30,000 for the Manpower Division, and $13,440 for the Food and Agriculture Division.[77] The consultants selected were from a variety of countries, e.g., the United Kingdom, the Netherlands, Switzerland, Sweden, Denmark, Norway, and Belgium.[78] The program had obvious advantages. Travel arrangements were easier, and money outlay was less than for trans-Atlantic trips. Far more important, however, was the relative absence of cultural barriers, due to greater similarities in institutional systems, geographic conditions, languages, and general European cultural background.

The marked increase in size from 1948 to 1949 was due to a decision by Dr. Alonzo Grace, head of the Education and Cultural Relations Division, who recognized the importance of cultural affinities in the selection of foreign experts. At the second Berchtesgaden Conference in October 1948, Dr. Grace announced that it would be his policy in the future to bring to Germany fewer American experts and to rely more heavily on experts from surrounding European countries, thereby drawing more directly on the great wealth of resources available on the Continent.[79]

Notes

CHAPTER I

1. *Germany, 1947–1949, The Story in Documents*, Dept. of State, publ. 3556, (Washington, D.C.: U.S. Government Printing Office, Mar. 1950), pp. 21, 47 ff.; Dept. of State press releases 479, 480, June 5, 1945, Dept. of State Library.
2. *Germany, 1947–1949, op. cit.*, pp. 21 ff.
3. *The Axis in Defeat, A Collection of Documents on American Policy Toward Germany and Japan*, Dept. of State (Washington, D.C.: U.S. Government Printing Office, 1945), pp. 62–70.
4. *Ibid.*, p. 69.
5. *Germany, 1947–1949, op. cit.*, pp. 21–33.
6. *Ibid.*, p. 23.
7. *Ibid.*, p. 34.
8. Roger Morgan, *The United States and West Germany, 1945–1973: A Study in Alliance Politics* (London: Oxford Univ. Press, 1974), p. 20.
9. *Germany, 1947–1949, op. cit.*, pp. 3–8.
10. See *ibid.*, p. 59.
11. *Ibid.*
12. John Edward Smith, ed., *The Papers of General Lucius D. Clay, Germany, 1945–1949*, 2 vols. (Indianapolis: Indiana Univ. Press, 1974), I, Item No. 157.
13. Full text in *Germany, 1947–1949, op.cit.*, pp. 34–41.
14. *Ibid.*, pp. 356–359.
15. *Ibid.*, pp. 541–542.
16. *Ibid.*, pp. 33–41, 180.
17. *Ibid.*, pp. 550–551.
18. Reactions were not negative throughout. When a few years later American educational programs were cut back, German teachers raised their voices

in protest against what they felt was a premature retreat from their declared stand on behalf of educational reform. In an article in the *Allgemeine Lehrerzeitung* of Mar. 15, 1952, Dr. Karl Bungardt, member of the Executive Committee of the Federal Association of Teachers, wrote: "It was not an effort but a pleasure, to study again Directive #54 . . . Again we were pleased, even enthusiastic about the wealth of progressive ideas expressed in it . . . Only evil-minded or uninformed people can pretend that the realization of such a program would mean the Americanization of German education. It contains the best ideas of the German school reform movement, even after a detour through America."

19. Hans Speier, "Social Order and the Risks of War," *Papers in Political Sociology* (George W. Stewart, Publisher, Inc., 1952). Chap. 30: "Re-education—The U.S. Policy," pp. 398–399. Speier points out that "the idea of re-education grew out of the division of the world into good and evil nations, with the good nations united to conquer evil." However, Speier argues, "strong moral convictions lead to neglect of time and circumstances," the circumstances being, *inter alia*, the rapid collapse of the unity of the conquerors and reeducation becoming a relativistic element determined by those who exercise control in the territory or zone of their governance. *Ibid.*, pp. 400–401.

20. *Ibid.*, p. 402; O/FADRC, RG 59, 58 D 373, Box 1659.

21. Report of U.S. Education Mission to Germany, submitted by letter from George F. Zook, Chairman, to Lt. Gen. Lucius D. Clay, Deputy Military Governor, Sept. 20, 1946; file: "Education Mission, Alphabetical Subject Files, Community Activities Branch—Youth Activities, Public Affairs," Education and Cultural Relations Division, Headquarters Military Government for Germany (U.S.); WNRC, RG 260, Box 295 2/5.

22. Comment on Report of U.S. Education Mission to Germany, addressed to Director, Civil Affairs Commission, War Department, Attention Maj. Gen. O.P. Echols, Office of Military Government for Germany. *Ibid.*

23. *The Papers of General Lucius D. Clay*, *op.cit.*, I, Item No. 137.

24. Included information centers, registration of copyrights, press and magazine publications, *ibid.*, Item No. 190.

25. *Ibid.*

26. Appendix to Memorandum No. 1059 of U.S. Political Adviser, Aug. 20, 1947, NA, 811.42762 SE/8-2047, copy in CU/H.

27. The full text of the policy is to be found in *Germany, 1947–1949*, *op.cit.*, pp. 611–612.

28. Dept. of State press release 267, U.S. Dept. of State Library.

29. See Appendix I.

30. Among the most active sponsors were the American Friends Service Committee, the Mennonite Central Committee, the National Catholic Welfare Conference, and the World Council of Churches.

31. For further details, see Henry P. Pilgert, *The West German Educational System* (Historical Division, Office of the U.S. High Commissioner for Germany, 1953).

32. O/FADRC, 58 D 373, Box 1659.

33. (Unsigned) message of visiting Army officer to War Department, Jan. 24, 1947. NA, CAD 350, Case 5.

34. Memorandum from Henry J. Kellermann to William T. Stone, Oct. 21, 1947, listing points to be covered by Charles E. Saltzman, Assistant Secretary for Occupied Areas, in his forthcoming talks with General Clay. O/FADRC, RG 59, 1258 56 D 12 and 57 D 22; copy in CU/H.

CULTURAL RELATIONS—INSTRUMENT OF FOREIGN POLICY

35. *The Papers of General Lucius D. Clay, op.cit.*, I, Item No. 244, Aug. 7, 1947.
36. Memorandum from D.C. Stone to James R. Sundquist, Nov. 15, 1947, summarizing meeting with Dr. Herman Wells, NA, RG 165; copy in CU/H.
37. Report on Wells Mission, May 4, 1948, Dept. of State, O/FADRC, 58 D 373, Box 1659.
38. *Ibid.*
39. *News Bulletin*, Institute of International Education, XXIII (May 1, 1948), p. 3.
40. *Ibid.*
41. Information relating to this paragraph supplied by Dr. Herman Wells in letter to author, Dec. 3, 1975; copy in CU/H.
42. It should be recorded, however, that the increase was not reflected in a corresponding growth of the budget. Allocations for reorientation expenditures, it is true, had been raised to $1,944,437, but most of this money had been earmarked for film production and acquisition with only $208,178 set aside for American experts and consultants. To this total had been added the revenues from the sale of publications produced by OMGUS which were actually plowed back into the rest of the program. However, these profits had become negligible, largely as the result of the recent currency reform. The funds for exchanges thus came mostly from private sources.
43. For both statements, see *Germany: 1947-1949, op. cit.*, p. 614; Dr. Grace's statement was incorporated as an objective in the "Regulations Governing the Function and Operation of the Education and Cultural Relations Division," Sept. 8, 1949.
44. "The Cumulative Report of Cultural Affairs Covering the Period 1 May 1948 – 30 April 1949"; file: "Cumulative Report," Alphabetical Subject Files, Exchange Branch—Student Exchange, Public Affairs—Education and Cultural Relations Division, Headquarters Military Government for Germany (U.S.); WNRC, RG 260, Box 335 3/5.
45. "The Cultural Exchange Program of the Office of Military Government for Germany (U.S.)." First draft of a Foreword on the "Role of Cultural Exchange in Military Government for Germany (U.S.)"; file: "Reorientation-Cultural Exchange, Analysis and Planning Sec., Alphabetical Subject Files, Management and Budget Branch, Control Division MG. Headquarters Military Government for Germany (U.S.); WNRC, RG 260, Box 257 2/5.
46. SWNCC 269/11, NA, RG 353; copy in CU/H.
47. Letter from Robert P. Patterson, Secretary of War, to the Secretary of State, June 12, 1947, NA, 811.42762, SE/6-1247; copy in CU/H.
48. "Procedures for Interchange of Persons under Reorientation Programs," submitted to the Secretary of State by letter of transmittal from the Secretary of War, June 12, 1947; "S.O.P. for Sending German Experts to the United States," issued on July 26, 1947. The criteria established by this S.O.P. were largely adopted by HICOG; copies in CU/H.
49. Letter from Gilbert White, President of Haverford College, to General Draper, Dec. 8, 1947. WNRC, CAD 350, Box 5.
50. Internal State Department memorandum from O'Sullivan to General Hilldring, Oct. 28, 1946. NA, 811.4276, SE/1-147-6.3047.
51. "The Cumulative Report of Cultural Affairs Covering the Period 1 May 1948 – 30 April 1949," see above; WNRC, RG 260, Box 335 3/5.
52. An especially prestigious group of seven leading administrators arrived in early 1949. It included, among others, Dr. Gerhard Mueller, Director

of the Chancery of Wuerttemberg-Hohenzollern who later became Chief Justice of the Constitutional Court of the Federal Republic, and Dr. Karl Mommer, then member of the Peace Bureau. Press release, Public Information Office, OMGUS, 24 Jan. 1949, file: "German Consultants—Budget Bureau Project, CAD," Office of the Chief, Alphabetical Subject Files, Exchange Branch, "Public Affairs"—Education and Cultural Relations Division, Headquarters Military Government for Germany (U.S.) ; WNRC, RG 260, Box 335 3/5.

53. Among the journalists traveling to the United States during 1949 were some of Germany's most outstanding editors, such as Werner Friedmann, Karl Gerold, Eugen Kogon, Franz Karl Maier, Oscar W. Reschke. OMGUS cables, Apr. 28, 1949, file: "German Consultants—ISD," *ibid.*
54. Press release, Public Information Office, OMGUS, Mar. 17, 1949, *ibid.*
55. OMGUS cable, Mar. 10, 1949: file: "German Consultants—CAD cables, *ibid.*
56. The Cumulative Report of Cultural Affairs, May 1, 1948–Apr. 30, 1949, *ibid.*
57. Procedures for Interchange of Persons Under Reorientation Program, transmitted by letter of June 12, 1947, from Secretary of War to Secretary of State, NA, 811/42762 SE/6–1247 ; copy in CU/H.
58. Letter from General Noce to Congressman Case, May 25, 1948, and enclosed memorandum on student exchanges ; copy in CU/H.
59. *Ibid.*
60. "Standard Operating Procedure for Student Exchange, 28 October 1948." File: "Reorientation-Cultural Exchanges," Analysis and Planning Section, Alphabetical Subject Files, Management and Budget Branch, Control Division MG, Headquarters Military Government for Germany (U.S.). WNRC, RG 260, Box 357 2/5 ; copy in CU/H.
61. "The American College and the German Student Exchange Program," report of the Education and Religious Affairs Branch, Internal Affairs and Communication Division, OMGUS, Nov. 4, 1947, O/FADRC, RG 59, 66 A 363, Box 752; copy in CU/H. Also, Alphabetical Subject Files, Exchange Branch-Student Exchange, "Public Affairs," Education and Cultural Relations Division, Headquarters Military Government for Germany (U.S.) ; WNRC, RG 260, Box 335 3/5 ; copy in CU/H.
62. In the appendix to the letter to Congressman Case (see above) General Noce pointed out that funds for exchange of German students had actually been requested for FY 1948 but had been refused by Congress. A similar proposal had then been made for 1949. H.R. 6801 had thereupon included an item of $220,000 for exchanges.
63. The reader will notice discrepancies when comparing the data in this chart with statistics quoted elsewhere in this study. Data vary indeed slightly though not sufficiently to distort overall trends. The inconsistencies are due to the fact that in computing totals HICOG and the Dept. often used different criteria, i.e., proposed or estimated exchange grants, grants actually given and actual arrivals or returnees.
64. Henry P. Pilgert, *The Exchange of Persons Program in Western Germany* (Historical Division, Office of the U.S. High Commissioner for Germany, 1951), *op. cit.,* pp. 66–67.
65. Standard Operating Procedure for Visiting Artists Program, issued by Headquarters, European Command, Office of the Commander-in-Chief, Berlin, May 3, 1948; file: "Reorientation— Cultural Exchanges," Analysis and Planning Sec., Alphabetical Subject Files, Management and Budget

Branch, Control Division MG, Headquarters Military Government for Germany (U.S.) ; WNRC, RG 260, Box 257 2/5 ; copy in CU/H.
66. O/FADRC, 12582, 56 D 21, 57 D 22–WNRC, RG 306, 63 A 190, Boxes 652–653.
67. Announcement, Office of Military Government for Germany (U.S.), Public Information Office (OMGUS–3–C–76), Berlin, Germany, Mar. 25, 1948. NA, RG 331 ; copy in CU/H.
68. General Lucius D. Clay, *Decision in Germany* (New York: Doubleday & Co., Inc., 1960), p. 301.
69. "Standard Order of Procedure on Administration of Foreign Students to German Universities in U.S. Zone of Occupation of April 27, 1948," file: "Admission of Foreign Students to German Universities," Alphabetical Subject Files, Exchange Branch-Student Exchange, "Public Affairs"—Education and Cultural Relations Division, Headquarters Military Government for Germany (U.S.) ; WNRC, RG 260, Box 335 3/5.
70. Statistics are somewhat contradictory. According to our best source, 80 graduate nurses went to Switzerland in 1947 for a 6-month training course, and elementary school teachers were sent to Sweden to study modern teaching methods. Conceivably, some of the programs were financed from funds other than those of the U.S. Government. (Pilgert, *The Exchange of Persons Program in Western Germany, op. cit.*, p. 31).
71. Memorandum by James R. Sundquist, Control Officer, OMGUS, Apr. 5, 1949, WNRC, RG 331 (OMGUS), AG 23.2 (CO) ; copy in CU/H.
72. *Ibid.*
73. WNRC, RG 331 (OMGUS) ; copy in CU/H.
74. *Ibid.*
75. Issued by the Inter-Divisional Reorientation Committee (IRC) of OMGUS on Mar. 17, 1949. *Ibid.*
76. *Ibid.*
77. Weekly Newsletter 2, Oct. 4, 1948, Education and Cultural Relations Division, Cultural Affairs Branch, Nuremberg, WNRC, RC 331 (OMGUS) ; copy in CU/H.
78. See Pilgert, *The Exchange of Persons Program in Western Germany, op. cit.*, p. 32.
79. "Out of the Rubble," Address on the Reorientation of the German People—The Berchtesgaden Conference—by Alonzo G. Grace, Director, Education and Cultural Relations Division. Analysis and Planning Sec., Alphabetical Subject Files, Management and Budget Branch, Headquarters Military Government for Germany (U.S.). WNRC, RG 260, Box 257 2/5.

CHAPTER II

Administration of the OMGUS Program

Functional Responsibility—The Project Approach

The development of projects that made up the total exchange program was strictly the responsibility of each of the OMGUS divisions directly concerned; it also was their function to solicit sponsors in the United States.[1] It was this arrangement more than anything else that established and shaped the character of the exchange program as one dictated by substantive rather than logistical considerations. Further, it gave the program its proper focus, format, and content. The mandate of each office and division determined the selection of projects and candidates. The authority of the various functional units, in turn, stemmed from directives and regulations issued by the Allied Control Council and by the Military Governments in each of the zones of occupation. The directives had to do with such problems as school reform, administration and supervision of education, political activities, courts and judicial procedures, government institutions and elections. Each of the major offices, divisions, and branches was assigned responsibility for the execution of one or more of these directives and nearly every unit soon seized upon the exchange program as a means of enlisting German participation in one form or another in the implementation of its programs.[2] To do so was both logical and practical. Given the conditions prevailing in Germany in 1947, 1948, and 1949, with public and private institutions only slowly recovering from physical destruction and political corruption, with professional and technical manpower at a premium—in short, with a critical shortage of resources in the face of overwhelming demands for expertise and guidance, assistance was needed from the outside. OMGUS' efforts had to be supplemented and, in time, superseded by efforts from within, that is, by Germans who had observed and studied democracy in action outside Germany proper. The exchange program offered the opportunity for them to do so. It came to be recognized as the long arm of the reorientation effort.

55

The bulk of exchanges sponsored by Military Government in the early years fell upon the Education and Religious Affairs Branch (see Appendix VI). The objective of the Branch was to bring about a democratic reform of the German educational system on all levels in accordance with the principles stipulated in Allied Control Council Directive 54. To achieve equal educational opportunity (Principle 1), it demanded that "German education . . . must be so organized and so conducted as to give continuous opportunity and guidance to each individual to develop to the best of his ability, irrespective of race, color, creed, financial condition or political belief . . ."[3] This meant freedom of teaching and learning. The policy enunciated by Dr. Grace in October 1948, for the Education and Cultural Relations Division, deemphasized the technical aspects of educational reform and raised policy to the level of broad humanitarian principles, e.g., "dignity and rights of the individual, deference to the personal conviction of others and to universal opinion, freedom of thought and expression, and liberal social attitudes." The resources of the Division were to be used as a means of achieving a reform of German society *in toto* through a broad change in social concepts, attitudes, and institutions.[4]

The diversified structure of the Division entrusted this task to a number of subdivisions and branches pursuing the objectives in critical sectors of German society. The Religious Affairs Branch was concerned with the restoration of organized religion. Taking its guidance from a statement by the State-War-Navy Coordinating Committee and issued as Directive 12 by the European Advisory Committee and JCS 1143 by the Joint Chiefs of Staff, the policy of OMGUS assured freedom of worship according to the dictates of the individual, protection and fair treatment to all religious elements; and was so proclaimed by General Eisenhower in April 1945.[5] The policy was dictated by humanitarian and practical considerations. OMGUS relied heavily on the prestige of the church and, in particular, on those elements within the Catholic and Protestant communities which had a proven record of resistance to National Socialism.

The Community Education Branch had as its principal objective the development of grass roots support for democratic institutions and processes through group initiative and cooperative action of voluntary organizations, community councils, and the like. The purpose was to stimulate citizen participation, individual responsibility, and tolerance in civic and social life—qualities whose absence at critical moments in German history had proved fatal to political stability and democratic reform.[6]

Adult education classes, as postulated by Control Council Directive 56,[7] October 28, 1947, "to prepare active workers for the democratic education of Germany," now offered a chance to supplement school training. SWNCC 269/9 of February 4, 1947,[8] singled out youth as a special group to be reoriented, and encouraged "initiative and active participation of German Youth in the reconstruction of German community life." Ninety percent of the young people left school in their early teens after consuming a scholastic diet that was highly deficient in civic education.

Women received special attention. They outnumbered men by 7½ million, yet they were still struggling for liberation from a deeply underprivileged status in professional and civic life. In 1948, a special Women's Affairs Section in OMGUS was established "to aid, advise and encourage individual German women to assume their full responsibility as citizens in the building of a democratic society and to assist voluntary associations of women to exercise a constructive role in developing democratic attitudes and democratic principles in community life." [9]

Other HICOG divisions equally concerned with reorientation also used exchanges as a means of accomplishing their objectives. The Civil Administration Division, e.g., devoted its efforts to helping create a democratic cadre of political and civic leaders who could be relied upon to rebuild the civil service, legislative, and other key institutions greatly depleted by the necessity for de-Nazification, war casualties, and the exodus of many members of the prewar elite. The Division's aim was to create "a lively citizen-government relationship which will strengthen the cause of civic responsibility and give life to the democratic structure and procedure." [10] To do so involved, among other things, the development of local self-government, the protection of civil liberties, and the exercise of the franchise by periodic and free elections.[11]

The Legal Division was principally concerned with the restoration of a viable democratic judiciary. This required not merely inducement to introduce democratic principles into the legal system, but a major effort to insure acceptance and support of a totally reformed legal system by the German public. Another program feature of major importance was a systematic attempt to broaden the scope of legal training and the horizon of law students by a new emphasis on ethical and social issues.[12]

The objectives of the Manpower Division were the restoration of democratic trade unions and the creation of an effective working relationship between labor and management and labor and government.[13] The Labor-Management Techniques Branch of that Division was especially concerned with the establishment of relations between German trade unions and their counterparts in the United States, in order to bridge the gap caused by 12 years of isolation that had left even what remained of the German labor movement wholly uninformed of developments in unionism on the outside.

The Information Services Division saw as its principal function the rehabilitation and democratization of German information media, partly through the creation of media, e.g., RIAS (Radio in the American Sector of Berlin), *Der Monat*, a monthly magazine, *Die Neue Zeitung*, a daily paper which at one time had a circulation of 1.6 million, under OMGUS auspices; and partly by a systematic attempt to familiarize German editors, columnists, commentators, reporters, news broadcasters, and other media technicians with democratic practices, and new techniques of printing and the like. The purpose of this program was to help German media specialists to modernize their output and to improve their professional and technical skills, as well as to demonstrate to them the importance of vigilance and independence vis-a-vis encroachments by official authorities and pressure groups.[14]

Finally, the Food and Agriculture Division was concerned with both the political and occupational status of the farmer. It introduced organizational reforms and new production and consumption concepts and techniques. Special attention was given to the training of young farmers.

A new procedure was developed to regulate the initiation and clearance of projects originating outside OMGUS headquarters. Responsibility for the development of projects was charged to each of the substantive divisions but could be launched at the Land (State) level. Land offices submitted their proposals to the corresponding OMGUS division at the zonal level which in turn placed them, along with proposals of their own, before the Interdivisional Reorientation Committee. The latter made the ultimate decision—approval or disapproval.[15]

These, then, were the functional units and their multiple purposes which gave exchanges under OMGUS their special content. The complexity of the objectives pursued by each called for a type of organization which broke each division or branch program into individual projects and which grouped leaders and specialists selected for exchange visits around such projects. This was, indeed, the way in which OMGUS proceeded.

Most of the projects were developed by the Education and Religious Affairs Branch and subsequently, after the organizational change already noted, by the Education and Cultural Relations Division. The program moved slowly at first. Early budgets contained proposals for visits of groups organized according to occupation (professors, teachers, administrators) or professional specialization (e.g., subject matter: education, literature, history, psychology, sociology).[16] The final budget proposed by OMGUS in 1949 for fiscal year 1950 foresaw a total of 241 individual projects under 33 different titles sponsored by the Education and Cultural Relations Division. Most of the projects involved the visits of German educators (1,255) to the United States and of American educational experts (88) to Germany. All projects addressed critical needs in the fields of elementary, secondary, higher and vocational education, and teacher training. Examples were: the use of audio-visual aid equipment in classroom teaching, research in child growth and development, educational psychology, citizenship training, social studies, vocational guidance, education for the handicapped, curriculum improvement, textbook writing, and comparative education. The purpose behind the selection of these subjects was to enable educators to deal with some of the most notorious deficiencies in the German system by studying theory and practice of education in other (American and European) countries. Comparison, it was hoped, might encourage German educators to come to grips with fundamental weaknesses inherent in the philosophy and structure of the German system, among others, the segregation at the age of ten, of the gifted and socially advantaged, the upper-crust children, from the less endowed ones and, in so doing, to reserve solely for the former admission to secondary and higher education and eventually to the professions.

Other projects were designed to remedy "flaws" in the German training of teachers and school administrators by having these persons observe the organization, administration, operation, and the architecture of schools in the United States.

Still other projects were intended to free German schools from their isolation within the community by demonstrating the benefits of lay participation and local initiative in supervision and planning, e.g., through parent-teacher associations and cooperation with other community groups. Finally, various projects were devoted to the encouragement of teacher and student initiative in forming organizations representing their interests and in practicing self government.[17]

Other OMGUS divisions and branches followed the example of the Education and Cultural Relations Division although on a somewhat lesser scale. The Civil Administration Division proposed a total of 47 projects under 9 titles labeled governmental affairs, political parties, civil service, books, films, city planning, social science, public welfare, and public health. They called for the visits of 613 Germans to the United States and of 55 Americans to Germany. The Legal Division listed 3 projects involving the exchange of 155 Germans and of 16 American experts. The Manpower Division had 2 projects in which 155 Germans and 19 Americans were to participate. The Information Services Division presented only one project for 52 representatives of the German press. The Food and Agriculture Division, on the other hand, proposed a total of 42 projects grouped under 4 titles: technical assistance, agricultural extension, home economics, and student exchanges. These involved a total of 558 Germans and 12 Americans.[18]

How many of these projects actually got off the ground is difficult to determine from available records. Educators were among the first to arrive in the United States, some as early as 1948. As far as the other groups were concerned, it appears that most of the more significant projects did not move forward until 1949 when seven high-ranking German administrators visited the United States under the auspices of the Bureau of the Budget. They were followed in relatively short order by similar groups of federal, state, and local officials, mayors, county executives, city planners, women leaders, journalists, and other media experts. The first major group of students came in the fall of 1949.

Moreover, under OMGUS even the project approach remained by and large a concept that was never fully realized and, in fact, not completely accepted. It even came under fire. In a memorandum to his Land directors of March 23, 1949,[19] Major General George P. Hays, the Deputy Military Governor, sharply criticized what appeared to him a waste of money and motion on behalf of reorientation and democratization. "While it is not intended," Hays said, "to criticize our present program as being unworthy in any respect, we are scattering our efforts and our funds at present over a rather broad field with very little knowledge of the concrete results obtained from any project." Hays ordered that a survey be made to identify the accomplishments up to then and to determine what was valuable enough to be continued. A survey of this kind, he suggested, would assure optimum use of funds and manpower, even if it might involve the termination of certain projects, once a German Government had been established.

General Hays' criticism was shared by officers of the Department of State who had felt for some time that existing machinery at the disposal of Military Government and the Department of the Army was not adequate to administer an expanding and increasingly sophisticated program and to do justice to the multitude of projects proposed or contemplated.[20] The project approach was a step in the right direction, but it seemed premature. Major changes in policy, organization, and funding were required before it could be expected to become an effective operational tool.

The Administrative Structure

The problem of finding a proper administrative structure to support a unique exchange program such as this one, with specific foreign policy goals, proved to be extremely difficult and was, in fact, never settled by OMGUS to the full satisfaction of all parties involved. As shown above, the exchange program had neither autonomy nor a substantive identity of its own, but was a service operation that took direction from a multitude of divisions and branches, all of which had reorientation functions and shared the reorientation funds and the services of the exchange operation. Instead of forming an independent unit, the exchange division was part of one of the functional divisions.

In the beginning, exchanges were handled by the Interchange-of-Persons Office which, in turn, was a sub-unit of the Education and Religious Affairs and Communications Division. The Education and Religious Affairs Branch was raised subsequently to the rank of Education and Cultural Relations Division. It was ably led and staffed by distinguished educators, such as Thomas Alexander and John Taylor of Columbia University, Edward Y. Hartshorne, Jr. of Harvard, and A. E. Zucker of the University of Maryland.

In 1946 the staff of the Education and Religious Affairs unit numbered 55. Exchange programs were assigned to the Cultural Affairs Branch, one of the Division's units, the others being the Education Branch, the Religious Affairs Branch, and the Group Activities Branch. The responsibility of the Cultural Affairs Branch was to oversee policies and procedures regarding international cultural exchanges between Germany and other countries. Its major operational function included, *inter alia*, the selection, processing, and program administration of all German nationals traveling to the United States and other countries on a cultural mission, and the coordination of program planning and budgeting for all expert consultants going to Germany from the United States or other countries on a reorientation project under the sponsorship of the U.S. Government.[21]

The services of the Cultural Affairs Branch were available not only to the Education and Cultural Relations Division but also to the Civil Administration Division, the Legal Division, the Manpower Division, the Information Services Division, and the Food and Agriculture Division to assist them in performing the reorientation aspects of their programs. There was collaboration among these divisions, especially between the Education and Cultural Relations Division and the Civil Administration Division which together, for all practical purposes, formed the nucleus of the OMGUS reorientation program. The number of sponsors in the United States, the multitude of projects, and the relative paucity of funds that had to be equitably shared, called for tighter arrangements insuring stronger and regularized coordination.

In response to this need OMGUS created in July 1948 [22] an Interdivisional Reorientation Committee (IRC) which was given the job of coordinating the programs of the several divisions, of developing plans and procedures for implementing all aspects of the reorientation program and, to that end, of enlisting the interest of all offices and divisions. Furthermore, IRC was to establish criteria for the evaluation of projects, i.e., to coordinate projects and procedures for soliciting private funds, materials, and services and to review and approve all projects suggested by any one of the component groups of the IRC, and make appropriate recommendations. The Committee (IRC) was composed of the Director of the Education and Cultural Relations Division acting as chairman, the Director of the Civil Administration Division, the Director of the Information Services Division, the Control Officer, and the Chief of the Cultural Affairs Branch or anyone whom the Division chief had designated as his proxy. Representatives of other divisions, such as the Legal, Manpower, or Food and Agriculture Divisions would attend meetings at which projects of direct concern to them were discussed. Responsibility for the budget and fiscal aspects was assigned to the Control Office of OMGUS. The establishment of IRC marked considerable progress in comparison to the situation existing before; but the IRC did not succeed altogether in terminating competition among sponsoring units for funds, through firm priorities or quota allocations, nor did it reduce the flood of projects proposed by various divisions and branches.

The horizontal layout of controls at headquarters level was supported by a vertical structure consisting of field offices at the Land level. These field offices were advised by Interdivisional Reorientation or Cultural Exchange Committees on the selection of experts and students. Attached to each Committee were groups of persons (panels) representing the interests of the various functional divisions concerned, e.g., the Education and Cultural Relations Division, the Civil Administration Division, and so on. Other panels could be added, as circumstances warranted. The panels received and reviewed applications, made preliminary selections, and submitted their choices with evaluative comments to the Land military government office.[23]

The responsibilities of the Land offices were rather comprehensive as far as students were concerned. They included selection and appointment of the so-called Committees on Selection, oral interviews with candidates, chairing the Committees on Selection, evaluating the Committees' nominations, formulating policy at the Land level, and forwarding recommendations for program improvement to OMGUS, et al.[24]

Compared to the OMGUS operation, the organization in the United States in the early days was relatively small but, despite its modest size, fairly complicated. Essentially, stateside agencies provided policy direction and technical and logistic support, so-called "backstopping." From 1945–1949 the State-War-Navy Coordinating Committee (SWNCC) exercised overall responsibility for policy. Later this function was returned to the separate agencies in Washington and in the period which followed the program was supervised by the Department of State in close cooperation with the War Department, which then became the Department of the Army. Within the Department of State responsibility for matters relating to Occupied Germany devolved upon the Bureau of Public Affairs under Assistant Secretary William Benton, followed by Howland H. Sargeant (Acting), up to 1948, and upon the Bureau for Occupied Areas, under General John H. Hilldring, and later Charles E. Saltzman, each of whom consulted with the appropriate geographic desks on significant policies and programs. The principal liaison officer in the Bureau for Occupied Areas was Benjamin O'Sullivan. Central responsibility for the initiation, coordination, and supervision of policy was assigned to the Area Division for Occupied Areas (ADO) under the direction of Henry P. Leverich, later of Hans Speier, followed by the author. ADO, later renamed Public Affairs Overseas Program Staff (POS), was a staff unit under the Assistant Secretary of State for Public Affairs. The Division (ADO) approved or disapproved applications of candidates and sponsors and projects.

All operational functions, i.e., chiefly backstopping activities, were discharged by the Reorientation Branch of the Civil Affairs Division of the War (Army) Department under Colonel Robert B. McRae, and subsequently Colonels Bernard B. McMahon and Leon P. Irvin. The Reorientation Branch was responsible, among other things, for establishing program policy (jointly with the Department of State), performing liaison between all interested parties and agencies involved, approving projects requested by the Theater Commander or private sponsors, evaluating security clearances, employing the services of the Institute of International Education to administer the student program, and arranging the transfer of funds to the International Exchange of Persons Division of the Department of State to act as agent for the administration of programs for visiting American experts and specialists. The Personnel and Training Branch of CAD was assigned the function of recruiting and processing all individuals as requested by the Reorientation

Branch for service under the exchange program provided that such individuals passed the security investigatiton and met minimum requirements to qualify as experts.[25]

Private Support

The governmental organization functioned well considering the extremely complicated mechanism created to administer the program. As the program grew at an ever-increasing pace, however, it became apparent that in the absence of adequate funds through Congressional appropriations, the Government lacked the resources to run an effective program. Dr. Wells had been quick to recognize this dilemma. Quite evidently upon his initiative, the Office of the Cultural Adviser, Headquarters, European Command, wrote a memorandum in which it pointed out that the Department of the Army was simply unable to approach private institutions, foundations, and individuals with requests for money or for contributions of personnel and materials to aid its exchange program in Germany.[26]

The Civil Affairs Division in Washington had indicated that it did not possess the funds nor the personnel to recruit individuals to serve as visiting experts and artists in Germany, to say nothing of the far more complicated and absorbing process of developing private resources for programming the vists of German visitors to the United States. Consequently, the memorandum went on to say, the problem had devolved upon OMGUS itself. Yet distance and lack of direct contact had slowed down progress. It was "manifestly difficult, if not impossible," to achieve any measurable success under these conditions. What was needed was "some kind of supporting organization" in the United States, more specifically, an "officially recognized nonprofit organization of private citizens and affiliated institutions in the United States which would take the initiative in raising financial support, stimulating interest in this program in governmental and civilian circles, encouraging and selecting experts to come to Germany, and encouraging sponsorship by appropriate stateside organizations of visits to the United States by governmental and private leaders." Such an organization, the memo suggested, "would be invaluable for coordinating and implementing in the United States the democratization programs projected by Military Government for Germany."

The organization, Dr. Wells proposed,[27] should be directed by "a group of noted, public-spirited citizens who are distinguished leaders in their respective fields, persons whose reputations and influence would enable them to work *with* and *through* existing foundations, councils, and institutions in the interest of German reeducation."

Actually, considering the meager resources at the disposal of the Army, the latter had done a most creditable job in alerting the educational and philanthropic community to the importance of the program and in enlisting the interest of key organizations and institutions. It had approached the Institute of International Education as early as 1946 to secure its cooperation in bringing German students to the United States. The Institute, in turn, had written to more than 100 colleges and universities asking them to provide for incoming German students full maintenance and scholarships,[28] once it became clear that governmental funds were not available. IIE had received favorable replies from such institutions as the Universities of Georgia and Notre Dame, Oberlin College, Pendle Hill (a Quaker college near Philadelphia), Union Theological Seminary, and Washington State University at Pullman. After the program had grown to major proportions in the late forties, the Institute, under contract to the War Department, assumed responsibility for the administration of the student program, including raising funds for travel in the U.S. and incidental expenses.

Following the release of SWNNC 269/8, the Civil Affairs Division sent identical letters to 31 organizations and institutions, including the Rockefeller Foundation, the Carnegie Endowment for International Peace, the National Education Association, the American Council on Education, the Institute of International Education, and many church and cultural, religious, social and civic organizations, calling attention to the new policy and emphasizing that the program in Germany was entirely dependent on private support.[29] Such private support, the letters pointed out, might consist of scholarships, training opportunities for specialists and experts, funds for maintenance and transportation, or any other special project considered appropriate for the program.[30] The response was wide and varied. The University of Chicago, for example, offered to release eight to ten of its faculty members to work as a group at a German university for one or two semesters, and, moreover, promised to obtain the necessary funds to do so. Columbia University indicated that it had obtained $25,000 to bring six German broadcasters to the United States for a 6-months' orientation period. The American Friends Service Committee offered to revive and expand its school affiliation program by including 25 30 German schools beginning in the fall of 1947. The Experiment in International Living of Putney, Vermont, declared itself ready to send 30 college students to Germany and Austria to reestablish contacts with their counterparts in these and other countries to help in jobs of physical reconstruction.[31]

But the Army lacked the necessary capability for a follow-up and for full exploitation of the opportunities afforded them by generous donors. Private organizations complained that correspondence remained unanswered and that projects got bogged down in bureaucratic details.[32] Corrective action was needed to deal with what appeared to be a critical deficiency in the organization of the program and what threatened to become a serious public relations problem.

Washington acted with dispatch. The Department of State approved Dr. Wells' plan of establishing a nonprofit organization of private citizens in the United States to assist the Government in furthering cultural interchange with Germany. The Department, moreover, while declaring that operational responsibility within the Government should remain with the Army, offered to render all assistance possible under the circumstances and proposed that the work of establishing the requisite organization on the governmental and nongovernmental side start as soon as possible. The element of urgency was suggested by the approaching beginning of the academic year and the anticipated transfer of operational responsibilities in Germany from the auspices of the Army to the Department of State, then scheduled for July 1, 1948.[33] In its reply the Department of the Army expressed its gratification over the readiness of the Department of State to accept the plan and proposed, in turn, that the Department should assume responsibility for establishing the nongovernmental unit and perfecting plans for implementation under its control.[34]

As a result, an Advisory Committee on Cultural and Educational Relations was created in the fall of 1948 under the auspices of the American Council on Education with the help of a grant from the Rockefeller Foundation. It was composed of representatives of leading U.S. cultural and educational organizations and interests. Its name was later changed to Commission on the Occupied Areas (COA). Dr. Wells assumed the chairmanship and Harold E. Snyder, who was directing several international projects for the American Council on Education, became its director.

The COA's stated purpose was "to develop and strengthen sound approaches to cultural and educational affairs in the occupied countries (i.e., Japan, Austria, and Germany), stressing particularly the establishment of mutual relations between institutions and organizations in the United States and those in the occupied areas." Primary emphasis was to be placed on "the promotion of such activities in the educational and cultural fields as will encourage the development of democracy in these areas." [35]

COA's specific functions were listed as follows: (1) review of program policy in consultation with U.S. Government departments and agencies, concerning educational and related activities in occupied areas; (2) negotiation with independent organizations for services required to implement educational programs; (3) assistance in recommending qualified American personnel for overseas service;

(4) stimulation and coordination of voluntary reconstruction aid to supplement government funds; (5) assistance in arrangements for foreign personnel coming to the United States; (6) establishment of technical panels to advise military government in special fields as needed; and (7) preparation of reports and recommendations to governmental and nongovernmental agencies directly concerned.[36]

The primary role of COA was that of acting as adviser to the Government on private support for the reorientation program and of opening up additional private resources to supplement the capabilities of the government, not so much as regards funds, although in 1948 such were still badly needed, as in terms of much greater professional and technical know-how and institutional sponsorship for German exchange students and visitors. As OMGUS control functions over the total program shrank and were gradually replaced by private advice and assistance, eventually by cooperation, the role of voluntary agencies in the reorientation effort gained greater momentum. The members of COA were firmly convinced that "cooperation between government and the voluntary groups, with the latter assuming an ever-increasing share of the joint responsibility, would maximize the likelihood that the influence on Germany . . . would be constructive, effective, and persistent." [37]

The creation of COA gave a decisive boost to the exchange program if for no other reason than that of placing the prestige of some of the leading representatives in the fields of culture and education behind a government program critically in need of public and private support. COA was relatively short-lived (1948-1951). The Commission insisted that it was a short-term organization and that long-range responsibility whenever possible should be left with existing permanent operating agencies.

COA completed an impressive number of assignments. The first year was spent on a review of federal policy, vigorous representations for adequate governmental programs, recruitment of personnel for service overseas, organization of a series of technical panels, and arrangements for exchange of persons. The second year witnessed an increased promotional effort to stimulate and coordinate the work of voluntary agencies, notably of national organizations. COA furthermore developed standards for the visits of foreign nationals and even organized some exchanges through four of its panels. It also established and operated an orientation center for German leaders (described in Chapter V, below).

In support of these activities the Commission organized major national conferences, held meetings with government consultants, created a clearing house to exchange information among government agencies and voluntary organizations, undertook field investigations by sending missions to Japan and to Germany, actually operated, under contract with the government, some leader exchange programs, and published reports, studies, and recommendations. In addition, COA gave assistance to a number of specific projects, such as the Harvard-Salzburg International Seminar, the affiliation of American universities with German counterparts (e.g., Columbia University and Swarthmore College with the Free University of Berlin), the Unitarian Service Committee medical teaching missions, the American Association of Colleges for Teacher Education in helping sponsor the visits of German educators, and many more. One of the Commission's most successful ventures was the establishment of technical panels in the following fields: the arts, community activities, governmental affairs and the social sciences, higher education, humanities, legal affairs, natural sciences, public education, teacher education, religious affairs, rural affairs, and women's activities. Most of the panels were placed under the auspices of a sponsoring organization and had as their members some of the most outstanding members of the professions which they represented.[38] Their function was, *inter alia*, to encourage contacts and reciprocal relations with corresponding organizations in the occupied countries, to propose policy, programs and projects to government agencies and private groups, to evaluate, place, and assist with the operation of programs and in some cases to conduct exchange projects.[39] Due in no small part to the efforts of COA, there were eventually 167 private institutions which sponsored student programs alone.

OMGUS had made a beginning. It had introduced the concept of exchanges as an instrument of policy important to the realization of reorientation which had become an overall objective of OMGUS' mission. While it had succeeded in achieving a certain measure of coordination among its various functional units concerned with aspects of the reorientation, it fell short of creating a fully integrated program with a distinct focal point under unified high-level direction. Specifically, it had been unable to provide the organizational, administrative, and, above all, financial wherewithal needed to achieve its objective. Nevertheless, OMGUS, thanks to the effort of many highly qualified staff members, left a legacy of ideas, structures, and procedures which, with appropriate adaptations and improvements, set the stage for the full evolution of the exchange program under the Office of the High Commissioner.

Notes

CHAPTER II

1. Standard Operating Procedure for Sending German Experts to the United States, July 21, 1949, issued on July 26, 1949; WNRC, RG 331 (OMGUS).
2. OMGUS policy summarized in a draft on "The Cultural Exchange Program of the Office of Military Government for Germany" authorized each division to send to the United States as visitors, singly and in groups, a limited number of German technicians and other experts for training in various fields. The underlying purpose was described as "to enable the visitors to extend their knowledge and usefulness in their chosen fields, become acquainted with American practices and ways of life and upon their return with a widened professional and social outlook, to communicate their experience to their colleagues and fellow countrymen." File: Cultural Exchange Program," Administration, Alphabetical Subject Files, Religious Affairs Branch, "Public Affairs," Education and Cultural Relations Division, Headquarters Military Government for Germany (U.S.); WNRC, RG 260, Box 339 1/5.
3. "Regulations Governing the Functions and Operations of the Education and Cultural Relations Division," transmitted to Ralph A. Nicholson, Director, Office of Public Affairs, by letter from Alonzo G. Grace, Sept. 28, 1949"; File: "Objectives and Programs," Alphabetical Subject Files, Community Affairs Branch, "Public Affairs"—Education and Cultural Relations Division, Headquarters Military Government for Germany (U.S.); WNRC, RG 260, Box 293 1/5.
4. *Ibid.*
5. Beryl R. McCloskey, *The History of U.S. Policy and Programs in the Field of Religious Affairs Under the Office of the U.S. High Commissioner for Germany* (Historical Division, Office of the U.S. High Commissioner for Germany, Feb. 1951), pp. 16–17.
6. For details, see "The Aims, Goals and Program of the Community Education Branch," file: "Objectives and Programs," Alphabetical Subject Files, Community Affairs Branch, "Public Affairs," Education and Cultural Relations Division, Headquarters Military Government for Germany (U.S.); WNRC, RG 260, Box 293 1/5.
7. For full text, see *Germany, 1947–1949, The Story in Documents*, Dept. of State, publ. 3556, Mar. 1950 (Washington, D.C.: U.S. Government Printing Office), pp. 550–551.
8. Copy in CU/H.
9. "Memorandum on Women's Affairs, 9 September 1949," file: "Objectives and Programs," Alphabetical Subject Files, Community Affairs Branch, "Public Affairs," Education and Cultural Relations Division, Headquarters Military Government for Germany (U.S.); WNRC, RG 260, Box 293 1/5.
10. "The Cultural Exchange Program of the Office of Military Government for Germany (U.S.)" (draft). File: "Cultural Exchange Program," Administration, Alphabetical Subject Files, Religious Affairs, "Public Affairs," Education and Cultural Relations Division, Headquarters Military Government for Germany (U.S.); WNRC, RG 260, Box 339 1/5; copy in CU/H.

70   CULTURAL RELATIONS—INSTRUMENT OF FOREIGN POLICY

11. *Ibid.*
12. *Ibid.*
13. *Ibid.*
14. *Ibid.*
15. "The Cumulative Report of Cultural Affairs," see above; WNRC, RG 260, Box 335 3/5.
16. OMGUS Budget for Reorientation, FY 1947–48; copy in CU/H.
17. Proposals by Education Branch for FY 1950; copy in CU/H.
18. Proposed OMGUS Reorientation Budget for FY 1950; copy in CU/H.
19. WNRC, RG 331 (OMGUS); copy in CU/H.
20. Memorandum from Henry J. Kellermann to J. Franklin Ray, Bureau for Occupied Areas, Dec. 6, 1948. NA 811.42762/12–648. Copy in CU/H.
21. "Functions and Activities of the Cultural Exchange Office," file: "Exchange of Persons Procedures," Alphabetical Subject Files, Exchange Branch—Student Exchange, "Public Affairs"—Education and Cultural Relations Division, Headquarters Military Government for Germany (U.S.); WNRC, RG 260, Box 335 3/5.
22. General Order No. 29, 1948: "The Establishment of the Inter-Divisional Reorientation Committee," file: "Exchange of Persons Procedures," Alphabetical Subject Files, Exchange Branch—Student Exchange, "Public Affairs," Education and Cultural Relations Division, Headquarters Military Government for Germany (U.S.), *ibid.* Copy in CU/H.
23. "The American College and the German Student Exchange Program," brochure published by the Educational and Religious Affairs Branch, OMGUS, Nov. 4, 1947; WNRC, RG 59, 66 A 363, Box 752; copy in CU/H.
24. "Functions of OMGUS, ERA, and of Land, ERA on Interchange of Persons Program as it Relates to Student Exchange to the United States," *ibid.*
25. "Procedures for Interchange of Persons Under Reorientation Program," attachment to letter from Secretary of War to Secretary of State, June 12, 1947, NA, 811.42762, SE 6–124; copy in CU/H.
26. Memorandum of Jan. 27, 1948, on "The Development of an Organization in the United States to Support a Cultural Exchange of Persons Program for Germany. Headquarters European Command, Office of the Cultural Affairs Adviser." File: "Reorientation—Cultural Exchange—Analysis and Planning Sec., Alphabetical Subject File, Management and Budget Branch, Control Division, MG, Headquarters Military Government for Germany (U.S.). WNRC, RG 260, Box 257 2/5; copy in CU/H.
27. *News Bulletin*, Institute of International Education, XXIII (May 1, 1948), pp. 3–4.
28. Letter from Laurence Duggan, Director of Institute of International Education, to Robert P. Patterson, Secretary of War, June 10, 1947, and letter to Brig. Gen. G. L. Eberle, Acting Chief, CAD, July 18, 1947; NA, 811.42762, SE/6–1247; copies in CU/H.
29. Memorandum from Henry J. Kellermann to William T. Stone, Oct. 21, 1947, and attachments; copies in CU/H.
30. Letter of June 26, 1947, signed by Howard C. Peterson, Assistant Secretary of War; WNRC, RG 319, CAD 350; copy in CU/H.
31. Letters in WNRC, RC 165, CAD 350, Sc 5; copies in CU/H.
32. Letter from Edgar J. Fisher, Assistant Director, IIE, to Secretary of War Patterson, June 10, 1947; copy in CU/H.
33. Letter from Frank G. Wisner, Deputy to the Assistant Secretary of State for Occupied Areas, to William H. Draper, Under Secretary of the Army,

ADMINISTRATION OF OMGUS PROGRAM

Feb. 19, 1948, and appendix. WNRC, RG 165, CAD 350, Sc 5; copy in CU/H.
34. Hand-carried letter from Draper to Wisner of Mar. 8, 1948. *Ibid.*
35. Harold E. Snyder and George E. Beauchamp, *An Experiment in International Cultural Relations*, A report of the Staff of the Commission on the Occupied Areas, American Council on Education Studies, Washington, D.C., Series I, No. 49, Vol. XV, Aug. 1951, pp. 11–12.
36. *Ibid.*
37. "The Role of American Voluntary Agencies in Germany and Austria," Report by Karl W. Bigelow, Bernice Bridges, Msgr. William E. McManus, team sent by the Commission on the Occupied Areas (COA) at the request of the U.S. Dept. of State. Published by COA, American Council on Education, 1951.
38. The sponsors were: for community activities—the National Social Welfare Assembly; for governmental affairs and the social sciences—the American Political Science Association; for higher education—the American Council on Education; for the humanities—the American Council of Learned Societies; for legal affairs—the American Bar Association, the Association of American Law Schools, and the International Bar Association; for natural sciences—the National Research Council; for public education—the National Education Association; for teacher education—the Council on Cooperation in Teacher Education; for religious affairs—the National Conference of Christians and Jews; for rural affairs—the International Federation of Agricultural Producers; and for women's activities—the American Council on Education.
39. For a more detailed description of the panel's structure and functions, see Chapter V.

The Climax

CHAPTER III

Transition from OMGUS to HICOG: Reeducation to Reorientation

A Question of Survival of Policy

The ascendance of educational exchange to its level of importance and to its unprecedented size under HICOG was the logical sequence of the elevation of the Reorientation Program, of which exchanges were a key element, to the rank of top priority. But, as will be shown, this achievement did not come about without a struggle. There were in fact moments when both programs (i.e., reorientation and exchange) appeared to be in jeopardy—partly due to changes in policy reflected in the legal instruments defining Allied responsibilities, and partly due to changes in attitude on the part of policymakers and program operators.

The establishment of the High Commissions by each of the Allies was one of a series of steps that manifested the transition of Germany from a country under foreign curatorship to that of a sovereign state. In General Clay's words, 1949 witnessed "the termination of the negative phase of United States occupation policy and the beginning of a constructive policy." That year also foreshadowed Germany's restoration to a position of partnership in the council of European and Atlantic nations. Secretary of State Acheson declared: "It is the ultimate objective of the United States that the German people, or as large a part of them as possible, be integrated into a new common structure of the free peoples of Europe." [1]

The legal and political framework for the new policy was created by several major agreements among the three Western Allies: on an Occupation Statute for Western Germany; on the economic and political merger of the three military governments into High Commissions; and on a revision of the reparations program.

These agreements were accompanied on the German side, in May 1949, by the adoption of a new German Constitution, the so-called Basic Law. It was promptly approved by the three Military Gov-

75

ernors. On May 18, 1949 John J. McCloy was appointed U.S. High Commissioner in Germany; on May 19, André François-Poncet, French High Commissioner; and on June 1, Sir Brian Robertson, British High Commissioner. Konrad Adenauer was elected Federal Chancellor on September 15, and a few days later established the first postwar cabinet.

The following year (1950) saw Germany move more closely to political, economic, and military alliance with the West. 1951 witnessed the revision of the Occupation Statute of April 8, 1949, and the proposal to replace the Statute by contractual agreements. This development culminated in May 1952 in a treaty regulating the relations between the Federal Republic and the three Western Powers, the so-called "Bonn Convention."

Such changes in the political climate could not but have had a strong and significant impact on U.S. cultural relations with Germany. The Occupation Statute created an immediate problem. Until its enactment, controls over education and cultural affairs had been inherent in the supreme powers of Military Government. The controls constituted a legitimate instrument to bring about the reeducation of the German people as an integral part of U.S. policy. The Occupation Statute revised the relationship between the occupying powers and Germany opening the way toward a gradual relaxation of Allied control over internal affairs. Relaxation of controls, in turn, required a redefinition of those to be reserved and of those to be abandoned by the occupying powers. Education, cultural relations, and information were no longer listed among activities to be "reserved" to insure the accomplishment of the basic purpose of the occupation. Indeed, the policy directive to the U.S. High Commissioner confirmed explicitly that reorientation and public information were examples *par excellence* of those fields in which no powers of control were to be retained by the High Commissioners, notwithstanding the fact that these activities were of continuing critical concern to the Allied Powers. Lacking authority over these educational and cultural programs, the Allied Powers had no power to direct legislative, executive, or judicial action by the German Government in these fields; nor did they have any further right to arrogate to themselves such competencies.[2]

Accordingly, the proposed Charter of the Allied High Commission did not include a committee on information or cultural affairs on a par with the key tripartite committees which determined political and economic policies under the High Commission, but rather subordinated concerns about information and culture to the Political Affairs Committee.[3] The basic philosophy behind this policy was in line with General Clay's own thinking as well as with that of policymakers in other parts of the Government who had long advocated that "reorientation," if it was to be a realistic program in the first place, had to be left to German initiative rather than being "imposed" from without—hence, General Clay's earlier policy of restraining U.S. efforts in this field and limiting requests for Congressional funding. The U.S. Military Government (OMGUS) in its final days actually suggested the reduction and eventual phase-out of the educational program altogether. Concentration on the exercise of the explicitly reserved powers and, in particular, on the task of economic reconstruction was declared to be paramount.

It must be recorded, though, that this change of pace appears to have originated with officials in the entourage of the Military Governor rather than with General Clay himself. Despite his previous reluctance to accord top priority to education, and to request Congressional support for exchanges, Clay eventually modified his views. His change of mind may be attributed to Dr. Wells' persuasive powers. Not only did Clay take great personal satisfaction from the fact that he had "laid the foundation for one of the most basic reforms in our scheme of objectives," that is, for education,[4] and that the exchange program had been "one of the great programs of Military Government,"[5] but he also expressed the hope that the educational staff would carry on its friendly advisory role as long as the occupation lasted and specifically that arrangements would be made to continue the exchange program.[6] However, in the critical spring days of 1949, General Clay's influence was on the wane. Understandably, uncertainties created by the transition then underway and speculation regarding the intentions of the Department of State produced an atmosphere of uneasiness within OMGUS about the future of the reorientation program, including cultural and education exchanges, resulted in a serious problem of morale within the OMGUS staff.

The possibility of elimination of a program which, thanks notably to the efforts of Dr. Wells, had just begun to come into its own, caused great concern in interested circles inside and outside the U.S. Government.[7] Dr. Alonzo G. Grace, Chief of the Education and Cultural Relations Division, OMGUS, protested in a letter to the educational community in the United States that "the United States cannot afford to spend billions on economic reconstruction without a more valiant effort in the field of education and cultural relations . . . If we have merely an advisor to the High Commissioner and an exchange program of diminished proportions," wrote Grace, "we will have lost everything that we had planned." Grace urged a major public effort to create a favorable climate of opinion in the United States.[8]

Officials in Washington, rushing to the aid of Grace, pointed out that an earlier draft of the Occupation Statute had stipulated, quite clearly, that the occupation authorities would continue to have a specific responsibility "to observe, advise and assist the Federal Republic and its Laender (States) in regard to democratization of political life, social relations and education of the German people." This paragraph had been interpreted and welcomed by the United States educational community as a source of authority for HICOG to exercize such powers of persuasion as might be needed to assist German officials and functionaries with their own effort to achieve a reorientation of the German education system. It was believed that the omission of this stipulation which had been given wide dissemination in Germany and in the United States would seriously retard, if not altogether scuttle, the reorientation effort. A "thorough study" of OMGUS operations was urged.[9]

Sharp protests came from the American educational community. Criticism of OMGUS' efforts in favor of a stronger education program had never come quite to rest during the OMGUS period. Such criticism now gained momentum. Dr. George F. Zook, President of the American Council on Education and head of the U.S. Education Mission to Germany of 1946, and Dr. Herman B Wells, now representing the Advisory Committee on Cultural and Educational Relations with the Occupied Areas warned against the suggested phaseout of the program first by personal appearance in the Department of State and subsequently by a letter of April 29, 1949 addressed to the Secretary of State in which they quoted Dr. Grace's noted apprehension with "deep concern."

Drs. Zook and Wells insisted that, while they did not advocate the direct supervision of German education over a long period of time, they felt that the responsibility to "observe, advise and assist," as agreed upon previously by the occupying powers, "must be maintained for some time to come." "We believe," they wrote, "that to view the problem of Germany in purely political and economic terms is to leave out of consideration the spiritual and psychological factors which are at least of equal importance." Zook and Wells urged reconsideration of the Occupation Statute or at least as broad an interpretation of the Statute as possible, to permit the maintenance of an adequate program of education and cultural relations.[10] Subsequently, the Commission on the Occupied Areas released a statement in which it noted with concern that neither the Occupation Statute of April 8 nor the Agreement on Tripartite Controls released on April 25, 1949 had referred specifically to the important role of education and cultural affairs in achieving a stable and democratic nation. The Commission made three recommendations: "1. that an early agreement be reached by the occupying powers emphasizing the high priority of education and cultural affairs among the continuing functions of the occupation in Germany; 2. that responsible United States agencies continue to maintain competent professional staff of at least the present size to observe, advise, and assist German educational agencies; and 3. that increased emphasis be placed upon cultural exchanges between Germany, the United States, and other countries to the end that the emerging democratic leadership of Germany may be encouraged and strengthened." [11]

The letter of April 29, 1949 to the Secretary of State, jointly with the statement of the Commission, had the desired effect and strengthened the stand of officials in the Department of State who believed strongly that the reorientation program not only needed to be continued but, if anything, had to be expanded. In his reply to the letter, the author over the signature of Acting Secretary of State James E. Webb assured Drs. Zook and Wells that the "omission of any direct reference to education [in the Occupation Statute] was not intended to reflect upon the importance of the reorientation program [nor] to prejudice the continuity of this Government's interest to observe, advise and assist the German people in their efforts to bring about in ever-increasing measure the democratization of public life." Consequently, the letter said, since the Occupation Statute did not preclude the inauguration or continuation of educational programs, a reconsideration of the Statute was not required.

The following passages of the Acting Secretary's reply deserve direct quotation, since they laid the foundation for the policy pursued by HICOG in the years to come:

"You are assured," the Acting Secretary stated, "that there is fundamental agreement within the Department with the thesis cited in your letter that the United States cannot afford to spend billions on economic reconstruction without a valiant effort in the field of education and cultural relations. It has been the basic principle underlying this Government's policy for Germany that 'the reeducation of the German people is an integral part of policies intended to help develop a democratic form of government and to restore a stable and peaceful economy.' This principle has lost none of its importance and its application must remain in force. The Department has recognized quite early and has so stated that the task of educating the German people away from authoritarianism and aggression and toward democracy and peace remains the hardest and longest of all our responsibilities in Germany and, in the long run, the most decisive. The United States Government would have failed the American people no less than the democratic elements in Germany in their justified hope for lasting security, if this task were to be regarded as consummated with the establishment of a government by democratic processes, and if it desisted from further efforts to advise and assist the German people in the proper and effective use of their new freedom and of the democratic institutions and tools which it helped provide for them." [12] (Underlining supplied.)

The Department pointed out that democratization would have to employ methods different from those applied during the punitive and restrictive period. It proposed that this task be performed increasingly by the educator and information specialist within the framework of the reorientation program, and it expressed the hope that the role of the Advisory Committee in encouraging, sponsoring, and facilitating educational and cultural programs under private auspices would gain momentum and would supplement more and more the efforts of the Government.

The State Department Survey Missions (1948–1949)

To prepare for an orderly transition from military to civilian control and to pave the way for an organizational structure and program more in tune with reality, the Department of State sent two missions to Germany, one in 1948 and another in 1949.[13] The 1948 "mission" came to an abrupt halt when the Soviet Government blockaded Berlin. The group completed its report as a plan on which to draw in the case of a future transfer from military to civilian auspices, but the changeover originally contemplated for July 1, 1948 was considered "inadvisable" in the light of the situation created by Soviet conduct.[14]

The second survey mission went to Germany more than a year later, in 1949, after the blockade had ended. This time a team consisting exclusively of Department of State officials concerned with information and cultural affairs was formed. Their assignment was "to secure the information necessary for the transfer of the administration of the reorientation activities of OMGUS to the Department of State and for the preparation by the Department for the support of the reorientation program in Germany."[15] The mission was "to develop details of organizational staffing . . . to be transmitted to the U.S. High Commissioner for his consideration . . ."[16] In accordance with its mandate the second mission surveyed such programs as exchange of persons, libraries, motion pictures, radio broadcasting, news and press services from the policy and operational point of view.

The members of the mission found OMGUS in a state of considerable confusion, disarray, and low morale. A memorandum from General Clay's Assistant had recommended discontinuation of vital parts of the program.[17] On the day of the mission's arrival,

96 members of the staff had been given notice of dismissal, among them all members of the public opinion survey unit. There was considerable internal friction among members of the staff, quite specifically between the educational and the informational units. In the view of Lloyd Lehrbas, chairman of the 1949 survey mission, the organization (created by OMGUS) seemed to be disintegrating.[18]

The members of the mission soon discovered that, while some of OMGUS' operations had been deficient, others had been of high quality. They were determined to salvage as many activities as were needed to build a strong and viable program along the lines developed in the letter of the Acting Secretary of State. The organization of HICOG had to have the required capability for continuing a broad reorientation program with a staff fully qualified to observe, advise, and assist the Germans in their endeavor to build democratic institutions.

But the mission was equally convinced that a new organizational pattern, wholly different from that which existed under OMGUS, was needed. What was required was a *command* structure which consolidated the multiple features of the reorientation program under firm leadership and unified control. It also proposed elevation of the program to a level high enough to assure direct access to the High Commissioner; and on a par with the other key functions (e.g. political, economic, legal) of HICOG. It recommended specifically: (1) that a Public Affairs Officer be appointed to be responsible for all reorientation programs and activities carried out by any unit of HICOG; (2) that the Public Affairs Officer preside over the Interdivisional Reorientation Committee and that the status and functions of the Committee be reexamined from the point of view of raising the status of the Committee to that of a Reorientation Program Board responsible for overall policy and program planning; and (3) that the Public Affairs Office be responsible for insuring full and effective coordination of the reorientation program with the comprehensive policies of the U.S. Government and HICOG.[19]

Other recommendations asked for the appointment of a Survey Mission consisting of outstanding experts in the fields of education and information to study reorientation in all its aspects and to submit a report to the Secretary of State and the High Commissioner. The findings of the Mission were to be considered by the High Commissioner in directing such changes in organization and programs as he might deem necessary and desirable.[20] With the recommendations for changes of the overall structure went a proposal to integrate the reorientation budget with that of the total occupation budget for Government and Relief in Occupied Areas (GARIOA) of the Department of the Army.

Among the substantive program changes proposed by the survey mission was an increased exchange program with heavy emphasis on the exchange of younger persons, especially students, and of community leaders. To extend the exchange program to the grass-roots level and especially to rural areas, the author urged the addition of the nearly 200 so-called liaison and security officers (later renamed "Kreis (County) Resident Officers") residing in counties and hamlets, to the reorientation program staff to assist in particular with the selection of exchangees.

Most of the recommendations of the survey mission were adopted. The Policy Directive for the U.S. High Commissioner explicitly instructed him to "keep informed of all important developments in these matters [i.e., reorientation and public information] and work in conjunction with the German authorities by giving them such advice and assistance as may be required." It confirmed, as the "basic purpose of the occupation," the reorientation of the German people toward democracy and peace. It enjoined the High Commissioner specifically

> "to advise and assist the German people with respect to the democratization of social relations and institutions, education, public information, and civic life, including the provision of equal opportunities for men and women in the political, economic and educational fields." [21]

The program, moreover, was extended to the two other Western (i.e., British and French) Zones of Occupation with the three Allied powers granting to each other "complete and unrestricted liberty of action" in respect to cultural activities in the three allied zones.[22]

The reorientation program was transferred from the Department of the Army to the Department of State in the summer of 1949. U.S. High Commissioner John J. McCloy had a perfect understanding of his mandate. He was profoundly convinced of the validity of the reorientation program as a keystone of his mission in Germany. In one of his early statements of policy, McCloy had this to say to an audience in Stuttgart on February 6, 1950:

> "Let me emphasize . . . and this I say particularly to the political leaders of Germany: we Americans are not here exclusively to feed the German people and to promote economic recovery. Nor merely to see that tanks and planes are not built. Our main purpose is to help Germany achieve political recovery. By that I mean, to help the German people establish a political democracy in which they can live as free men and enjoy the benefits of their freedom." [23]

Political reconstruction and democratization remained the basic theme of U.S. policy in Germany and the main purpose of the reorientation program throughout the HICOG period, but it underwent a series of modifications each of which reflected a deliberate and careful attempt to adapt policy and program to the new realities of the early fifties. The trend toward German sovereignty and rapprochement with Western nations was a major modifier of policies. It was now accelerated by the increasing intensity of the Cold War. In addition to being an incentive for internal reform, democracy became a militant issue to be defended in the form of two-front resistance toward totalitarianism from the right and the left (see Chapter IV). The highlight statement of the 1950 budget presentation to Congress defined the four objectives of the public affairs program as follows: (1) to strengthen in the German people the will for and knowledge of democratic self-government and repugnance for authoritarian rule, whether from the left or from the right; (2) to contain and counter the propaganda of Communist and extreme nationalists hostile to democracy and to Allied and United States purposes in Western Germany; (3) to explain and to gain acceptance and support of United States policy, especially as it concerns the political integration of Germany into Western Europe and the economic objectives of the European Recovery Program; and (4) to promote better understanding and friendship between the United States and a reconstituted Germany.[24]

Thus while there was no fundamental change in policy, there were changes in emphasis, scale, and methods of such significance that one could justifiably speak of an almost totally new program. When HICOG took over, some key officials of OMGUS, as was noted, felt that the job had largely been done. The Department of State, in contrast, believed that the reorientation program not only had to be continued—and so instructed the High Commissioner—but that its importance was increasing. The progressive loss of direct controls, the Department reasoned, necessitated a shift from coercion to persuasion through a strengthened and far more sophisticated public affairs program. The program had to be given greater authority, its standards of performance had to be raised, and it had to be expanded. This expansion was to be accomplished by elevating the status of the program within the organizational structure of HICOG to office level, by enlarging and improving the quality of the staff through more careful selection, and by requesting substantial appropriations from the Congress. All this was done during the period of HICOG's existence—1949–1953.

New Program Criteria

The shift to new programs necessitated a change of criteria which eventually gave the HICOG's public affairs program its distinctive character: (1) it was *massive* both in terms of persons and funds to be involved; (2) it was *target oriented*, aimed at the critical segments of German society; (3) it was highly *stratified*, ranging from grassroots to persons at the summit of political and civic responsibility, in short all strata and factions of German society; (4) it was *innovative*, introducing such new features into German political, social, and cultural life as would be apt to assist in democratic reconstruction; (5) it was *participatory*, in that it permitted increasing German influence in the shaping of the program; and (6) it was *interzonal*, extending gradually to the British and French Zones of Occupation, but, of course, one must be reminded, not the Russian Zone, which the Soviets were rapidly turning into the People's Republic of Germany.

Massive

Under HICOG, the Public Affairs Program, where the reorientation effort was anchored, became the largest undertaking of its kind ever conducted by the United States in any country. At its peak in 1952, 3,415 persons were involved in that Program (Appendix III) and its budget was in the neighborhood of $48 million, i.e., nearly one-half of the total HICOG budget of $102 million. Of this $48 million, $6 million went into exchange of persons. A fourth of all American staff members and almost one-half of all locals were directly engaged in public affairs activities.[25] It should be noted that these sums did not include the so-called McCloy Fund, i.e., German mark counterpart revenue from the sale of American equipment, much of which was spent for purposes directly or indirectly related to public affairs. Nor did it include voluntary contributions of private American or German organizations in support of cultural exchanges. The HICOG staff in 1951 numbered 8,511.

Target Oriented

Focus on well-selected persons was stipulated in the directive which instructed the High Commission "to concentrate increasingly on those groups, organizations and institutions which have demonstrated their devotion to democratic ideals and practices, on individuals who are in a position of leadership or are likely to take a responsible part in the reconstruction of German community life, and on individuals and groups which have been exposed to anti-democratic influence or which are in need of guidance and assistance to withstand such influence."[26]

Stratified

The broad and extensive character of the program was manifest in the choice of devices employed to reach into every geographical and social area of Germany, particularly into rural communities, and to address people on various levels of intellectual sophistication, political authority, and community activities, ranging from mass audience appeal to tailor-made projects for special groups. A most useful element in implementing this multidimensional character of the program proved to be the use of the Kreis (County) Resident Officers who helped extend its benefits to the grassroots level.

Innovative

The introduction of new political, social, and cultural concepts and practices had started under OMGUS, notably in the area of school reform. A number of program features, designed to assist German Government officials wrestling with legislative and administrative reforms and other groups dealing with pressing problems of civil rights, education, social welfare, public health, community organization, and the like, were now introduced in addition to activities begun by OMGUS.

Participatory

The participatory character of the program had its modest beginnings under OMGUS when, among other things, Germans were invited to take part in the preliminary selection of prospective exchangees. This feature was now given greater emphasis and broader scope by the Policy Directive which enjoined the High Commissioner

"with the development of Germany toward a status of self-government . . . [to] encourage and facilitate the active and responsible participation of Germans in the formulation of programs conducted so far exclusively under American public and private auspices, including projects under joint auspices."

Interzonal

With respect to interzonal activities, progress was more gradual, although here, too, informal but limited contacts had preceded the actual enunciation of policy. In accordance with the terms of the Tripartite Agreement cited above, the Directive authorized the High Commissioner

"to determine, together with your British and French colleagues, the nature of projects which may be undertaken in cooperation with them . . . and to seek to obtain agreement with your British and French colleagues which will permit coordination of existing programs and services, as far as desirable, and which will allow each power to conduct certain programs in the other occupation zones."

Relationships among the three Western powers were good, and in the course of events became more active, although each zonal occupation authority maintained its separate identity with regard to policy, program, and organization. One of the main reasons for this autonomy within the zones lay in the difference in philosophy that guided each, especially with respect to educational and cultural affairs. The British assumed rather early a fairly relaxed attitude on matters of reorientation, whereas the French for a much longer time maintained a strict "reformist" approach involving direct intervention in German domestic affairs. The American position lay somewhere in between. Consequently, few joint projects resulted, although consultation became more frequent and intensive.

Reorganization

One of the secrets of the success of the Public Affairs Program under HICOG, and perhaps one of its most significant features, was its restructuring both in Washington and in Germany. Essentially the new structure rested on four key pillars: (1) full integration of the public affairs policy in the Department's Bureau of German Affairs, on a par with the political and economic policies; (2) day-by-day coordination of policy with the Department's organization responsible for the administration of the worldwide educational exchange program, i.e., the Office of Educational Exchanges followed by the International Educational Exchange Service under the Assistant Secretary for Public Affairs; (3) consolidation of the scattered parts of the reorientation program of OMGUS into one Office of Public Affairs of HICOG, equal in rank to the offices for political, economic, and legal affairs and with direct access to the High Commissioner (see Appendix II); and (4) clear channels of command and communication between Washington and the field. It was the combination of these four elements, more than anything else, that gave the reorientation program, or as it was now increasingly referred to, the Public Affairs Program, the status of *primus inter pares* and, with it, higher prestige, visibility, and more impact than it ever attained under OMGUS. It must indeed be doubted whether a program of lesser rank and scope would have attracted in equal measure the attention and support of leading officials, of Congress and of the American public.[27]

The Washington setup in the Department of State was unusual in many respects, so many in fact that it has been doubted whether it could ever serve as a model for future programs. Given the special situation occurring in Germany in those years, with the U.S. Government serving first as proxy for, and later as an adviser to and overseer of, the Government of the Federal Republic, the extraordinary circumstances indeed seem to exclude duplication of the model. However, they do not necessarily diminish the value of practices such as close cooperation between geographic desks responsible for the conduct of foreign policy and others concerned with the development of cultural exchange programs.

Policy direction and planning in the Department of State was centered in the Office, later the Bureau, of German Affairs (GER), headed by a director with the rank of Assistant Secretary of State and equal in status to the other geographic and functional bureaus of the Department of State. Robert D. Murphy was the first director, subsequently Henry A. Byroade, who in turn was succeeded by James W. Riddleberger. The Bureau was responsible for the formulation of policy, for interagency and intergovernmental relationships, and for the provision of policy guidance to the Office of the U.S. High Commissioner. In addition, it performed a wide range of operational tasks in connection with the occupation. Furthermore, it coordinated the efforts of all Departmental offices concerned with the program for Germany.[28] The Bureau consisted of the Office of the Director, the Office of the Executive Director, the Office of German Political Affairs, the Office of German Economic Affairs, and the Office of German and Austrian Public Affairs (GAI), which was directed by the author.[29]

As a focal point for public affairs policy and program planning, the Office of German and Austrian Public Affairs discharged several key responsibilities with respect to information, education, and domestic (U.S.) public affairs activities concerning Germany. They included the formulation of public affairs policy to guide and assist the Office of the High Commissioner in the day-by-day operation of the program and the coordination of public affairs policy in Germany with occupation policy and U.S. foreign policy in general.[30] These functions, in turn, entailed a series of implementary activities, such as participation in program planning, supervision, review and evaluation in terms of program effectiveness.[31] Later the Office assisted in the briefing of German leaders on matters regarding U.S. foreign policy and German-American relations (see below). Of these responsibilities participation in the development of total U.S. policy toward Germany and formulation of public affairs policy for Germany were by far the most significant ones. As one of the three offices of the Bureau, equal in status to the political and economic offices, the Office of German and Austrian Public Affairs was a party to important decisions affecting U.S. policy for Germany; and it provided advice and service on many decisions. The staff of GAI in those days numbered 26.[32]

For the performance of all strictly operational functions, GAI relied on the competent offices under the Bureau of Public Affairs headed by the Assistant Secretary of State for Public Affairs. From 1948 to 1953, George V. Allen, Edward W. Barrett, and Howland H. Sargeant occupied that office. The Bureau had overall responsibility for the development of policies governing the International Information and Educational Exchange Program (USIE). This

Bureau acted with the advice of the regional bureaus, in the case of Germany with GER, and other geographic offices of the Department, as appropriate; it directed the conduct of international information and educational exchange activities, subject to the review of the regional or geographic bureaus, and it post-audited the execution of the programs.[33] The key operating unit within the Bureau for exchanges was the Office of Educational Exchange (OEX) under the direction of William C. Johnstone, Jr. Of the 155 staff members assigned to work on German public affairs, 129 worked in the Bureau of Public Affairs (P) but were paid from funds appropriated to the Office of German and Austrian Public Affairs.

The arrangement insured close coordination on the policy level between German public affairs and the U.S. worldwide public affairs program. On the operational level the activities carried on by the Bureau of Public Affairs on behalf of Germany remained subject to policy guidance and overall program planning by the Bureau of German Affairs (GER), through its Office of German and Austrian Public Affairs (GAI), and the Office of Public Affairs in HICOG. Conversely, worldwide policies of the Department's Bureau of Public Affairs were gradually introduced in the German program and many established activities, including the Voice of America, informational materials, press releases, magazines, motion pictures, and the like were used with appropriate adaptation to conditions in Germany. As for exchange, the institutional resources and machinery of USIE, used for programs on a worldwide scale, proved to be major assets in conducting the stateside part of the German program. In the fall of 1949, the Division of International Exchange of Persons (IEP) of OEX assumed active program responsibilities for the HICOG exchange of persons program.

The organization in Germany did not fall as easily into place as that in Washington. On the tripartite level the Allied High Commission charter, as we noted, denied information and cultural functions equal rank with political and economic affairs and relegated the former to subcommittee status. However, within HICOG the proposal of the 1949 survey mission prevailed. The Office of Public Affairs was created directly under the High Commissioner and on a par with the other major program offices. It united under single leadership the various aspects of the reorientation program.

The first director of this office was Ralph Nicholson, a prominent newspaper publisher, radio station director, and public relations executive from New Orleans. His deputy was Shepard Stone, assistant editor of the *New York Times Magazine* who assumed the directorship after Mr. Nicholson's departure.[34] His deputy in turn was Frederick Burkhardt who had been President of Bennington College and later became President of the American Council of Learned Societies.

The office had two sub-units—the Division of Education and Cultural Relations and the Division of Information. James Morgan Read, previously Foreign Secretary of the American Friends Service Committee, and subsequently U.N. Deputy High Commissioner for Refugees, headed the former which, among other programs, sheltered the Exchange of Persons Branch (see below for details). Field offices handled public affairs activities in various zones.

In 1950 the total staff of the Public Affairs Program numbered 1,183 persons, of whom 503 were Americans and the rest Germans. In 1951 the total had risen to 8,511 and 567, respectively. In 1952 the American contingent climbed to 594 but the total force dropped slightly to 7,046. Thereafter both categories underwent a gradual reduction in force. The sharpest decline of nearly 50 percent occurred in 1953, because of decreases in the total program. Still, in 1954 the total was 2,538, a larger group than was serving in any other country.

The priority of its objectives, the very scale of its operations, but specifically the supportive nature of its activities, which served the interests of other offices in HICOG, made the Office of Public Affairs the focal point for reorientation on the operational side in HICOG. Taking its cue from the now defunct Interdivisional Reorientation Committee of OMGUS, the Office of Public Affairs eventually regularized its coordinating function through the establishment of an interoffice committee (PEPCO) under the chairmanship of Director Shepard Stone, on which all major HICOG offices were represented.

The effectiveness of the organization established in Washington and in Germany depended on the quality of communications between the two elements, and on a clear understanding by both of their relationship and of the nature of their respective responsibilities within that framework. The instructions given the Public Affairs Office of HICOG by the Department spelled it out. They stipulated

> "that arrangements be made to insure constant maintenance of closest coordination in matters of policy and programs between the Department of State and the Public Affairs Officer (HICOG) and his organization under the established system. whereby the Department formulates policy, issues guidance and does broad program planning for all public affairs operations of the Department in the United States and abroad to insure consistency of policy and program in each area with those of other areas and with overall U.S. objectives."

Accordingly, they provided

> "that the Public Affairs Officer (HICOG) establish procedures whereby policy and program recommendations may be transmitted from the field for the consideration of the Department,"

and, in turn,

"that the Department, in cooperation with the appropriate government and private agencies and organizations, assume responsibility for and provide such backstopping services as will be required by the Public Affairs officer in the performance of his functions."

Furthermore, the instructions made it clear that in conformance with these arrangements the long-range and day-by-day programs under the jurisdiction of the Public Affairs Officer "continue to be performed in accordance with policy guidance issued by the Department" and that the Department "will make available to the Public Affairs Officer guidances which will reflect the official position of the Department." [35]

The arrangements proved to be sound and effective. They profited in no minor degree from the high caliber of leadership shown by the Public Affairs Officer and his staff and the excellent personal relations that existed between key personnel in the Department and HICOG. Furthermore, officers in Washington and in the field were in constant working contact with each other, facilitated by almost daily telecons* and frequent visits. Arrangements were kept flexible to permit changes in policy, programs, and procedures as demanded by a political situation that remained in constant flux.

It should be noted for the record that some HICOG officers had viewed the takeover by the Department of State with a degree of concern. They had feared that the Department's preoccupation with problems of global reach would work to the disadvantage of the German program and reduce it in importance and size to the level of other country programs. But after having touched base with the key policy and program planners in the Department in December 1949, Sam H. Linch, one of the principal officers on the staff of the late Dr. Ralph A. Burns, the chief of HICOG's exchange program, sent home this message: "We do not need to worry about the Department considering Germany in the same way as it does the rest of the world. They fully realize here that the occupation areas represent particular and unique reorientation problems." [36] It was indeed the quasi-governmental nature of the U.S. Government's authority in Germany vested in the Bureau of German Affairs and in the High Commissioner's office that gave GER and HICOG powers of control not exercised by any other bureau and that correspondingly required policies different from those developed for other countries.

---

*A telecon (teleconference) was a conference conducted by radio transmitted signals to a teletype, with the messages coming and going being thrown onto a screen similar to a television screen. They were analyzed on both sides by officers of IEP and GAI in the Department of State, and HICOG's public affairs staff.

Notes

CHAPTER III

1. Address of Apr. 28, 1949, "The Current Situation of Germany," reprinted in *Germany, 1947-1949, The Story in Documents* (Washington, D.C.: Dept. of State publ. 3556, 1950), pp. 16–17.
2. Policy Directive for U.S. High Commissioner, Dept. of State, copy in CU/H.
3. O/FADRC, 56 D 12, 57 D 221, Box 12582.
4. Statement by General Lucius D. Clay, Jan. 1949, reprinted in *Germany, 1947-1949, op. cit.*, p. 14. Clay was even more positive in his memoirs, *Decision in Germany* (New York: Doubleday and Company, Inc., 1950). Although he conceded that the results of the educational exchange program were intangible and that evidence was hard to produce, he expressed his "deep conviction that our work in the field of education is taking hold and that it may indeed succeed in creating a people more conscious of their rights and freedom." *Ibid.*, p. 303.
5. *Germany, 1947-1949, op. cit.*, p. 15.
6. *Decision in Germany, op. cit.*, p. 303.
7. It was also shared by representatives of the French Government and its High Commissioner who had conducted a vigorous education program in their zone and who considered the contemplated change of pace premature.
8. Letter partially reprinted in Harold E. Snyder and George E. Beauchamp, *An Experiment in International Cultural Relations*, a report of the Staff of the Commission on the Occupied Areas, American Council on Education, Washington, D.C., Aug. 1951, p. 28.
9. Dept. of State memorandum from Henry J. Kellermann to Robert Murphy, Apr. 13, 1949. O/FADRC, RG 59, 70 A 4521, Box 403. In a separate memorandum to Robert Murphy, the author pointed out that the relegation of information and cultural affairs to a subcommittee under the Political Affairs Committee, as proposed in the Charter of the Allied High Commission, was in conflict with the declared intention of the Department of State to guarantee adequate status to the reorientation program and would raise serious doubts on the part of the American public regarding future official policy. But, while parity was achieved within the U.S. structure, both in Washington and in the field, no changes were made in the Charter itself. See O/FADRC 56 D 12 and 57 D 221, Box 12582.
10. Reprinted in Snyder and Beauchamp, *An Experiment in International Cultural Relations, op. cit.*, p. 28.
11. *Ibid.*
12. *Ibid.*, pp. 31–32; also *Germany, 1947-1949, op. cit.*, pp. 544–545.
13. The author was a member of both missions.
14. War Department message of Mar. 24, 1948, and appendix, NA, RG 165, CAD 321, Sec. 3; copies in CU/H.
15. See Henry P. Pilgert, *The Exchange of Persons Program in Western Germany* (Historical Division, Office of the U.S. High Commissioner for Germany, 1951), p. 10.
16. Internal Departmental memorandum from Richard Cook to Assistant

Secretary of State George V. Allen, 1949. O/FADRC, RG 59, 70 A 4521, Box 403.
17. General Clay himself does not appear to have shared the opinion of his Assistant. In his memoirs (*Decision in Germany, op. cit.*, p. 305) he reports that because of his personal belief in the educational program the personnel engaged in these activities formed the only group that was not reduced in number.
18. Statement of Lloyd Lehrbas, Director of the Office of International Information in the Department's Bureau of Public Affairs, before the U.S. Advisory Commission on Information, Aug. 4, 1949. Lehrbas actually said: "The chief problem was . . . the fact that the organization was bad. Under the Army set-up we had too many headquarters for people to report to, too many channels to go through . . . It was not in any sense a streamlined organization and didn't function well . . ." O/FADRC, RG 59, 4521, Box 403.
19. Pilgert, *op. cit.*, p. 11.
20. *Ibid.*, pp. 11–12.
21. Policy Directive to the High Commissioner, Feb. 6, 1950. Copy in CU/H.
22. Meeting of the Information and Cultural Affairs Subcommittee of the Interdivisional Reorientation Committee, Dec. 1, 1949. Copy in CU/H.
23. Address delivered at Stuttgart on Feb. 6, 1950. Copy of abstracts in CU/H.
24. NARS, RG 59, 63 A 217, Box 313. Copy in CU/H.
25. Guy Lee, "Report on HICOG Public Affairs—Policy, Organization and Programs," 1953. O/FADRC, 58 D 372, Box 3000.
26. See note 24, above. The so-called "country paper" for public affairs developed by the Office of German (and Austrian) Public Affairs in the Department of State broke down the so-called "target groups" into primary and secondary targets.

Primary targets were defined as:

1. Persons in positions of public responsibility, e.g., government officials, political leaders, legislators, and the like.

2. Persons not in a status of public authority, but in a position of public influence, e.g., teachers, labor leaders, editors, and others directly concerned with public information.

3. Persons concerned with the initiation and development of democratic institutions, movements and projects, e.g., civil liberties, parent-teachers associations, school reform, 4–H clubs.

4. Persons leading or representing groups or professions of critical importance for democratic reconstruction and reform, e.g., women's groups, youth organizations, trade unions, farm cooperatives, etc.

5. Young persons of promise preparing themselves for public service careers.

Secondary targets were defined as:

1. Persons not in a position of leadership or major influence but belonging to groups which have shown sympathy and devotion to democratic concepts, and whose loyalty deserves recognition, encouragement, and support, e.g., labor, independent press, victims of Nazi persecution.

2. Persons not in a position of leadership of major influence but belonging to groups which have shown little interest in democratic reform but,

if reoriented, would constitute an element of considerable importance within a democratic community, e.g., professional and wage-earning women, intelligentsia and students, civil servants, organized and unorganized youth in general.

3. Persons belonging to groups of undeclared loyalties who, if left alone, may fall victim to anti-democratic influence, e.g., unemployed, expellees, young intellectuals, including university graduates without definite professional prospects. These are the elements most likely to be influenced by blandishments from the radical right or left; and

4. Persons in vocations needy of reform assistance and international contact, e.g., scientists, church leaders, etc.

It would appear that these nine categories by themselves covered practically every political, professional or social group, and in point of fact they did. Whoever remained outside these categories was most likely reached by U.S. sponsored mass media. Nevertheless, the categories may have proved useful to HICOG officials who needed criteria to differentiate between major and minor groups to be reached.

27. In fact, the author, who defended the budget before Congress, cannot recall a single hearing at which members of the Senate or House ever raised serious objections to a critical line item or, for that matter, to the spending level.
28. GOAG budget justification, 1950–51, O/FADRC, RG 59, 63 A 217, Box 313.
29. The Austrian program was later transferred to the Bureau of European Affairs, and the office became responsible exclusively for German Public Affairs.
30. GOAG budget justification 1950–51, *op. cit.* The Manual of Regulations and Procedures, Vol. II, Organization, U.S. Dept. of State, Washington, D.C., Jan. 25, 1950, specified the functions of GAI as follows:

1. "Plans programs and develops guidances, subject to the responsibility of the public affairs area for overall information and educational exchange policy and activities, for the United States High Commissioner in Germany in pursuance of the United States Government's policy to assist in the reorientation of the German people towards democracy and peace.

2. "Develops public affairs programs in cooperation with the public affairs area based on the specific requirements of the reorientation program and designed to support the efforts of the United States High Commissioner in Germany in this respect." Copy in CU/H.

31. As Director of the Office of German Public Affairs, the author frequently used the services of the Research Staff of HICOG's Office of Public Affairs under Leo Crespi to probe into attitudinal changes of returned exchanges. For details, see Chapter VIII.
32. GOAG budget justification 1950–51, *op. cit.*
33. Manual of Regulations and Procedures, *op. cit.*
34. He was succeeded by Alfred V. (Mickey) Boerner.
35. Instructions to the Director of Public Affairs, HICOG, Briefing Book, 1949; O/FADRC, RG 59, 70 A 4521, Box 403.
36. Telecon, Dec. 13, 1949, WA–16, Linch to Burns, WNRC, CC 14–15.

CHAPTER IV

The HICOG Exchange Program: 1949-1953

Criteria and Terms of Reference

With the takeover of the OMGUS exchange program by the Department of State, the ultimate and long-range objectives "to promote better understanding of the United States" and "to increase mutual understanding between the people of the United States and the people of other countries," [1] which governed all other exchange programs, applied automatically to Germany.

First and foremost, however, the German exchange program continued to pursue the immediate and short-term objectives set by U.S. policy for Germany, that is, to help achieve the goals of the reorientation program. Those responsible for fashioning the Public Affairs Program realized that cultural and educational exchanges offered the most appropriate and also the most promising instrument for a policy of reform by indirection, namely, an effective do-it-yourself approach to reorientation. Moreover, they believed that the six criteria which determined the scope and method of the Public Affairs Program as a whole (see pp. 83-86) were singularly applicable to the exchange of persons program. The time for a middling, haphazard, trial-and-error effort depending largely on the good will of private contributors had passed. The exchange program had to be placed on a firm and regular basis, and had to involve enough persons moving in each direction to assure broad impact. In short, what was needed was a *massive* breakthrough sustained by governmental instrumentalities and supported by adequate funds from the Congress. In fact, governmental capabilities had to be tested beyond precedents set by OMGUS and the worldwide exchange program.

The groups in the Department which met under the chairmanship of the author in the fall of 1949 decided to aim at an annual total of 3,500 persons coming and going, the highest figure ever proposed for any country exchange program.[2] To realize this expansion, the budget had to be increased accordingly, i.e., to $6,619,049 in 1950

95

and to $7,489,686 in 1951, i.e., the equivalent of one-third of the worldwide total for exchanges.

The criteria used in shaping the Reorientation Program as a whole applied with special relevance to the exchange program. It had to be *massive*, that is, a multiple of the OMGUS model. To avoid scattering of funds, however, it had to be *target oriented*, to wit, sharply focused on specific individuals and groups who by virtue of their position or potential of leadership or in view of their critical role in German society could be expected to use the benefits derived from their exchange experience to maximum advantage.

The approach involved a major risk. Emphasis on leadership could have reintroduced traditional criteria of elitism still prevalent in Germany. But, as noted earlier, in order not to cater to such tendencies, the program had to be *stratified* and made multidimensional; it had to be extended to all segments of German society regardless of political affiliation (with the exception of ultrarightist or extreme leftist elements), economic or social status, religious belief, sex, or age. In other words, it had to demonstrate democracy by its very process of selection.

At the same time the program could not be permitted to institute exchange for exchange sake. It had to be *innovative* in the sense that it not only introduced new features in the exchange program itself, but provided the returning participant with a series of options for innovative action at home—through followup programs.

The *participatory* nature of exchanges inherent in the very concept of the program was to be reaffirmed by the proviso that the responsibility of German nationals was gradually to be applied beyond mere assistance in the selection of candidates to areas of program planning and execution.

Finally, with the accelerating trend toward political unification of Western Germany, operating programs solely within the confines of occupation zones had to give way to *interzonal* arrangements permitting German nationals from the British and French Zones to compete on an equal basis for participation in the U.S. Government exchange program,[3] and vice versa.

The basic terms of reference for the Exchange of Persons Program under HICOG, aside from the Smith-Mundt Act, were laid down in the Directive to the U.S. High Commissioner, in the instructions to the Public Affairs Officer, in the HICOG Manual of Organization, Section 5, and in the language of the GOAG (Government in Occupied Area of Germany) budget justifications. They were later supplemented by the provisions of the Fulbright agreement and by a special delegation of authority to the chief of the Exchange of Persons Branch, as authorized in Section 4 of Public Law 73 (81st Congress).

The Directive to the High Commissioner was explicit. It assigned to the exchange program a central function in pursuit of U.S. policy to end the political and cultural isolation of Germany by restoring binational relations and to encourage democratic reconstruction. It instructed the High Commissioner to

"stimulate and facilitate direct contact between civic and professional groups in Germany and corresponding groups abroad, notably in the United States, [to] make use of such private resources, in the United States and elsewhere, as your Government may enlist for the purpose of actively supporting the reorientation program [and to] develop a broad and effective program of cultural exchange, aiming especially at the participation of those groups which are likely to promote the future democratic leadership in Germany." [4]

The January 1950 issue of the HICOG *Information Bulletin* recognized specifically the exchange program as a vital and integral part of the HICOG program. It said:

"The Exchange of Persons program is one of the most important activities of the Office of Public Affairs. The program is conducted in cooperation with all offices of HICOG in order to make sure that promising individuals and influential persons from all walks of life and occupations in Germany are given the benefit of seeing democracy at work in the United States." [5]

Accordingly, the instructions given to the Public Affairs Officer placed the exchange program directly within the context of HICOG's overall mission. They defined the program

"as a means of stimulating and promoting the development of a democratic German state and society, fostering in the German people a feeling of community with other democratic countries, increasing American prestige and the respect for American traditions and achievements, and overcoming antidemocratic tendencies and influences." [6]

The HICOG Manual and Technical Instruction 11, issued by the Office of Public Affairs in 1953, sharpened the focus by emphasis on the political and social aspects as the primary objectives of the program. They declared the program's fundamental purpose to be that of

"giving exchangees an opportunity to experience a democratic environment which contributes to a cooperative way of life, and to stimulate the free interchange of ideas between free nations."

The instructions made it equally clear that it was not the purpose of exchange visits to serve the personal interest of the individual through the acquisition of academic or cultural knowledge or technical skills, nor to help reestablish family or business contacts. If such benefits were derived incidentally, so much the better. They did not justify, however, consideration under the program and, if found to constitute the primary motive of prospective participants, could actually jeopardize their candidacy.[7]

The above terms of reference set the tone of the program. They established its character as an instrument of U.S. foreign policy. They also described its structure and format.

HICOG had inherited from OMGUS some of the categories which identified principal groups sharing certain interests and characteristics. They were: Germans going to the United States, specifically German leaders and specialists,[8] and German students and trainees; and American specialists going to Germany.[9] (Exchanges with European countries were discontinued during the first 2 years of HICOG but later resumed in response to a change of emphasis in overall policy.)

These were the key types of participants that were maintained and substantially expanded in number. The expansion was a deliberate effort to ensure a maximum return on the U.S. investment within a relatively short period.[10] But expansion in the number of persons coming to the United States demanded that there had to be appropriate differentiation among the thousands of participants according to their age, status, occupation, professional interests, and personal qualifications. The "project approach" now came into its own. Special projects were developed for different categories of participants. Categories, in turn, were divided in two major groups: competitive, e.g., teachers, students and teenagers, and noncompetitive, i.e., leaders.

Germans to the United States

The Leader Exchange Program

In terms of optimum political impact the leader exchange was without doubt the most significant of all programs. It was aimed at those persons in public life and in the professions who by their very position could be expected to have an immediate as well as a long-range influence on the German scene.[11]

In accordance with the comprehensive character of the exchange program as a whole, the definition of leader was kept intentionally broad to permit selection of representatives from all social and professional strata. Leaders were therefore defined as "persons of outstanding leadership, influence and prominence, [including]:

—those holding high official positions in federal or Land (State) governments;
—those leading or representing on a national level, groups or professions of critical importance in democratic reorientation and reform;
—other outstanding persons in unique fields of endeavor in which the number of qualified candidates is limited." [12]

Subsequently, HICOG's Office of Public Affairs refined and broadened the definition by adapting it to the primary target list developed for the Reorientation Program as a whole.[13]

Leader exchanges remained the largest single program with slight variations throughout most of the HICOG period. The climax came in 1950 when it rose (from 557 in 1949) to 1,181. In 1951 it decreased slightly to 981, climbed back to 1,058 in 1952, to drop again to 725 in 1953. Thereafter, it declined sharply to 450 in 1954 and to 364 in 1955. These figures do not include German leaders going to other European countries. Available data indicate that of the latter, 681 went in 1951 and 1,074 in 1975 (Appendix III).

Leaders were grouped according to their professions and interests. The HICOG budgets for 1951–1953 list 14 categories of German leaders and specialists: namely, in order of magnitude, education (885), politics and government (819), labor (679), information media (368), youth (314), cooperative action teams (288), agriculture (260), women's affairs (259), community activities (233), law (185), public health (123), libraries and museums (67), religion (52), and social workers (24).[14] These were pivotal groups expected to shape the future of Germany. Their representatives sat at the political controls, were the managers of national institutions, and were the heads of various professional and civic organizations. Many of them were engaged in activities aiming at fundamental reform and were therefore believed to be on the lookout for new ideas and models applicable to domestic problems. They operated on different levels of authority and in a variety of political and social settings. They comprised, for instance, members of the Cabinet, top-level administrators, legislators and judges, trade union leaders, social agency executives, school administrators, teachers on all levels of education, women leaders, and youth leaders. As a rule, leaders came in groups formed on the basis of common interests.

The "project approach" recommended itself as a particularly effective method in programming leader visits. By trimming the itinerary down to the bare essentials it allowed leaders to concentrate on problems of direct interest to them, often of critical importance to political and social reform in Germany, and to study institutions and resources developed in the United States to determine their applicability to identical or similar domestic problems. Leaders were extremely busy people. Their stay in the United States was relatively short, as a rule no more than 45 to 90 days. By definition they were persons in high level, sensitive positions with pressing obligations and tight schedules. Prolonged absence from Germany could easily create major problems for them and their colleagues and constituents at home. To make the visits profitable, they had to be planned with particular care and related as closely as possible to the specific situation or preoccupations of the visitors.

The exchange program for 1950 listed a total of 156 project titles with nearly two-thirds (96) in education, including religious education, followed by food and agriculture, government and civic affairs, labor, law, and information media. In 1951 the total number of titles declined to 95 with the largest bulk, more than one-half, still in education.

By and large, HICOG found the list of project proposals developed by OMGUS useful and adopted much of it—but with a difference. Whereas OMGUS had relied heavily on foreign consultants, American as well as European, to guide and implement the projects, HICOG, in line with the new policy directive, shifted the emphasis to German participants as the responsible agents of project execution. The various leader projects were sponsored by most of the major offices and divisions of HICOG and their subunits, that is, by the Office of Political Affairs, the Office of Economic Affairs, the Office of Legal Affairs, the Office of Labor Affairs and, the largest number, by the Office of Public Affairs which organized no less than 10 out of a total of 14 leader categories, involving 2,613 out of a total of 4,556 persons for the years 1951–1953.

Education Leaders

The change of emphasis as between OMGUS and HICOG on German participation was particularly evident in the area of education where the ratio of foreign (American and European) experts—not counting OMGUS officials—to German leader and specialist exchangees had been on the order of two to one in favor of the former. Under OMGUS American officials had instructed German authorities how to reform the school system, how to write new textbooks, what textbook and teaching material to use or not to use, how to teach or not teach certain subjects. Americans had run education service centers, conferences, and workshops where German teachers were introduced to new methods and techniques developed in Western countries, e.g., for teacher training, counseling and guidance, classroom education, and the like. Only a limited number of German teachers had gone to the United States in 1949. Their visits had been arranged in instances where American institutions had achieved professional breakthroughs and where on-the-spot observation promised the best results.[15]

With the arrival of James M. Read,[16] the new chief of the Education and Cultural Relations Division, the situation changed radically. In the introductory statement to his first budget proposal, for fiscal year 1950, Read stated, "... It is hoped to impress individuals at all levels of community and professional endeavor with the need of democratic reform and the recognition of modern concepts and techniques in the fields of education, social welfare, youth work, community organization, religious affairs, women's affairs, public health, and the operation of information and education centers and libraries. To accomplish this, a continuing program has been devised to expose national leaders and qualified persons from various areas of civic life to democratic experiences and training in the United States and European countries under the HICOG Exchange Program." [17]

There were other significant changes. The program was larger not only in number of persons but of projects as well. It was more clearly structured. The projects were adapted to the HICOG programs concerned with education, community activities, information centers, religious affairs, women's affairs, and public health and welfare. Not all projects called for the use of exchanges, but a very large number did.

A series of new projects was added to those previously proposed by OMGUS. The organization and administration of school libraries which involved radical changes of traditional concepts was an example. On the premise that child development was not the monopoly of formal education, greater emphasis was placed on child guidance, preschool education, and out-of-school treatment of children. The traditional German system of education made little or no allowance for any one of these programs. Not all projects of HICOG were original. What distinguished them from those of OMGUS was less the choice of subject matter or problem area than the broader gauge and degree of sophistication employed in their selection and application.

Government Officials and Political Leaders [18]

This group included, first, members of the executive and legislative branches at the federal and state level, as well as a goodly number of municipal and county officials, all selected on a nonpartisan basis. Projects corresponded to the statutory functions or major area of competence of the candidates.

The first group of legislators, for instance, was intensely interested in studying the Legislative Reference Service of the Library of Congress. Lack of a similar institution in Germany had made the German Parliament unduly dependent on the resources and the cooperation of the executive branch even in matters which were its primary responsibility under the Constitution, namely national legislation. The creation of a library and research facility under the jurisdiction of the Bundestag (House of Representatives), the legislators hoped, would materially strengthen the position of the legislative vis-a-vis the executive branch of government. It would thereby correct an historical imbalance of power which, in the past, had led to excesses of the executive.

Another group was the Security Committee of the Bundestag, which was engaged in drafting a law for the new German defense forces. The group wished to study the American system, specifically the way in which the United States had dealt with the problem of civilian control over the military. This project was without doubt one of the most significant projects undertaken under the auspices of the exchange program. Among other things, it brought outstanding figures in German political life in touch with their American counterparts, policy makers, and administrators. Further, it produced a most progressive piece of legislation in Germany. (For details on the results of the above two visits by members of the German Bundestag, see Chapter VIII.)

Aside from such special projects, Bundestag members were given ample opportunities to observe Congress and state legislatures in action, the purpose of these arranged visits being to aid German legislators in their efforts to increase the prestige and authority of the German legislature on the Federal and Land (State) level and to improve the efficiency of legislative processes. Over the years a very substantial portion of Bundestag and Landtag (State legislatures) members availed themselves of this opportunity.

In the case of public administrators representing various levels of the executive branch, a principal objective of the Department of State and HICOG was to assist with ongoing efforts to overhaul and modernize the German civil service which in the past had long resisted attempts at democratic reform. While its members were not necessarily Nazis, many exhibited the traditional traits and trappings of German bureaucratic authoritarianism. This group of visitors was introduced to American methods of training and education for public service in a number of ways, through visits with their American counterparts, lengthy discussions with officials of the Bureau of the Budget, frequently including a period of training.

By and large, the HICOG projects demonstrated a deliberate attempt to provide information in specific problem areas. For instance, projects for the government and political leaders included the study of "Legislative Organization and Procedures" (devised in 1950 for a group of 31 members of the German parliament), "State and Federal Governments," "Liberalization of the Civil Service System," "Political Parties and Electoral Systems," "Training for Public Administration," "Local Governments," "City Planning," "Civil Liberties," and "Citizen Participation in Government."

Special attention was given to police officials, a sector of the German administration which had had in many states a history of strongly authoritarian practices. A project entitled "Police Policy and Administration" had the purpose of showing German police officials "the advantages of a system which limits the authority and jurisdiction of the police and which protects the individual citizen from arbitrary police action." The observation and training programs organized in the United States were thus assigned to give police officials a perspective on American police administration and to acquaint them with current U.S. techniques of organization, operation, and training. In 1950, for example, a group of 12 police officials attended a 4-month course on police methods and administrative procedures at Michigan State University with one month devoted to class instruction and 3 months to field inspection where the Germans worked with the local police on a day-to-day basis.

Labor Leaders

The selection of a relatively large number of labor leaders was not accidental. It represented a well-organized effort to help restore relationships between the American trade union movement and its counterpart in Germany, interrupted by 12 years of Nazism. The title "labor leaders," incidentally, was somewhat misleading since the group included managers as well. Another purpose of the program was therefore to acquaint both industrial and labor leaders with American principles, techniques, and procedures governing the "Organization and Administration of Trade Unions," "Standards and Methods of Collective Negotiation," "Labor Management Relations," "Public Service in the Labor Field," "Labor Education and Occupational Training," and "Fact Finding and Research Methods in the Labor Field," to name the most important projects sponsored by HICOG in 1950 and 1951. Two-thirds of the 156 leaders sent to the United States in 1951 were members of the German Trade Union League (DGB). The rest were representatives of the German Employees Union, labor educators, industrial managers, and officials of the labor ministries of the states and cities. A substantial number were young trade unionists. Some of them were grouped in teams of ten, composed of local officers, work counselors, women, and youth belonging to the same industry. Their visits were scheduled to last

90 days. Special programs were planned for 50 young labor leaders not over 25 years of age who were sent in groups of 25 each to the United States for 9 or 10 months of study at universities, such as Wisconsin and Cornell, which had schools or departments of labor-management relations. They took regular courses, visited industrial plants, and attended union meetings. Similar groups were sent in the following years. The director of HICOG's Office of Labor Affairs considered the exchange program "as the most important part of the labor reorientation effort." [19] (See trainee program, below.)

Information Media Leaders

This program represented a deliberate and careful attempt to strengthen the newly-created democratic press and radio as well as to open to the German people through the German media a steady flow of accurate information about the United States. The media had to be rebuilt practically from the ground up. They needed contact, professional advice, and technical assistance. Visits to the United States were to provide just that. Totaling 368 from 1951–1953, journalists and broadcasters constituted one of the larger groups of U.S. Government-sponsored German visitors. Practically every editor-in-chief and radio station director participated in the program. They were among the first to visit this country. They came for a variety of reasons. In the early days under OMGUS they had come to plead the case of a democratic press starved for newsprint in an effort to get General Clay's restrictions lifted and they were successful. Later groups were interested in learning more about American methods and techniques in running newspapers and radio stations. The American Press Institute at Columbia University in 1954 arranged a program for 25 journalists which provided for seminars with leading members of the American press and short internships with various leading newspapers. The Bureau of Applied Social Research at Columbia University organized a program for 40 radio broadcasters, announcers, program directors, and the like, which included seminars and observations at network headquarters and local stations. Another project was planned for five German opinion pollsters by the Survey Research Center of the University of Michigan.[20]

But, most important, nearly all were given a full opportunity to converse with officials of the Truman Administration, Representatives and Senators, and other prominent political figures, such as governors and mayors. The talks were extensive, covering not only German-American relations but other key issues as well. Conversations and interviews were profitable for both sides. They did not always result in an agreement but they produced broad and, on balance, favorable coverage in reports and commentaries for the benefit of the German public. (See also trainee program, below.)

Farm Leaders

A substantial part of the exchange program was aimed at farmers and rural community leaders (260 from 1951–1953). The reason was not so much a strongly-felt need to familiarize Germans with American farming techniques, many of which would not have been applicable to conditions in Germany; it was rather an attempt to extend the benefits of international contact to the rural population, a stronghold of conservatism and often of political isolation and reaction, and to explain to the rural population its role in participating in a democratic society. Projects were therefore oriented toward political, economic, managerial, and some international aspects, addressing such problems as the "Functioning of Free Farmers' Organizations in the U.S.," "Administration of Marketing Regulations in the Field of Food and Agriculture," "Farm Organization, Management and Mechanization," "U.S. Programs for Rural Welfare," "Development of Social Sciences in Agricultural Education," and also "International Aspects of Agrarian and Forest Planning." A number of projects were devoted to the study of "Home Economics" with emphasis on research, extension, and teaching. The educational and technical parts of the study program may have been a success, but surveys taken after their return showed that the political impact was less significant than in the case of other groups. Not altogether surprisingly, farmers still appeared to be a core of resistance to democratic reform (see Chapter VIII).

Women Leaders

Women in postwar Germany outnumbered men by substantial percentages, according to HICOG counts by 18 percent, reflecting the loss of manpower in World War II. But while women had the vote, many of them had entered the professions and even politics (women were members of the Bundestag), and, while, above all, more German women than ever had become wage earners, the average woman continued to lack the interest, the preparation, and especially the social recognition which could have enabled her to compete successfully with men in civic and professional life. HICOG's objective, as set forth in the program proposals of the Education and Cultural Relations Division (ECRD) for fiscal year 1951, was therefore declared to be:

> "to help equip German women to play a more effective role as citizens fully participating in civic life through leadership in community activities, in women's organizations, in professional

and religious organizations and in political parties [and] as an active individual citizen in rural areas, small towns and cities.[21]

To accomplish this purpose, ECRD proposed to provide opportunities for German women leaders for study and for personal experience in the United States and to invite prominent American women leaders to go to Germany to share their knowledge with their German counterparts. Among the problems singled out for special attention was the legal status of women, which involved a revision of the Civil Law Code, and participation of women in political life, in journalism, in adult education, in voluntary organizations, in voluntary and professional social work, in citizen safety programs, in social action, in the teaching of civics, in United Nations affairs, and the like. Serving such purposes were projects on "Women's Participation in Trade Unions," and "The Preparation of Women as Effective Citizens in Economic Life," the latter a subject of considerable urgency in view of the increasing number of women breadwinners. Another project, titled "Assistance in Improving the Position of German Women in Higher Education," was designed to help German women redress the unfavorable balance in academic life where the proportion of women students was little more than 20 percent and that of faculty members scarcely 4 percent. A third project, "German Women's Organization," addressed the need for women to get organized and to increase the effectiveness of their organization by studying and, wherever appropriate, by adopting some of the methods used by American women's groups. Among the first 50 women who came to the United States under the HICOG program, 28 were members of the Bundestag.

In subsequent years programs became more ramified, extending to areas such as "Labor-Management Relations," and "United Nations Specialized Agencies," and giving special attention to the training of young German women in politics and citizenship. Each of these projects was carefully organized, with well worked out itineraries, including briefing sessions by the sponsoring agency—chiefly the Women's Bureau of the Department of Labor—and ample opportunities provided for consultation, discussion and observation on the spot. Participation, as a rule, was limited to women between 20 and 40 years of age who had completed high school education and had had work experience in their specific fields of interest. A modest followup program was foreseen upon their return to Germany.

Community Leaders

This group was somewhat amorphous. Moreover, many of those in the above categories had engaged in community action, and had become community leaders. By definition, its members represented voluntary groups and institutions concerned with informal education of adults and young people for enlightened citizenship. The purpose of the Group Activities Branch of the Division of Education and Cultural Relations which sponsored these visits was "to encourage the development of voluntary and public organizations which provide programs of education for responsible citizenship . . . [and] to encourage the development of cooperative planning programs and projects to achieve a maximum of citizen participation in public affairs." It was another and perhaps the most general of HICOG's many efforts to enlist greater citizen participation at the grass roots in the democratic process in an attempt to supplement its approach to top-level groups. At least in the beginning this group included a large number of youth leaders. The rest consisted of adult education specialists and community organizers concerned with cooperative planning and leadership training. Community activities projects, aside from those devoted to youth programs, included, among others, "Aid to Local Adult Education Organizations," "Adult Education Programs in Rural Areas," "Family Advisory Centers," Community Councils and Citizens Councils," "Community Recreation and Sports," etc.

Legal Affairs Leaders

The study and practice of law in Germany has always been considered an "open sesame" to executive positions in government, industry, and management. It was simply a matter of political judgment for HICOG to choose jurists as another leader group deserving special attention.

Practically no attempt was made to persuade the German legal profession of the virtues of Anglo-Saxon and American law in preference to German or continental codes. One of the few exceptions was a project, launched in 1950, which provided for ten German jurists to study U.S. antitrust legislation and practices for 3 months. Selected for participation were senior members of the bar experienced in antitrust and decartelization matters and some outstanding young law graduates who received a thorough briefing by American attorneys and by the Decartelization Division of the Department of Justice. The project had political implications in view of the traditional structure of German industry and business.

Most other projects dealt with the administration of justice rather than with the practice of law. For example, one project was intended to introduce members of the legal profession to American principles of justice and law enforcement; another was to provide German prison and parole officials with an opportunity to study American methods used in prison administration, social welfare programs for prisoners, rehabilitation services, and measures to combat juvenile delinquency.

Special attention was given to the training of young lawyers and legal trainees (Referendare), the group most likely to enter key positions in the public service, business, and industry. As a rule, that is, with the exception of law students, lawyers were not brought here to enroll at U.S. universities for regular study. Instead, they were attached to courts, various legal authorities (district attorneys and the like), and law offices where they were assigned to auxiliary duties. (See also trainee program, below.)

Public Health and Welfare Leaders

OMGUS had included several projects concerned with health and welfare in its 1950 program proposals. Under HICOG these projects were placed in an independent branch of the Education and Cultural Relations Division. The primary purpose of the new branch was to help bridge the gap created by the 12-year cut off from developments abroad where steady progress had been made in professional fields dealing specifically with the social and psychological needs of women and children. Never a public priority in Germany, these problems had now reached significant proportions as a result of war devastation and postwar deprivation which had produced a sharp increase in infant mortality and communicable diseases. Projects developed under this title were concerned with the modernization of "Maternal and Child Welfare Services." They involved greater emphasis on the preventive and mental hygiene aspects of maternal and child care through appropriate training of physicians, nurses, midwives, and welfare workers. Other projects promoted modern programs on "Mental Health Practices."[22] Their purpose was to develop principles and practices in the field of mental hygiene, psychiatric social work, and related fields. Progress in these areas had been seriously retarded by the Nazis but it had now become an urgent necessity to deal with thousands of borderline psychiatric cases—a legacy of World War II.

A third type of project dealt with "Medical and Public Health Practices," a field that far from being deficient had had in fact a proud tradition in pre-Nazi Germany. The principal problem here was to bring German institutions and practices up to date. A total of 123 German leaders in these fields visited the United States between 1951 and 1953. Some of these visitors studied in public health schools, and obtained field training in local, state, or federal institutions.

Religious Leaders

In pre-Nazi days organized religion had been a significant factor in German political life. Under nazism many churches of various denominations either went into internal exile or into resistance. No wonder then that at the end of the war the churches emerged as one of the least contaminated and discredited elements in German society and reasonably well-equipped to aid in the work of reconstruction. In recognition of their record and potential, the Religious Affairs Branch of HICOG declared as its objective to "utilize the spiritual and moral resources of church organizations and interfaith groups in the establishment of a free society based on social justice, [and] a recognition of the dignity of man;" and to assist and encourage "German elements promoting freedom of religion, interfaith understanding and cooperation in international religious relations." [23]

Church leaders, as noted earlier, were among the first to visit the United States—just as American churches were among the first to sponsor these visits. OMGUS had started the program. Under HICOG the exchange of church leaders became one of the most important, if not indeed the most important, activity in the field of religious affairs. Its primary purpose was "to integrate German religious activities into those of the world community" and also "to afford the present and the future German leadership an opportunity to learn of new trends in world church affairs and new methods and techniques which have developed elsewhere . . ." [24]

Projects organized for religious leaders were therefore not focused on religious subjects *per se*, but on civic responsibility and on interfaith relations. Examples of the former were: "Development of Leadership and Improvement of Program Content in Religious Adult Education," "Development of Religious School Action in Relation to Individual Responsibility and Community Needs," "Development of Mass Media of Religious Interpretation," "Development of Leadership and Improvement of Program Content in Religious Youth Work," "Vitalization of Jewish Community Leadership," and the like. Examples of the latter were such projects as "Education for Democratic Interfaith and Intergroup Relations through Councils of Christians and Jews." The establishment of councils was aimed in the main at combatting anti-semitism, eliminating interreligious tensions, and training citizens "in the use of modern techniques of intercultural integration."

Youth Leaders

Youth leaders were at first part of the larger category of Community Leaders; thereafter in view of their special significance as the logical reservoir for future leadership, they received special attention. In 1952, a program was organized for young people 14–25 years of age. This group constituted about 15 percent of the population in the U.S. Zone.[25] It presented serious problems for the Germans as well as for the occupation powers. Most of the young people had completed their formal education, whatever it might have consisted of—apprenticeships, baccalaureate (Abitur), or graduation from universities. Many of those who had been uprooted by the war had returned from military service or prisoner of war camps or were refugees from East Germany. More than 10 percent were without gainful employment. Many were still imbued with the vestiges of National-Socialist indoctrination; others were apathetic, demoralized, or totally adrift.

HICOG sponsored a large-scale diversified program for youth in Germany and, in recognition of the tradition of German youth to "do their own thing" in autonomous organizations, permitted the restoration of certain pre-Nazi youth groups. Directives were issued which listed as objectives:

> "to help youth realize the interrelationship between individual freedom and social responsibility . . .
> "to generate among German youth active resistance to totalitarianism of both the Right and the Left . . .
> "to stimulate interest and confidence in democratic governmental and political institutions and practices . . .
> "to interpret and increase the understanding of the American way of life . . .
> "to develop and strengthen the cultural, political, economic and social ties between Germany and Western democratic countries . . ." [26]

To help accomplish these objectives, especially the last two, HICOG developed exchange programs which were aimed primarily at the current leadership of organized youth but, beyond this, at young persons likely to emerge as future leaders in politics, civic life, and the professions. The latter programs involved the inauguration of a substantial exchange program for teenagers.

In keeping with American practices of youth work, but somewhat contrary to German tradition, the youth leadership exchange had a strong professional social work accent [27] and was, in fact, organized and supervised to a large extent by social agencies and social workers. It encompassed such projects as "Civic Education," "Social Group Work Training," "Leisure Time Recreation Programs," and "Youth Publications." The purpose of the project on "Civic Education" was "to observe and analyze the role played by American youth and youth leaders in civic and community services," and "to understand the importance of self-government within youth organizations." The Social Group Work Training project was intended to help Germans engaged in group leadership to "analyze and learn methods, techniques, science and philosophy underlying group work," as it was taught at graduate schools of social work in the United States, and to "observe its practical application toward the development of a cooperative social structure."

In truth these youth-oriented exchanges were more in the nature of a social training than a leadership program. Participants in the civic education projects were young persons between the ages of 21 and 35 years who had completed their education and had been either professionally or voluntarily engaged in "group leadership" programs. Contrary to the usual requirements for leader exchangees, those undergoing social group work training had to commit themselves to a two-semester study (270 days) program at a university in the United States offering graduate courses in group work. Those selected for civic education projects would enroll for the same period at universities offering courses in government, political science, or social philosophy.

Both groups had to do a certain amount of field work. Social group work trainees observed group work programs as practiced in public and private social agencies. Those studying civic education visited citizens councils, political parties, labor unions, consumer cooperatives, youth leagues, and the like, to learn how civic and political institutions in this country were launched, programs activated, and information disseminated. In particular, they observed the organization and operation of political parties, their relationship to the government, the effect of political pressure, neighborhood initiative on city hall, and the like.

Upon their return to Germany, youth leaders who had been trained for social group work jobs, in particular, were expected to train other group workers, work with youth leadership centers, and contribute to the program of professional (socio-pedagogic) institutions. Those trained in civic education, it was hoped, would serve as leaders of public forums and civic committees, train volunteer leaders in civic and political education, undertake public speaking engagements, and assist in organizing youth events, including international camps and European youth rallies.[27] With a total of 314 participants between 1951 and 1953, programs for youth leaders were one of the more significant segments of the exchange program.[28]

Cooperative Action Teams

In 1951–1952, HICOG added a new leader category to the existing ones: the so-called "Cooperative Action Teams." The inauguration of this project has been described occasionally as signifying a departure from the reorientation purposes toward more general objectives.[29] The point is debatable. The Cooperative Action Teams had, at least implicitly, a reorientation purpose, namely, to demonstrate and stimulate nonpartisan citizen initiative in community affairs. German municipal administration has often been characterized by a high degree of bureaucratization and politicization. Party politics had dominated appointments and decisions. The influence of voluntary elements in the community had been relatively weak, if not totally missing. So had been cooperation based on citizens' participation. The objectives for the Cooperative Action Team project, as stated in an evaluation study of 1953, were:

> "to afford carefully selected German leaders representing various areas of community interest the opportunity to observe and study the operations of citizens' groups in American cities comparable in size to those cities from which the various teams originate in Germany." [30]

The ultimate purpose of the visits was to promote cooperation between civic authorities and citizens and to strengthen the hand of voluntary groups in exercising, through cooperative action, a modicum of influence in community affairs. It was hoped, as this study put it, that,

> "through the experience gained . . . these teams upon their return to Germany may stimulate their respective communities to take cooperative corrective steps through democratic community action to solve civic problems, such as housing, public welfare, public health, education, city government, and other facets of community life." [31]

In short, these teams represented still another approach to developing democracy at the grass roots.

To achieve broadest community participation, teams consisted, in addition to members of city administrations and city councils, of representatives of labor (trade unions), management, business, press and other information media, churches, education, social welfare, women's groups and other citizens' associations, youth, farmer groups, and political parties. Not each of these elements was included in every team. On the other hand, individual team members generally represented more than one civic group. As a rule, fewer than ten persons composed a team.

Altogether, 50 Cooperative Action Teams were sent to the United States between 1951 and 1955. Between September 1952 and April 1953 alone, 135 community leaders from 16 German cities visited the United States in teams. They were men and women with a wide range of interests, representing all age groups (with the bulk between 30 and 50 years of age) and the three major political parties, and coming mostly from the middle to upper socioeconomic strata. The first six teams arrived in the spring of 1951. They were chosen from six cities in the three western zones. They included men and women constituting a cross section of each community.

Their program in the United States was planned and organized by the Governmental Affairs Institute [32] under direction of the Department of State. Three localities were selected by the Institute to serve as study centers—a large city in the East, e.g., Philadelphia; a rural area in the Midwest, e.g., the Grand Traverse area of Michigan; a university town on the Pacific Coast, e.g., Berkeley, California. Each team spent 3 weeks at each center to observe various facets of citizen participation in community activities and, as the Institute stipulated,[33] to gain a broader understanding of citizen responsibility in community affairs. Eventually the projects were trimmed down from 90 to 60 days with visits limited to two instead of three centers. The curtailment permitted the inclusion of a higher caliber of community leaders who because of pressure of business at home would otherwise have been prevented from participation.[34] Initially most groups spent several days in Washington, D.C., for general orientation purposes, and for a final session at the end of their trip. At the centers, members of the team, depending on their interests and functions, would visit city halls, schools, newspaper headquarters, industrial plants, civic, labor and youth organizations, churches, and similar institutions, where they interviewed the principal officials. Each team member received a per diem of $10. Transportation between cities was arranged and financed by the Governmental Affairs Institute which received the necessary funds from the Department of State. In addition, sponsoring agencies in each of the three centers were given a sum of $300 to help cover local expenses.[35]

On balance, the Cooperative Action Teams proved to be an innovative feature that was well received by German and American participants alike. Its effectiveness was incontestable as far as its public relations aspects were concerned. To what extent it helped to accomplish the avowed purpose of civic reform in German communities, is less certain (see below, Chapter VIII).[36]

Other Categories

HICOG's reports and budget proposals listed a number of additional types of persons who fell into the category of specialists rather than leaders. These included social service workers, librarians, and museologists. Social service specialists were small in number (24), but performed a mission which in postwar Germany filled a sensitive void. Social work had been practiced in Germany largely on a voluntary basis. Existing institutes for "social pedagogics," corresponding roughly to our own schools of social work, did not have full academic status. Modern social work techniques, notably case and group work, which had been developed in the United States to a high level of professionalism, were widely unknown. With such problems as juvenile delinquency, the breakdown of social institutions, including the family, mass uprooting of persons of all classes, and economic distress dominating the German scene in the late forties and fifties, social service workers faced a seemingly unanswerable challenge. American social work with its professional approach and tested techniques provided valuable assistance. It helped increase the efficiency of the German welfare apparatus. (See also trainee program, below.)

Librarians were anxious to reform the antiquated German libraries and found at least part of the answer in the "open shelf" system. Models could be observed in the libraries of the America Houses in Germany, and the American Memorial Library in Berlin, where the system was introduced primarily on the initiative of the late Edgar Breitenbach, a consultant to HICOG on loan from the Library of Congress.

Two summary statements may be made about the visits of German leaders to the United States under the exchange program: (1) they helped restore and strengthen German capability of self-rehabilitation, and (2) they assured the infusion of new ideas and methods into critical sectors of German society (for further details, see Chapter VIII).

The Student and Trainee Program

The Student Exchange Program accented youth as one of HICOG's primary target groups.[37] OMGUS had recognized the importance of student exchanges but, as was pointed out previously, had failed to provide the organizational and, above all, the financial resources needed to give its intentions substance and reality. The OMGUS proposal for fiscal year 1950 had foreseen supplementary assistance in the amount of $206,680 at an average rate of $218 per student for 943 students receiving scholarships from private institutions. The Institute of International Education, as noted earlier, under its contract with the Department of the Army was unable to obtain more than 125 full or partial scholarships. Supplementary assistance in the amount of $600 per German student was necessary to enable them to take advantage of the program.

The Department of State, accepting the recommendation of the Survey Mission of 1949, proposed a total of $550,000 to cover the expenses of 250 German students and of $1,100,000 for so-called junior experts and trainees.[38] The amount requested permitted an average grant of $2,200 for each student, covering tuition, maintenance, books and incidentals, travel in the United States, shipboard maintenance, and head tax. This "minimum" number of grants had to be supplemented by scholarships offered by American institutions and organizations. Those were the 1949 proposals. An earlier initiative by the Army to send so-called junior experts for special study programs to the United States at a cost of $4,000 per participant had been rejected as extravagant and likely to provoke harmful repercussions in Congress and from the American public.

In actual fact, the number of students and trainees going to the United States differed slightly from earlier estimates (see Appendix III). The total for students was about 239 in 1949. It nearly doubled in 1950, dropped by 10 percent in 1951, and by another 50 percent in 1952, then remained through 1955 at an annual level of about 180. Trainees, on the whole, stayed below the number of students, except from 1951 to 1953 when they exceeded the latter by substantial amounts. Altogether, approximately 1,891 students and 1,823 trainees came to the United States between 1949 and 1955 under HICOG, with the largest groups, e.g., 1,055 and 1,253, respectively, in the three HICOG years 1950 through 1952. The peak year for German students was 1950 and for trainees 1951. After 1952, students came under the Fulbright program (discussed in Chapter VII, below).

The distinction made between the two groups was not always evident. Both students and trainees studied at various accredited institutions in fields of declared preference. Essentially, the difference was one of age and state of advancement. By HICOG's definition, students were "young people already studying or about to enter universities who were given a year's scholarship to an American college or university." Trainees, on the other hand, were "young men and women who had completed their formal education and were just beginning their chosen careers." [39] They were given an opportunity "to become acquainted with special cooperative and/or group concepts and techniques, as practiced in a democratic setting through practical experience in the United States." [40]

Both student and trainee programs were carefully designed to fit the students' needs and interests and, at the same time, to provide exposure to the American scene outside the academic field. Apart from that, student exchange programs were intended to make up for deficiencies in the academic training of all students and in the case of graduates and postgraduates to help prepare them for certain critical professions.

Student Programs and Projects

Among the student projects, the study of student government and of nonacademic student activities by selected teams figured most prominently. The idea sprang from a series of assumptions, namely, that there was a notorious lack of organized student participation in German university affairs; that this fact, in turn, tended to indulge the authoritarian habits of the university administration and faculty; that there was little emphasis in the academic training on social issues and studies; that the very concept of "campus life" allowing for a variety of extracurricular activities was missing; and that, as a result of all these deficiencies, there had always been a total lack of democratic tradition, to say nothing of the indoctrination of faculties and students under nazism.

Conditions in German universities, it was believed even after denazification, reaffirmed and perpetuated a system which produced topnotch professionals, highly qualified to perform with distinction in their field of specialization, but rarely inclined and ill-equipped to shoulder the broader responsibilities of citizenship. The projects, developed as early as 1950, were intended to stimulate student initiative in university reform, using American models as far as practicable. As spelled out by HICOG their purposes were:

—to help German youth to understand the effectiveness of student government activities;
—to orient German university student leaders in aspects of community concepts of university life;
—to permit German youth leaders to discover the place of extracurricular activities as a part of the broad educational program;
—to enable German university youth leaders to study designs, functions, and youth uses of student union buildings with particular emphasis upon student participation in management and administration, (and)
—to gain ideas concerning the development and administration of scholarship and student welfare programs.[41]

Contracts concluded between universities and the Department of State stipulated as their purpose "to introduce German student leaders to student activities as they exist on an American campus, to provide an opportunity for German students to participate in these activities and learn, first hand, the functioning of a democratically organized student life." [42]

As the projects developed under HICOG, their focus became broader and more sophisticated. The University of Minnesota, which hosted one of the most mature and most critical student teams, adopted the earlier formula which was to introduce German students to the philosophy behind student activity programs and to foster a closer working relationship between faculty adviser and student. But, beyond this, the objective was defined as one of providing the visitors with clearer concepts of the purposes and role of higher education in the United States, the mechanisms by which these goals are approximated, and the relationship between both classroom and out-of-class experience in attaining these goals." [43]

A number of universities and colleges participated in the program, including Antioch, Carnegie Tech, Florida, Harvard, Indiana, Michigan, Minnesota, North Carolina, and Syracuse. Organization, content, and approach varied. In most cases faculty members, e.g., the Dean of Students, with the assistance of the student body and advisory committees, developed, administered, and operated the project, a fact which some of the German visitors found difficult to accept (see Chapter VIII). In other instances, e.g., at Harvard, the Student Council assumed full responsibility for the administration of the program. Some universities appointed "coordinators" to supervise the project.

As a rule, the German visitors were considered as "special students." They were expected or at least encouraged to enroll in regular courses, generally in fields of their personal interest. Their academic load, however, was kept lower than that of their American classmates, so that few were able to complete full course requirements. Consequently, with some exceptions, their class performance was not graded.[44] One such exception was Harvard where students were not only graded, but attendance was prescribed for selected courses in government and the social sciences (e.g., American constitutional development, American foreign policy, international law, growth of the American economy, etc.). Even here the academic program was second in importance to the study of campus institutions, such as the student government, student union, assembly, and extracurricular campus activities, and participation was urged, wherever practical, in such activities. The balance of the students' time was devoted to field trips to visit community institutions, civic organizations, industrial plants, neighboring campuses, and the like. Finally, provision was made for regular consultations and discussions with faculty members and students to sort out and to evaluate impressions gained.[45]

Whether the student government project accomplished its objective is hard to tell. To be sure, it was more successful in some universities than in others—Minnesota being an example of lesser impact. Given the different and often conflicting philosophy and conditions prevailing in American and German universities, it was unrealistic to hope for complete success, if "success" was understood to mean a wholesale transfer of American models to the German situation. On balance, the results were better than could be expected, considering the open criticism and resistance exhibited by some of the German participants. A number of German universities introduced a series of innovations in their structure, although caution must be exercised in tracing these changes to the influence of former exchangees.

An undeniable benefit of the project was a better understanding, even where the visitors were critical, of American campus life. A number of students, moreover, carried away very positive impressions along with the resolve to apply their experience, with appropriate adaptations, to the situation at home.

Other projects that were focused on specific technical subjects were highly successful. This applied especially to studies in such fields as law, industrial relations, journalism, agriculture, agricultural economics, and home economics. Requirements were similar to those mentioned above but course selection was, as a rule, highly specialized with emphasis on technical rather than on broader liberal arts subjects. Nevertheless, here, too, the exposure to American campus life was strong enough to make an impact upon the visitors far beyond the acquisition of technical knowledge. It led to positive impressions of the American educational system, the American political scene, and the value of international contacts.

The bulk of students, i.e., those placed individually by the Institute of International Education, did not participate in group projects but pursued special academic studies on an individual basis. Yet, even in these cases policy prescribed that, regardless of the subject of specialization, the program had to include courses in the humanities and the social sciences, with special emphasis on political science, history, and sociology. Moreover, students were expected to participate in extracurricular activities, e.g., student government and other student functions, and to mix with American students. Arrangements to visit with American families were also made.[46] Among the students who participated, a number reached later positions of great prominence. Harvard student Klaus Schuetz was until recently the Governing Mayor of Berlin. Another who attended Harvard, Hildegard Hamm-Bruecher, became State Secretary in the Federal Government and an active promoter of educational reform.

Trainee Programs and Projects

More important and, perhaps, more successful were the projects developed for so-called trainees. They served basically two major purposes. The first, started by OMGUS and revived by Dr. Charles R. Cherington, professor of government at Harvard University, with the encouragement of the author in 1949,[47] was to supplement the highly specialized training received in German universities by postgraduate students about to enter government careers or other pursuits involving broad social and civic responsibilities. Participants were to be enrolled in courses in the social sciences and, on a selective basis, in courses related to their chosen professional careers. In addition, special seminars and field trips would be arranged. The second and overriding objective of these projects was to train a cadre of future leaders in professional fields which were of critical importance to the solution of some of Germany's postwar problems but for which German universities did not provide training opportunities on a sufficiently broad academic level, e.g., political and social sciences.

Quite consistently, HICOG Technical Instruction 2 of September 18, 1950 defined trainees as "persons who have completed all formal education necessary for entrance upon their field of activities but have not yet achieved positions of influence, who will go to the United States for periods from 3 months to a year for supervised study and training at one institution but with the opportunity for observation of activities in their field outside that institution."[48] Later the definition was broadened to include persons who "may have already practiced their vocation for a few years." Trainees, in fact, were described as "selected mature persons."[49] While this revision was meant to separate trainees from the bulk of students, though not necessarily graduate students, it blurred somewhat the lines of demarcation that separated them from young leaders and specialists, notably youth leaders.

The trainee program focused on a number of groups whose contributory role to democratic reform was of singular importance. The first group included the so-called "Referendare," that is, German law students who had passed their first state examination and were about to enter—or already had entered—3 years of practical internship.[50] Since as noted before, in Germany legal training has always been and still is considered as the normal preparation for the higher brackets in government, industry, and commerce, Referendare were potentially Germany's future administrators, executives, and managers. As such they constituted a priority group of great significance and required a tailor-made type of training. The Department of State, therefore, insisted and the office of the General Counsel of HICOG wholeheartedly agreed that this was not a student project, but a training project with high reorientation potential. Referendare were therefore not to be enrolled as regular students at legal institutions to work toward academic credits. Instead special programs were to be arranged for them in general jurisprudence, philosophy of law, public and comparative law, legal education, legal organizations and institutions and legal practices, as well as political theory, comparative government, and international relations. Special faculty advisers were to guide them in research in fields of special interest to them and related to reorientation objectives. HICOG subsequently recommended that this program be broadened to include younger judges, prosecutors, and other legal functionaries.[51]

The second group involved young professionals who had undergone training in Germany but who were anxious to catch up with developments outside that had occurred during 12 years of self-imposed isolation. Among them, journalists ranked most prominently. During the Empire and the Weimar Republic, German journalism had attained a level of excellence on a par with the best of the world press. It had been totally corrupted by nazism and needed to be rebuilt from the bottom up. OMGUS and HICOG had spent a great deal of effort and funds on resurrecting a democratic press and other media. Nevertheless, certain flaws persisted, such as the tendency to mix editorializing and straight news reporting. Furthermore, shut off from outside contacts during Nazi days, German journalists had not been able to profit from recent technical advances in printing processes, paper manufacture, and the like. An implicit purpose of this project was to provide German media specialists with a true and, it was hoped, favorable image of the United States so crudely distorted by Nazi propaganda.

A number of universities, e.g., Columbia, Kentucky, Missouri, Northwestern, and Oregon, organized special programs for groups of eight to ten journalists.[52] Again, these study programs were not limited to technical subjects, e.g., copy editing, composition, and modern printing techniques, but included a wide variety of academic disciplines, such as political science, economics, history, psychology, literature, art, speech, and languages. Requirements differed slightly at various universities but, as a rule, involved course enrollment, special seminars, and practice in professional writing. By its very design, the program enabled participants to form first-hand impressions of American journalism in action, of American institutions, and of American life in general.

Another group which added an innovative feature to the exchange program was the training project for social workers. As noted earlier the need for skilled professional performance in a country harassed by the breakdown of social relations and institutions was self-evident. The resources in Germany were scarce. Social work and social services were largely the monopoly of public agencies and private charity. None of the training schools in existence were fully accredited by academic institutions. Accordingly, the training lacked certain basic features endemic to the social work profession in a democratic environment. Casework methods, staff supervision, interagency cooperation, and the like were largely unknown, certainly unpracticed.[53]

The basic purpose of the training project was to enable German social workers showing potential for leadership to observe American institutions, philosophy, methods, and techniques with a view to adapting them as far as practicable to German conditions. The study program was carefully worked out by an Advisory Committee of the National Social Welfare Assembly under the leadership of the late Bernice Bridges. It foresaw regular study at nine accredited schools of social work, including the New York School of Social Work (Columbia University), St. Louis University, and Western Reserve University, and field visits to social agencies. The training ended with an intensive evaluation session of participants with sponsors to discuss prospects of applicability of the exchange experience to the situation in Germany.

Other trainee projects included study programs in industrial relations organized for young trade union leaders and potential managerial leaders. While Germany had a strong labor movement dating back to imperial days and flourishing in the Weimar Republic, it, too, had been destroyed by the Nazi regime. It was felt that American practices, specifically in the field of industrial, i.e., labor-management, relations might offer an adaptable model to German labor and industry in reviving a system of relationships appropriate to their own needs. The study program was worked out by the Department of State with universities, such as Chicago, Cornell, Illinois, and Wisconsin, which had special courses in industrial relations. Selected for study were courses in industrial management, methods of collective bargaining, handling of grievances, trade union organization, and the like. Again, special care was taken not to limit the program to classroom study of technical subjects but to include, though with somewhat minor emphasis, courses in American culture, history, political institutions, economics, education and minority problems, and to arrange field trips to industrial plants and the now customary visits with American families.[54]

Teenagers (Secondary School Students)

Programs for youth below college level started in 1949, when a group of 100 rural teenagers were invited to the United States upon the initiative and with the assistance of the Brethren Service Committee. Within the next few years the total increased substantially.[55] By 1956 a total of 2,283 German youths had participated in the program, their visits financed from public and private funds. The number of teenagers coming under governmental auspices was 2,246 (including 155 tentative openings for fiscal year 1956). Cost estimates foreseen or listed in HICOG budgets for fiscal years 1951 to 1953 ran to $1,113,880 (actual expenditures for 1951 were $383,400). The governmental program peaked in 1950 with a total of 495, then declined gradually through 1953, dropping in 1954 to less than half the 1950 figure (see Appendix III).

Participants in the teenage program were boys and girls of not less than 16 and not more than 18 years of age, generally secondary school students, from both urban and rural areas. Each was expected to spend a year in the United States living with American "foster" families, attending high schools and participating in the programs of local youth groups and community activities.[56] The original purpose of the teenage program had strongly humanitarian as well as practical purposes. The stay in the United States, it was hoped, would "heal the wounds of the war;"[57] but other purposes had specific reorientation aims, namely, "to instill a knowledge of and respect for the democratic way of life in the youth of those countries [Germany and Austria] who had been indoctrinated under the National Socialist regime and were isolated from [indeed had never been exposed to] democratic practices and thought." Subsequently, with the relaxation of Allied control and Germany's gradual return to independence and sovereignty, the program objectives shifted from reorientation to "increasing mutual understanding," [58] with the expectation that life in a typical American environment might help the youngsters correct prejudices and form new views of the United States, thus laying the groundwork for a mutually beneficial relationship between America and Germany.

The teenage program has been widely acclaimed as one of the most successful ventures in the history of exchanges. Whether it was or not (for details on its effectiveness see Chapter VIII), it was by all accounts highly popular. American sponsors, host families, and HICOG officials were enthusiastic, urging continuation from year to year despite the cost. A large part of the latter had to be borne by the "foster" parents and the private sponsors, such as the American Field Service, the Brethren Service Committee, the National Grange, the National 4–H Club Foundation, the National Catholic Welfare Conference, the Kiwanis Club of Georgia, Rotary International, the Ann Arbor Council of Churches, the National Conference of Christians and Jews, and other service oriented organizations. The Department of State accepted what appeared to be a general desire to proceed with the program but eventually proposed a gradual transition from partly governmental to fully private sponsorship, with the Department providing some assistance in the form of temporary grants-in-aid and logistic facilitation.[59]

Admittedly, the teenage program had a number of flaws which were partly technical defects and occurred mostly at the beginning. There were genuine complaints at first about faulty selection and careless placements.[60] Most of these difficulties were eliminated with growing experience on the part of the sponsoring organizations and the "foster" parents. Others, more fundamental, appear to have lingered on. Teenagers were enthusiastic admirers of the United States and equally enthusiastic reporters. They formed friendships and strong affinities to their host country. But their very enthusiasm created problems. For many, readjustment to life in still war-devastated Germany was difficult. The cultural shock of returning home proved too much for some. Of the 217 German participants in the exchange program who emigrated after their return to Germany, one-third were teenagers and two-thirds of the latter came to the United States.[61] Some of those who tried to tell the American story at home found it hard to get it across. Often adopted mannerisms, invidious comparisons, or sheer exuberance exhibited by them in their travel accounts caused misunderstandings and led to accusations that they had become "Americanized." In other instances, the tendency of German adults to put down the young denied them a bona fide audience altogether.[62]

On balance, however, the positive aspects of the program appear to have by far outweighed the negative. The teenagers proved to be good ambassadors of their country. On their return they were, in the judgment of HICOG officers, "constructive forces in their local communities in breaking down and preventing misunderstandings and misconceptions about the United States and its citizens as well as in promoting democratic processes in their own spheres of influence, such as their homes, schools and social organizations." [63]

Americans to Germany

At the beginning HICOG's program for American specialists visiting Germany was more or less a mere continuation of OMGUS' consultants' program, except that HICOG's consultants and specialists were expected to deal directly with their German counterparts rather than with HICOG officials. A HICOG instruction of September 1, 1950 defined U.S. specialists as "citizens of the United States highly qualified and professionally prominent, whose services are desired in Germany to confer and advise with German agencies on pertinent questions in their specific fields in conjunction with projects planned, according to indicated need, by various HICOG substantive divisions." [64] Reorientation remained the essence of their assignment, but it now became an auxiliary and advisory rather than an authoritative function. Consultants, or specialists as they were increasingly referred to, were to furnish "additional American expert assistance" and to "work with" German institutions and organizations for limited periods of time and to bring their expertise to bear on specific problems or projects. Within the confines of their mandate they were "to demonstrate the value of democratic concepts and techniques" for the benefit of their German counterparts. Beyond this, they were to assist "in establishing effective relationships between German and other Western groups and organizations." [65] No longer semi-employees of the U.S. Government, as they were under OMGUS, specialists were selected by the Department of State with the concurrence of HICOG's Exchange Division and subject to review by the German agency concerned. Projects on which specialists were to work were as a rule initiated by German agencies, but had to be approved by the HICOG exchange staff at headquarters.[66]

The program was different from that of OMGUS, but it certainly was not massive. By comparison with the number of Germans going to the United States, that of U.S. citizens traveling to Germany remained rather modest. The total of specialists from 1949 through 1955 was 689. In 1952 this number was increased by 330 so-called lecturers, scholars, and teachers, all but 27 of whom were Fulbrighters. (See Appendix III.) The rationale of this "exchange" reflected the lopsided nature of German-American relations in the early fifties when the United States still acted in the role of adviser and sponsor and Germany in that of client and recipient, but with the Americans performing their part on a steadily diminishing scale. Emphasis now was increasingly being placed on self-reorientation, so that Germans going to the United States in effect supplemented the American experts by providing their newly acquired knowledge to their fellow citizens upon their return.

The new arrangements required careful selection of subject areas and individuals. As far as the former were concerned, little if any difference was made between the areas of priority selected for Germans and American specialists. The first HICOG proposals of the Education and Cultural Relations Division for 1951 list between 70 and 80 American consultants distributed among education, community activities, information centers, women's affairs, public health, and welfare.[67] (The actual number processed was somewhat smaller, i.e., approximately 55). Other fields [68] included politics and government, youth activities, labor, information media, social services, law, agriculture, religious affairs, and libraries and museums.

Education remained the most important field, outnumbering the next highest category by nearly two to one. The rationale for selection of individuals was different from the one that governed the selection of Germans going to the United States. The emphasis for the latter was on study, observation, and training; in the case of American specialists the burden was, in accordance with established policy, on teaching, lecturing, counseling, and training, and on assisting the new leadership in Germany with the planning of political, administrative, and educational reforms and with the preparation of basic materials.

The American specialists' program had come under heavy fire when it was under OMGUS auspices. Under HICOG, voices of criticism were occasionally still heard. But, by and large, it gained in prestige and effectiveness, due primarily to the high caliber of American experts who were invited to participate.

A complete list of American specialists selected in the early HICOG years is no longer available, but a few samples for 1950 and 1951 give a good cross section of the level and scope of the selection made. In the governmental affairs area, the list included, among others, the names of Roger Baldwin, Chairman of the American Civil Liberties Union; Arnold Brecht, Professor of Political Science, New School for Social Research; Taylor Cole, Duke University;

Harold Dorr, Professor of Political Science, University of Michigan; Pendleton Herring, Director of the Social Science Research Council; Karl Loewenstein, Professor of Jurisprudence, Amherst College; Franz Neumann, Professor of Government, Columbia University (who was instrumental in promoting the study of political science at the Free University of Berlin and assisting with the creation of the new Institute for Political Science in Berlin); Sigmund Neumann, Professor of Sociology, Wesleyan College; James Pollock, Professor of Political Science, University of Michigan; Richard Scammon, at that time Chief, Division of Research for Western Europe, Department of State; Roger Wells, Professor of Political Science, Bryn Mawr College; and Quincy Wright, Professor of International Law, University of Chicago, to name just a few. Some of them had previously served on the OMGUS or HICOG staff. Among them were some distinguished German scholars in the United States who were exiles from Nazi Germany.

Those in religious affairs included Willard Johnson and Sterling Brown, both of whom served at one time as General Directors of the National Conference of Christians and Jews; Rev. Gilbert V. Hartke, Head of the Speech and Drama Department, Catholic University; and Rev. John LaFarge, Catholic Inter-Racial Council; in labor and agricultural affairs, S. Earl Grigsby of the Bureau of Agricultural Economics of the Department of Agriculture; in legal affairs, Max Rheinstein, Professor of Comparative Law, University of Chicago; and Richard A. McGee, Director of the California Department of Corrections. American women interested in helping in German women's affairs included Margaret Hickey, editor of the *Ladies Home Journal*, and a member of the executive board of the American Red Cross; Lilian Shapley of the Community Division of the YWCA; Mrs. Harold Dyke of the League of Women Voters of the United States; Mrs. Arthur Anderson, president of the National Board of the YWCA; Dr. Dorothy Ferebee, Medical Director of University Health Services at Howard University; and Dr. Minnie Maffett, surgeon and gynecologist, and former president of the National Federation of Business and Professional Women's Clubs.

American specialists in education included George A. Selke, Chancellor, University of Montana; Chris A. DeYoung, National Education Association; Hazel Hatcher, Professor of Home Economics, Pennsylvania State University; Edward G. Olsen, Supervisor of School and Community Relations, State of Washington; and Lucile Allard, supervisor and psychologist, New York Public Schools.

All consultants submitted reports to HICOG and to the Department of State upon their return which summarized, often quite critically, their major findings and concluded with specific recommendations. Unfortunately, most of the reports were subsequently lost or destroyed. Even more regrettably, there appears to be no record of the use that was made by HICOG of the recommendations. Undoubtedly, given the investment made in the program and the high quality of some reports, it is safe to assume that many of them were put into practice by HICOG or by German policy makers, administrators, civic leaders, and educators to whom they were addressed. But, aside from a few instances (see Chapter VIII), the influence of American experts cannot be documented.

There were practically no American student exchanges during the first HICOG years. A program of notable scale started only after the Fulbright agreement came into effect in 1953, which is discussed fully in Chapter VII, below. American students who attended German universities prior to the Fulbright agreement did so under private auspices.[69]

While the so-called project method was followed only to a degree in the case of Americans going to Germany, there were exceptions which deserve special mention. Among the first to volunteer assistance was a group of young men and women organized under the auspices of the Experiment in International Living who wished to participate in reconstruction work.

Nearly all other projects were in the field of art and music. As such, their reorientation value may have seemed negligible, at best indirect. But their projection of America as a center of artistic creation had an impact second to none. The major occasions were the Berlin Arts or Cultural Festivals in 1951 and 1952. The Department of State and HICOG decided to send to Germany some of the best musical and theatrical productions that were available at the time. HICOG provided the facilities and the Department contracted with the American National Theater and Academy (ANTA). It was the beginning of a long and useful relationship with that organization, which selected, managed, and presented, subject to the Department's approval, the individual events.

The idea underlying this singular undertaking was to demonstrate the high standards of American performing arts achievements and, by implication, to refute Nazi and Communist propaganda clichés of American cultural insensibility and sterility. The selection was done with skill and imagination. It included in 1951 a performance of "Medea" with Judith Anderson in the title role, guest appearances of soprano Astrid Varnay with the Berlin Opera Company, the Juilliard String Quartet, a presentation of "Oklahoma" with Celeste Holm, the Hall-Johnson Choir, a violin recital by

Maurice Wilk, and Angna Enters, dance-mime. The American participation was a success. Ernst Reuter, then Mayor of Berlin, spoke of the "superb" American contribution to the festival.

Yet the success of the American presence in the following year (1952) was nothing short of spectacular. The author decided to send Gershwin's "Porgy and Bess" to the festival, whence it was to go to other European capitals. Well-meaning friends advised against it. So did prominent members of the American black community, who feared that German or even any European audiences were not ready to appreciate the message and that the sordid misery of Catfish Alley would be taken to portray the normal life of the American black community. Yet the performance of a 65 all-black member cast was a triumph. It literally overwhelmed the Berlin audience. Comments in West Berlin were lyrical and not one critical note was heard from the Communist press in East Berlin. The success was similar in other cities. It was a major breakthrough of American black culture upon the European scene.

Other American participants in the festival were the New York City Ballet, Eugene Ormandy, and sopranos Astrid Varnay and Polyna Stoska. The combined effect of these contributions, according to HICOG, "did more to elevate American prestige in one month than anything else attempted in Germany in the past seven years." [70] During the same year the Boston Symphony Orchestra under the baton of Charles Munch and of Pierre Monteux played in Berlin and Frankfurt; as did the Paganini Quartet.

Germans to Other European Countries

Nearly from the very start of the exchange program provision was made for the travel of Germans to other Western European countries and for the use of European consultants, as noted in Chapter I. OMGUS policy was dictated largely by reasons of expediency, e.g., economy, cultural affinities, geographic proximity, and language. But during the first two HICOG years few Germans went to other countries. They were mostly sponsored by German agencies such as the European Exchange Service (Europaeischer Austausch dienst) and the International Council for Youth Self-Help (Internationaler Rat fuer Jugendselbsthilfe). In 1951 HICOG revived the program but this time for reasons of policy dictated by the new trend toward European unification (see Chapter VI).

Notes

CHAPTER IV

1. Public Law 402, 80th Cong., "United States Information and Educational Exchange Act of 1948" (Smith-Mundt Act). Subsequently, other policy objectives were added, such as "The Campaign of Truth" to counter the "Hate America" campaign launched by the Soviet Union. See Chapter VI below.
2. The number was actually never quite reached but nearly so in 1951 when the program peaked with a total of approximately 3,319 persons.
3. The Directive to the U.S. High Commissioner instructed him to "seek to obtain agreement with [his] British and French colleagues which will permit coordination of existing programs and services, so far as possible . . ." Copy in CU/H.
4. Copy in CU/H.
5. Copy in CU/H.
6. Copy in CU/H.
7. HICOG Manual, quoted in HICOG Report on Public Affairs, Vol. IV, Exchange of Persons, O/FADRC 58 D 372, Box 3000; Office of Public Affairs, Technical Instruction 11, Feb. 3, 1953, O/FADRC, RG 59, 64 A 200, Box 155.
8. The distinction between leaders and specialists was more technical than real. Leaders came for limited periods of time, normally not more than 90 days. Specialists stayed longer, i.e., for periods of 90–180 days. Technical Instruction 3 of Sept. 19, 1950, defined specialists as "persons who have achieved established positions in their professions or fields of specialization, who will be sent to the United States . . . to observe and confer with professional colleagues in private and governmental organizations and agencies." (Henry P. Pilgert, *The Exchange of Persons Program in Western Germany* (Historical Division, Office of the U.S. High Commissioner for Germany, 1951), p. 19. Eventually, however, the requirements were relaxed and the leader and specialist programs became, for all practical purposes, interchangeable. Aside from that, HICOG more or less adopted the leader or specialist categories used by OMGUS but added a few.
9. Under the Fulbright program, this part of the program was later broadened to include lecturers, research scholars, teachers, and students. See Chapter VII.
10. For names of participants who contributed to democratic reform or who subsequently attained a high level of prominence in German public life, see Chapter VIII.
11. The Exchange of Persons Manual, as quoted in HICOG's Report on Public Affairs, Vol. IV, "Exchange of Persons," May 1953, defined the purpose of leader exchange as to give Germans in positions of influence in fields of critical importance added stimulation for the promotion of Germany into the community of free nations, and an opportunity to observe democratic ideas, attitudes and techniques as practiced in the United States, specifically,

    "—to provide experiences for German leaders which will promote better understanding between Germany and the United States;

—to permit German leaders to observe how leaders in the United States fulfill their responsibility toward the society in which they live;
—to help establish a continuing exchange of ideas between important professional and occupational groups in Western democratic nations and corresponding groups in Germany; [and]
—to afford German leaders opportunities to observe the attitudes, concepts, practices and techniques of social, economic, and political agencies in the United States." O/FADRC, RG 59, 58 D 372, Box 3000.

12. Technical Instruction 4, Sept. 15, 1950, quoted in Pilgert, *op.cit.*, p. 20. The Manual quoted in HICOG Report on Public Affairs, Vol. IV, "Exchange of Persons," May 1953, rephrased these criteria somewhat by referring to "persons in positions of public responsibility, e.g., government officials, political leaders and legislators." It also stipulated that such individuals "must, upon their return to Germany, contribute the most toward realization of democratic principles." O/FADRC, RG 59, 58 D 372, Box 3000. Personal criteria, specifically professional qualifications, English language proficiency, age requirements, prospects of communication of the exchange experience to others, moderation in personal habits, political acceptability in terms of past and present political activities and affiliations, etc., were spelled out in Technical Instruction 3, Nov. 29, 1949, Appendix B. Copy in CU/H. The criteria were relatively lenient. No rigid standards were required as regards educational background except that the candidate had to be "well-qualified" in his particular field. A "working knowledge" of English commensurate with the requirements of the program was considered sufficient, but exceptions were granted.

13. Technical Instruction 11, Revised, Feb. 3, 1953, broke the leader category down as follows: (1) national leaders, or persons in positions of public responsibility and national influence, e.g., governmental officials, political leaders, legislators and the like; (2) leaders of national organizations, whose sphere of activity includes most or all of the Federal Republic, e.g., the German Red Cross; (3) local leaders, including political leaders and public officials as well as persons not in status of public authority, but in a position of public influence, e.g., teachers, labor leaders, editors, and others directly concerned with public information; also, persons concerned with the initiation and development of democratic institutions, groups, movements, and projects, e.g., community councils, parent-teacher associations, women's groups, youth organizations, trade unions, farm cooperatives, school development projects and the like. O/FADRC, RG 59, 64 A 200, Box 59.

14. The figures following each sub-category represent the 3-year total during the peak period 1951–1953. Compared to those given in the previous paragraph, they include grants to specialists as well as leaders, thus comprising a larger total. Some discrepancies are unavoidable due to the use of different yardsticks in computing totals, such as number of grants versus number of arrivals in the United States.

15. This applied to the fields of child growth and development, counseling and guidance, educational psychology, home economics, community participation in school affairs, school administration, school building planning.

16. At the time of his appointment he was Foreign Secretary, American Friends Service Committee.

17. Budget proposal for Cultural Exchange Projects, Fiscal Year 1951. Copy in CU/H.

18. For references on following leader programs, see O/FADRC, RG 59, 66 A 363, Box 752.

19. J.F.J. Gillen, *Labor Problems in West Germany* (Historical Division, Office of the Executive Secretary, Office of the U.S. High Commissioner for Germany, 1952), pp. 66 ff.
20. See also under trainees, pp. 119–120.
21. Program Proposal for FY 1951, Education and Cultural Relations Division, HICOG. Copy in CU/H.
22. In 1951 the Josiah Macy, Jr. Foundation, under the leadership of Dr. Frank Fremont-Smith, in cooperation with the World Federation for Mental Health, under the chairmanship of Dr. John R. Rees, organized an international conference in Germany which sparked a series of German initiatives for mental health programs. The Department of State and HICOG actively supported the conference and the follow-up programs. Betty Barton of the Office of German Public Affairs (GAI) was the principal officer responsible for introducing and developing this facet of the reorientation program.
23. Beryl R. McCloskey, *The History of U.S. Policy and Programs in the Field of Religious Affairs under the Office of the High Commissioner for Germany* (Historical Division, Office of the U.S. High Commissioner for Germany, 1951), p. 31.
24. *Ibid.*, p. 29.
25. For details see Henry P. Pilgert, *Community and Group Life in Western Germany* (Historical Division, Office of the U.S. High Commissioner for Germany, 1952), pp. 14 ff.
26. HICOG Policy Directive No. M-4, Oct. 26, 1951, quoted in *ibid.*, pp. 20–21.
27. It catered, to use the German terminology, more to "Jugendpflege," i.e., youth care or youth welfare, than to "Jugendbewegung," i.e., free and autonomous youth movement.
28. Dean Mahin, *The International Visitor Program*, 1974, Manuscript. Copy in CU/H.
29. "A Cooperative Action Team in Action, An Observer's Report on 90 Days with the Team from Freiburg, Germany." (Prepared for the International Educational Exchange Service, International Information Administration, Department of State, by International Public Opinion Research, Inc. (IPOR), New York, June 30, 1953). Copy in CU/H.
30. *Ibid.*, ii.
31. *Ibid.* See also "Cooperative Action Teams—A Study of Effectiveness" (International Public Opinion Research, Inc., New York, Jan. 1954). Copy in CU/H; H. Philip Mettger and Clifford P. Ketzel, "Viewing the U.S. Community in Action," *The Record*, Dept. of State (Nov.–Dec. 1951), pp. 11–18. Copy in CU/H.
32. See Chapter V, below.
33. "A Cooperative Action Team in Action," *op.cit.*, ii.
34. *Ibid.*, pp. iii–v; Mettger and Ketzel, *op.cit.*, *passim*.
35. *Ibid.*, "Cooperative Action Teams—A Study in Effectiveness," *op.cit.*, *passim*.
36. *Ibid., passim;* IES Semiannual Report, July 1–Dec. 31, 1953, O/FADRC, RG 59, 64 A 200, Box 154. According to some observers the reorientation objective was not necessarily advanced, but the Cooperative Action Teams proved extremely valuable in arousing German interest in American community affairs. WNRC, RG 59, 66 A 363, Box 752.
37. Technical Instruction 1 of Sept. 19, 1950 (cited in Pilgert, *The Exchange of Persons Program in Western Germany*, *op. cit.*, p. 19) defined students as "persons presently or within the past year engaged in formal academic training in German schools who will undertake further training at pre-

college, undergraduate or graduate (university) level at one institution in the United States for a full academic year."
38. Dept. of State instructions to the Public Affairs Officer, 1949, Appendix II. Copy in CU/H.
39. HICOG–OPA Report on "Examples of Effectiveness," attached to desp. No. 2110, Apr. 1, 1953. WNRC, RG 59, 64 A 200, Box 155.
40. Inter-Divisional Reorientation Committee, Form for Reporting Cultural Exchange Projects for 1950. WNRC, RG 59, 66 A 363, Box 752.
41. Sample: Contract concluded with the Univ. of Florida, 1952. WNRC, 64 A 200, Box 155.
42. Univ. of Minnesota, Report on Frankfurt Student Team, 1953. WNRC, RG 59, 63 A 217, Box 303.
43. Some of these procedures were changed when the Fulbright program came into operation. See Chapter VII.
44. For further details, see Chapter VIII.
45. IIE contract form. O/FADRC, 63 A 312.
46. Exchange of Persons Manual, quoted in HICOG Report on Public Affairs, Vol. IV, Exchange of Persons, May 1953. O/FADRC, 58 D 372, Box 3000.
47. Dept. of State, Memorandum of Conversation, Nov. 18, 1949. Copy in CU/H.
48. Pilgert, *The Exchange of Persons Program in Western Germany, op. cit.*, p. 19.
49. Technical Instruction 11 (Revised Feb. 3, 1953). O/FADRC, 58 D 372, Box 3000.
50. This group had already been singled out by OMGUS for special attention as representing the cadre of future civil servants and business executives. Memorandum of Nov. 13, 1948. Copy in CU/H.
51. State-HICOG telecon, Jan. 31, 1950, WNRC, RG 59, 63 A 217, Box 313; also, HICOG budget, 1951, p. 160, *ibid.*
52. These universities had been active in international journalist exchanges since the late thirties.
53. For a more detailed analysis, see Report by the National Welfare Assembly, 1951. WNRC, RG 59, 63 A 217, Box 303.
54. WNRC, RG 59, 63 A 217, Box 313.
55. Fifteenth Semiannual Report to the Congress by the United States Advisory Commission on Educational Exchange, Dept. of State, for the period July 1 to Dec. 31, 1955, 84th Cong., 2d sess., H. Doc. 335 (Washington, D.C.: U.S. Government Printing Office, Feb. 10, 1956), p. 8.
56. HICOG–OPA report on "Examples of Effectiveness," attached to desp. 2110, Apr. 1, 1953. WNRC, RG 59, 64 A 200, Box 155.
57. Report of the National Catholic Welfare Conference, 1952–53, Appendix. WNRC, RG 59, 63 A 217, Box 312.
58. Fifteenth Semiannual Report of the U.S. Advisory Commission, *op.cit.*, p. 9.
59. *Ibid.*
60. Pilgert, *The Exchange of Persons Program in Western Germany, op.cit.*, pp. 61–62.
61. O/FADRC, 58 D 372, Box 3000; status as of 1953.
62. Report of the National Catholic Welfare Conference, 1953. WNRC, RG 59, 64 A 200, Box 155.
63. Report by Marita Houlihan. WNRC, RG 59, 63 A 217, Box 312.
64. Technical Instruction 5, quoted by Pilgert, *The Exchange of Persons Program in Western Germany, op. cit.*, p. 20.
65. Technical Instruction 11 (Revised), quoted in HICOG Report on Public Affairs, Vol. IV, May 1953. O/FADRC, RG 59, 58 D 372, Box 3000.

66. *Ibid.*
67. Education and Cultural Relations Division, Program Proposals for 1951.
68. Listed in HICOG's summary budget reports for the years 1951–1953. O/FADRC, 63 A 217, Box 312. Copy in CU/H.
69. It will be recalled that OMGUS limited American student enrollment to one percent of the total student body. When this restriction was lifted is not clear from available sources. It may, however, have discouraged American participation well into the HICOG period.
70. Report of IES Voluntary Programs Branch, Leaders Division. WNRC, RG 59, 64 A 200, Box 154.

CHAPTER V

Administration of the HICOG Program

An extraordinary kind of administrative machinery was mounted on both sides of the Atlantic to develop and manage a program that had no precedent and no equal in the history of cultural and educational exchange. In the United States the Department of State assumed policy and program responsibility, with the cooperation of a large number of public and private agencies. In Germany, the Office of Public Affairs organized effective relations with other offices in HICOG and progressively encouraged the participation of German authorities and institutions in carrying out the program.

Operation of the Program in the United States

As in the case of the reorientation program as a whole, two major considerations determined the structure of the organization needed in the United States to guide and support HICOG operations. One was the establishment of clear channels of authority through the assumption by the Department of State of central responsibility for policy, program proposals, and suggestion of projects.[1] The second was the creation of intraagency and interagency arrangements that could be relied upon to give indepth support to HICOG operations. This was done in two ways: first, through close day-by-day coordination of activities between the policy-making and the program-executing units of the geographical bureau and the public affairs bureau, respectively; and, second, through the enlistment by the latter of the resources and facilities available in other government agencies and in the private sector.

The functions of the Department of State, notably its Division of International Exchange of Persons (IEP), were greatly expanded and exceeded by far those performed by the Department of the Army in OMGUS days. They encompassed, first of all, responsibility for general policy guidance, program proposals, and suggestion of projects. They included, furthermore, arrangements through

133

correspondence by phone with the public and private agencies, institutions, and individuals in the United States cooperating in the program on a contractual or voluntary basis, negotiation of contracts, control and supervision of services performed, for instance, by the Institute of International Education for German students; arrangement of sponsorship of German leaders, experts, specialists, and trainees by suitable public and private agencies and institutions in the United States; review and final approval of programs of observation, study or training arranged by such sponsoring agencies; security clearance of all participants; and, finally, reception and orientation of the Germans when they arrived.[2]

The Department of State was likewise responsible for the recruitment, selection, and briefing of American specialists going to Germany,[3] and for all arrangements and commitments incident thereto, as long as such visits were sponsored or funded by the Department. In cases of private sponsorship, approval by the Department after prior concurrence by HICOG's Exchanges Division was required.

The performance of these functions necessitated the pooling and coordination of all pertinent resources and facilities within the Department, but most specifically the Bureau of German Affairs and the Division of International Exchange of Persons in the Bureau of Public Affairs.

Again, as in the case of the Reorientation Program, general responsibility for policy guidance and program planning as regards exchange of persons was centered in the Office of German Public Affairs (GAI) of the Bureau of German Affairs.[4] Vaughn DeLong,[5] an educationist who had worked as an education officer in OMGUS, was appointed Officer-in-Charge of the Division of German Cultural and Social Affairs which handled the policy aspects of the exchange program. Under the direction of the author and in consultation with other substantive offices of the Bureau of German Affairs, and upon the recommendation of HICOG, he determined program priorities, especially with respect to the selection of American experts and German participants, and the choice of projects. As a member of the geographic bureau (GER), he was in the unique position of providing that Bureau and its offices with a practical tool for the execution of some of its policies while, at the same time, receiving constant guidance from them in the choice of candidates and projects. The location of total responsibility for policy and planning in the Bureau of German Affairs thus insured full integration of the exchange programs with U.S. policy for Germany.[6]

To be more specific about these complicated bureaucratic details, it should be mentioned that having no operational facilities of its own and wishing to draw on the resources and to relate, as closely as feasible, to the objectives of the Department's worldwide exchange program, the Bureau of German Affairs (GER) entered into convenient partnership with the U.S. International Information and Educational Exchange Program (USIE) which operated under the auspices of the Assistant Secretary of State for Public Affairs.[7] A general manager, Charles M. Hulten, administered the three major program units, one of which was the Office of Educational Exchange (OEX) under the direction of William C. Johnstone, Jr.

OEX, in turn, was subdivided in two divisions, the Division of Institutes and Libraries (ILI), and the Division of International Exchange of Persons (IEP) whose chief was Francis J. Colligan, and whose deputy chief was Frederic O. Bundy. The responsibility of IEP, which assigned a staff of 39—a number that was later increased—exclusively to the German program, was to carry out the domestic operations of the program, to establish basic procedures and operational policies, and to insure the full use of facilities of other cooperating agencies, public and private. It exercised complete final control over all exchanges. Finally, it selected and processed all American experts going to Germany. Salares for the IEP staff detailed to work on the German exchange program and for two additional posts in the Office of General Manager were entirely funded from the overall German Affairs GOAG budget which provided for all expenditures incurred by the Department and HICOG in execution of the U.S. mandate for Germany.[8]

The stateside division of labor between the Division of Cultural and Social Affairs of the Office of German Public Affairs (GAI), and its counterparts in USIE and OEX worked remarkably well. It gave GAI easy access to USIE and OEX program facilities, and at the same time insured that the exchange policies of the global USIE program were implemented to the extent possible in the program for Germany.[9] It also guaranteed that IEP facilities in the United States, e.g., reception and orientation centers, as well as the private and public agency resources contracted by IEP, were available for the execution of the program. Most importantly, the arrangements established the primacy of the geographical bureau, GER, in setting policies and presiding over the program. For, while USIE, as a rule, directed exchange programs subject to "review" and "advice" by the regional bureaus,[10] the special status and responsibilities of the United States in Germany required closer direction and supervision by the competent geographic bureau with the ultimate authority for policy formulation and guidance for all public affairs programs, including exchanges, resting with the Office of German Public Affairs. This was the overall administrative arrangement in the Department until 1952.

With the exception of certain leader programs for key government officials and legislators who were handled directly by GER/GAI, program execution was delegated to other government agencies and to private institutions, with IEP arranging the contracts and grants-in-aid, and retaining general supervisory functions. Selection of agencies and institutions was done in consideration of their special field of competence to meet the interests and needs of the different categories of exchangees. The terms of cooperation were spelled out in detailed guidelines which explained the objectives of the program, assignment procedure and criteria, reception and itinerary, coordination with government agencies, publicity, per diem and travel payments, travel arrangements, insurance, and other operational details. Among other things, the guidelines provided for a week of general orientation for each visitor in the Washington International Center.[11] They also stipulated greatest possible flexibility in designing the itinerary of each exchangee making certain that his avocational interests were met as fully as possible and at the same time that his observations and study were not limited to his field of specialization but encompassed a broad spectrum of American life. To achieve this, exchangees were to be permitted to participate fully in the formulation of their own programs. Furthermore, they were encouraged to establish contacts with Americans who were familiar with contemporary Germany, having been visitors or lecturers and specialists under the U.S.-German exchange program. Care was taken to limit visits to a relatively small number of communities rather than to permit hasty trips to a larger number, thus allowing for more intensive contacts with families and civic life. At the same time, the guidelines cautioned against a best-foot-forward approach that highlighted the most favorable aspects of American life; instead, they proposed a program that would give the visitor "a balanced view" of progress made and of problems yet to be solved.[12] The basic assumption appears to have been that "a balanced view" would in effect be favorable, with positive impressions outweighing the negative ones—an assumption that was by and large confirmed by subsequent surveys (see Chapter VIII).

A number of government agencies played a significant part in planning and organizing exchange projects for special leader categories. The Department of Labor handled several groups. Its Office of International Labor Affairs programmed the visits of labor and management leaders and others concerned with labor problems, e.g., trade union officials; chairmen of workers' councils; management representatives concerned with labor-management relations; government officials responsible for mediation and conciliation functions, employment services, labor standards, labor statistics, welfare, and insurance plans for workers; college and university faculty members specializing in labor problems; members of labor research institutes; and editors or staff members of labor newspapers and magazines.

The Women's Bureau of the Department of Labor assumed responsibility for projects of German women leaders. The Department of Agriculture arranged programs of farm leaders. The Federal Security Agency, through its Office of International Relations, the Office of Education, the Social Security Administration, especially its Children's Bureau, and the Public Health Service, looked after educational administrators, teachers, welfare workers, and health officials. Other cooperating agencies were the Department of Interior, the Bureau of the Budget, and the Housing and Home Finance Agency.[13]

But by far the largest number of cosponsors, acting under contract with the Department of State or other governmental agencies, were private organizations. As the Smith-Mundt Act required, these were organizations with reputable records of experience in the exchange field. Others were agencies experienced in specific fields which added sponsorship of exchange projects to their established functions. In some cases, where no appropriate private agencies could be found to deal with special categories of projects, *ad hoc* sponsoring groups were created.

Until 1951, when it ceased to exist, the Commission on Occupied Areas (COA) of the American Council on Education, thanks largely to the energetic efforts of Dr. Herman Wells, was one of the newly established cosponsors. The Department of State and HICOG considered COA as one of the prime promoters and coordinators of private interests and availed themselves extensively of its highly professional resources. Both State and HICOG participated actively in the three major national conferences arranged by COA in 1949 and 1950. As noted earlier (see Chapter II), professional panels, 12 altogether, were set up by COA, chaired by members of the Commission and composed of specialists, each of whom was a leading member in his or her profession. The panels were staffed with coordinators competent in the panels' functions. Their primary task was advisory, promotional, supervisory, and coordinative. But each panel was encouraged to initiate and carry through any projects and recommendations within its own area of interest.[14]

Thus the Community Activities Panel of COA sponsored programs for youth and community leaders; the Government Affairs and Social Sciences Panel for government officials and legislators; and the Legal Affairs Panel for judges, legislators, lawyers, criminologists, and police officials. In addition, the panels organized conferences in their specific fields of competence, and assisted in the development of contacts between American groups and their German counterparts. Three members of COA, Vice Chairman Karl W. Bigelow, Bernice Bridges, and Msgr. William E. McManus, were sent to Germany and Austria in 1950 to study the role of American voluntary agencies in these two countries and to report their findings to a national conference of hundreds of private sponsors. The team recommended, among other things, an increase in the participation by private organizations in the exchange of persons programs. "Such efforts," the report concluded, "contribute more importantly than any other kind to the strengthening of education and cultural relations with Germany and Austria." [15] It proposed a series of criteria to be observed by sponsoring agencies in developing programs, in selecting candidates, in providing the services of American experts, and in promoting affiliations between American universities, colleges, schools, churches, social and cultural agencies, study and research groups, and corresponding German and Austrian institutions.[16]

After the demise of COA, a number of governmental and nongovernmental agencies and organizations inherited exchange programs previously handled by COA panels. The lion's share for sponsoring public notables fell upon the Governmental Affairs Institute which, at first under the auspices of the American Political Science Association, but later as an independent incorporated organization, programmed the exchanges of political leaders from Germany and Austria.[17] The Institute had a small professional staff headed by H. Philip Mettger, a former OMGUS official, coordinator of COA's Panel on Governmental Affairs, and vice president of the Governmental Affairs Institute. In 1954 the Institute was reorganized and its responsibilities expanded. With the exception of projects so special that they had to be handled directly by the Department of State, and those conducted by the Office of International Labor Affairs of the Department of Labor, all exchange programs for government officials were transferred to the Governmental Affairs Institute. But the clientele of the Institute was soon greatly expanded. Under the terms of its contract with the Department of State, the Institute arranged the national itineraries of political leaders and government officials except for those of persons primarily interested in education, cultural affairs, youth, social welfare or labor matters; of newspaper publishers, editors, correspondents, and reporters, except for those interested in the aforementioned subjects; of radio and television writers, editors, broadcasters, and commentators primarily concerned with political, governmental, and international affairs; of leaders in important organizations primarily interested in civic (e.g., women in organizations comparable to the League of Women Voters), political, governmental, and international affairs; of university and college professors of political science, public administration, and international relations; of staff of research institutes publishing periodicals in the above subject areas; of important representatives of professional organizations in these fields; of leaders in the field of law, law enforcement, and penal affairs, including lawyers, prosecuting attorneys, judges, police officers, and prison officials except for those primarily interested in juvenile courts and correctional institutions for juvenile delinquents.[18]

As noted elsewhere in this study, various aspects of the planning for the experiences of German visitors to the United States resulted in the development of procedures that proved so effective that they have been continued and are used with the worldwide State Department Exchange of Persons Program. One example is the orientation program for foreign visitors.

As early as the forties special orientation programs were provided for foreign visitors arriving here on State Department grants. They were conducted primarily for students and trainees, and were held under various auspices at different localities throughout the country. When the large program with Germany got underway, however, the need for a regularized introduction to the United States for German leaders was recognized. Consequently, in 1950 the Commission on the Occupied Areas, with financial assistance from the Department, organized a general orientation program in Washington as a key activity in the plans for German and Austrian leaders coming here under the Department's auspices.[19]

The working group that organized the program included Mgr. William E. McManus and Bernice Bridges of the Commission, George E. Beauchamp of the Commission Staff, and Vaughn De-Long, the OMGUS liaison representative to the Commission. The program's offerings consisted of a week-long introduction to the United States presented at the Washington YWCA, first headquarters of what was to become the Washington International Center. The program itself consisted of an introduction to the United States—history, arts, letters, labor, religion, education, agriculture, and government. All decisions of the working group in planning the orientation sessions revolved around consideration of procedures that would best illustrate and set forth the American concept of citizenship in a democracy. Thus, the speakers for the orientation session on religion, for example, included one representative each of the Protestant, Catholic, and Jewish faiths.

Soon the YWCA quarters were outgrown, as the Center adapted its programs to serving the increasing number of Department-sponsored visitors from all parts of the world. The need for larger facilities resulted in several moves, culminating in the purchase of the handsome and spacious Meridian House in Washington, D.C., made possible by a grant from the Ford Foundation, where the now privately administered Washington International Center is located. It is of interest to note that there was much discussion from the very beginning about the relative merit of locating the orientation center in New York or Washington. The choice of Washington was based on the belief that a more effective orientation would be possible in the national capital.

Later, the Department of State turned to the American Council on Education for assistance in organizing tailor-made program arrangements and itineraries for leading personalities in the fields of education, arts, and culture. Specifically included were visits with college and university presidents, deans, professors; directors and staff members of special institutes, academies and seminaries; school principals and teachers on all levels of education; leaders in the field of adult education; leaders in the field of fine arts and cultural affairs; government officials; radio and television leaders, newspaper writers and editors if primarily concerned with education, the fine arts and cultural affairs; and those engaged in the production, distribution, and utilization of feature and documentary motion pictures.[20]

The National Academy of Science arranged opportunities for qualified visitors to teach, lecture, or undertake research at appropriate American institutions. The National Social Welfare Assembly, under the direction of the late Bernice Bridges, took command of programs for youth leaders and leaders in the field of community relations and social services.

As pointed out before, the social work field attracted a good deal of attention. Although the program itself was modest in scope, it was one of those in the private sector where a major innovative effort was called for to deal with such problems as child and family care and, above all, organized youth, all of which presented major social challenges in postwar German society. In response to this need an enlightened group of citizens in Cleveland, Ohio, under the leadership of a social service executive, Henry B. Ollendorff, started in 1956 a program for the training of 25 German youth leaders, with the encouragement and support of the Department of State. The purpose of the program was to bring the professionalism of American social work into a situation where the technical tools and human resources in this field were sadly lacking.

In the following year the program was named "The Cleveland International Program for Youth Leaders and Social Workers, Inc." (CIP). It soon became multinational and included youth leaders from other countries, and it added agencies in other Amer-

ADMINISTRATION OF HICOG PROGRAM   141

ican cities as cosponsors. Twenty years later, the number of participants had increased to 175. It then comprised social workers, youth workers, and volunteer youth leaders from 55 countries. Its objectives combined humanitarian and professional purposes, namely, "to increase mutual understanding among people and to increase professional knowledge in the fields of social work and youth work." Interestingly, over the years the number of German participants has remained among the highest.[21]

Many other examples of institutions concerned with international educational and cultural exchange could be cited which received a strong impetus from the type and magnitude of programs for German students and trainees arriving in the United States in the early fifties or were a direct outgrowth of these programs. One of these would surely be the program for foreign journalists which began at the School of Journalism at Northwestern University under Professor Floyd G. Arpan. He later transferred the program to Indiana University School of Journalism, and has been operating there ever since. Its 25th anniversary was celebrated in 1974, when the published record showed that young journalists from 70 countries had participated over that period, many of whom have since become outstanding journalists in their own countries. Newspapers in 39 States had cooperated in carrying out the program.

Another notable example is that of Youth for Understanding, which began with a very small number of German teenagers sponsored by the Ann Arbor Council of Churches under the direction of Mrs. Rachel Andresen. The program rapidly expanded into the state of Michigan under the auspices of the Michigan Council of Churches; it has now become worldwide and nationwide, and each year moves as many as 9,000 teenagers between their countries and the United States.

A similar example is that of the American Field Service International Scholarships program, which had begun on a small scale as a predominantly humanitarian gesture between France and the United States after World War I. But, with the infusion into the program of 300 German youngsters scattered about this country on farms and in city high schools in the early fifties the intrinsic and political value of such exchanges was suddenly discovered. It now sponsors about 2,500 secondary school students for a year each in American high schools and sends at least an equal number abroad for stays with foreign families.[22]

Other programs which grew less rapidly and on a smaller scale, but which began with the German program, evolved into permanent and worldwide programs for journalists, librarians, writers, museologists, and other specialists who received training in their fields aided by such institutions as the University of Pittsburgh, the University of Iowa, the Library of Congress, and the Association of American Museums. After a period of specialized training, the grantees then traveled about the United States on State Department funds.

With respect to university student exchanges, the Department continued to rely on the services of the Institute of International Education (IIE) which had previously been employed by the Department of the Army for programs with Germany. Under contract with the Department of State, IIE was responsible for placing students in as many areas of the United States as possible, as well as for guidance and counseling, for obtaining scholarships, tuition waivers, room and board or any combination, and for supplementing government funds. Often residence was provided by fraternities and sororities on campuses. IIE was expected to make semiannual reports to the Department on the students' progress. The German student program was by far the largest single program the IIE had ever handled. It, in turn, contracted for programs with American colleges and universities. In 1950, 23 colleges and universities participated in the program; by 1952 the number had reached a total of 52. Major subject matters differed from institution to institution.

In the early forties the Department of State had established Reception Centers in four major port cities—New York, Miami, New Orleans, and San Francisco—to receive and assist foreign visitors arriving in the United States. But in these and other cities throughout the country local contacts established over the years were not geared to take on the massive influx of German visitors arriving in the late forties and early fifties. What was needed were local sponsors who could mobilize on a much larger scale the professional and volunteer resources of the whole community. As a result, community organizations to provide programming and hospitality services to the visitors were established in about twenty of the most frequently visited American cities. Universities, colleges, schools, and other state and private agencies cooperated to help meet the challenge.

As was noted earlier, the OMGUS program was transferred to the Department of State under considerable pressure and in some haste. For instance, as regards the complications of transfer of funds and reorganization of personnel, the Department, beginning in January of 1950, had to complete a full fiscal year's program in 6 months—by June 30, 1950.

Fortunately, officers in the Department and private organizations across the country were ready to meet the emergency demands during the hectic changeover period. Had this not been so, the program would never have succeeded. A number of examples come to mind at once, such as a direct placement by the Department of State in approximately 60 colleges and universities of groups of Ger-

ADMINISTRATION OF HICOG PROGRAM 143

mans in such fields as foreign service, political and social science, law, industrial relations, police administration, home economics, agriculture, and the like. The Department showed marked flexibility in accommodating American sponsors. When the dean of a law school in January of 1950 was asked to accept 12 German advanced law students (Referendare), sight unseen, no names known, the Department was able to assure them that all their study expenses would be paid, and enough money would be available to pay for special courses, housing, community visits, and the like.

With respect to Americans going to Germany, private support was limited in view of the modest scope of the effort prior to the initiation of the Fulbright program. The Department's major contractor for artists was the American National Theater and Academy (ANTA) which arranged for American participation in the Berlin Cultural Festival and for the appearances of American artists in Western Germany (see above).

The above list of private cosponsors is not complete. It does not include, for instance, the large number of organizations, notably churches, which invited German leaders, specialists, students and trainees to visit the United States entirely under their auspices. Estimates of the number of Germans and Americans involved are impossible to obtain. A tentative guess would be neither accurate nor fair. It suffices to say that the American community, academic and nonacademic, rose nobly to the challenge. Without private support the exchange program would never have achieved the scope nor the impact that made the difference between success and failure.

Operation of the Program in Germany

Responsibility for program development operation and administration in HICOG was anchored in the Exchanges Division under the direction of Dr. Ralph A. Burns, a professor of education on leave from Dartmouth College. Dedicated to the concept of exchange as a "democratic catalyst" in the German social order, Burns believed that exchange would prove to be a significant factor in the process of democratic reform.[23] Under Burns' leadership the exchange program assumed division status, becoming one of the four divisions of the Office of Public Affairs, the others being Education and Cultural Relations, Information Services, and Public Relations. U.S. High Commission Staff Announcement 8 of September 21, 1949 [24] stipulated that the "Exchanges Division . . . controls and evaluates all programs for the exchange of persons and reorientation materials, advises on grants-in-aid or other types of assistance to German organizations cooperating in [the] reorientation program and maintains necessary liaison with budget and fiscal authorities to insure proper financial management of such programs." The mandate was comprehensive. It involved, among other things, the development of program plans, the preparation and management of a large budget ($6.3 million at its peak), supervision of operations and extensive coordination of selection of exchanges with substantive offices, such as the Offices of Political Affairs, Labor Affairs, the General Counsel, the Office of Economic Affairs,[25] with the Information Services Division, and, above all, with the Division of Education and Cultural Relations. As part of its managerial functions, the Exchanges Division developed a series of highly meticulous procedures for the allocation of exchange opportunities, for project preparation, processing and review, for the selection of candidates, for publicity review and followup.[26] The Division discharged its functions through two branches, a Personnel Exchange and a Materials Exchange Branch, and through exchange offices attached to 15 public affairs field centers, each headed by a regional public affairs officer (Land (State)/Exchange Branch).[27]

In 1951–1952, in tune with a general review of policy and a corresponding organizational adjustment in HICOG, the exchange program was integrated with cultural activities and became a branch within the Division of Cultural Affairs. Its principal function was that of advising the chief of the division on matters of policy, but it retained its previous responsibilities of controlling, administering, and evaluating the exchange of persons program. The Branch was subdivided into program implementation and evaluation sections operating under the supervision of the Office of the Chief, who was Everett G. Chapman. Field operations were handled by exchange officers attached to the public affairs staffs of the ten consulates general throughout the territory of the Federal Republic, i.e., all three zones of occupation.

Considering the magnitude and diversity of the program, the size of the staff was not inordinately large. The Exchanges Division in 1950 employed 21 U.S. citizens and 33 non-Americans. In 1951 the number of employees rose to 26 U.S. citizens and 85 non-Americans, in keeping with the organizational changes mentioned in the previous paragraph. It maintained about the same level throughout 1952 and 1953, whereupon it dropped proportionately as the program was reduced. To these figures, however, must be added the 181 so-called County (Kreis) Resident Officers whose duties included, on a part-time basis, facilitation of exchanges at the grass roots. To afford Germans an opportunity for responsible participation, HICOG continued a procedure initiated during the late OMGUS period. It set up selection panels at the Land level composed largely of German citizens. Orders went out[28] from zonal headquarters to establish in each Land and in the Berlin Sector German exchange or selection committees composed of no less than

5 and no more than 15 persons. Each committee was appointed by the Exchanges Division. It was chaired by an American, the Land Exchange Officer. Members were not appointed as representatives of any group but as civic-minded individuals. Their main responsibility was to screen candidates.

Furthermore, special panels were attached to each committee, representing the functional Land offices or divisions (e.g., agriculture, law, education) participating in exchange projects for leaders. While the committee examined the credentials of candidates in terms of their total fitness, their moral and personal qualifications, the panels would inquire into their academic and professional competence. Each special panel consisted of no more than five members, with an American official, representing the functional office or division, acting as chairman. Each panel member was selected by the Land Commissioner's office or division directly concerned. The very breadth of the program pervading most of the operating offices and divisions of HICOG required a kind of infrastructure with procedures that permitted a maximum of coordination on all levels. To this end, a policy board was established composed of the above-mentioned cooperative offices and divisions with the responsibility to recommended policies and priorities for the exchange program to the Public Affairs Officer. The function of this board was changed later to that of an advisory committee.[29]

The procedures developed by the Exchanges Division for German participants were complex and comprehensive. They were particularly exacting with respect to selection and processing of candidates. Each category had its own requirements and channels.

The leader program rules stipulated *inter alia* that eligibility for participation be based on "demonstrated leadership qualities" and on prospects of continued influence upon return to Germany.[30] Adopting most of the criteria developed by OMGUS, no rigid standards were to be applied regarding educational background or experience, language, and age (see above). Leaders, specialists, and trainees were fitted into projects proposed either by the HICOG office, the division concerned, or by the Department of State. The Exchanges Division in consultation with its Advisory Committee thereupon developed the total annual program within established budgetary limits and in accordance with policy directives of the Department of State and the appropriate HICOG offices or divisions, and the proposal was recommended to HICOG's Office of Public Affairs for transmission to the Department of State which had responsibility for final review and approval.[31] All arrangements for sponsorship of projects in the United States were the exclusive domain of the Department.

Activation of individual projects after approval of the whole program was the responsibility of the Exchanges Division in HICOG upon request of the substantive office or division concerned and upon clearance and concurrence by the Department of State.

The selection process of candidates started at the Land level where the County (Kreis) Resident Officers distributed application blanks, received from the Land Exchange Branch or officer, to interested parties in the county. Executed forms were returned to the Land Exchange Branch or officer who thereupon made them available to the appropriate panel. Candidates would appear before the panel for interviews. The panel would review the applications, make its choice, and submit its recommendations with a suitable number of alternates for each opening and with a written evaluation of each candidate, showing order of preference, to its HICOG headquarters office. After the latter's approval, the panel would forward the approved application to the full Land Exchange Committee.[32] Candidates from the British or French Zones appeared before local panels. Their recommendations were passed on to the U.S. Land selection committees located in Bremen for the British and in Stuttgart for the French Zone.[33] Recommendations of names were limited to the original list of candidates presented to the panel and approved by the competent HICOG office or division. They had to be submitted to the full Land Exchange Committee with the chairman of the panel or his designee in attendance.[34] It should be noted, though, that except for the leader program, essentially a "noncompetitive" category, the Land Exchange Branch or officer was expected to utilize fully the advice and services of his colleagues and of German citizens of influence in soliciting names of suitable candidates. By 1952 the exchange staff had accumulated a roster of prospects amounting to the equivalent of a *Who's Who in Germany*.[35]

Procedures for students were similar with regard to personal requirements but differed in that no provision was made for the kind of project proposal and approval that characterized the leader program. Responsibility for developing the annual student program was left exclusively with the Exchanges Division within established budget limits and policy directives. The Division was expected to specify allocation of funds, including estimates of unit costs, and of minimum number of students with indication of field and level of study.

The selection process for students resembled that of others. Candidates had to appear before the student panel of the Land Exchange or Selection Committee. Their eligibility would be determined in the light of the criteria established for leaders and other participants.[36] Acceptable candidates would be grouped according to their particular fields of study and recommendations. Full biographical details would then be forwarded by the Exchanges Division to the Department of State for final clearance and approval.

At a relatively early time, allowance was made for the inclusion of students from the British and French Zones. Preliminary selection of these students was carried out on a competitive basis under arrangements worked out between the Exchange Division of HICOG and their British and French counterparts. Here, too, intensive use was made of German selection committees.

The procedures established for the visits of Americans going to Germany reflected, at least in the early days of HICOG, the nature of their mission as an auxiliary force to HICOG operations. Project proposals originated either with the interested HICOG office or division or with the Department of State and recommendations were made to HICOG's Exchange Division which, in turn, consulted its Advisory Committee before developing the annual program.[37] Subsequently, the Exchanges Division would recommend the program to the Department of State for review and approval. Activation of projects was the responsibility of the Exchanges Division upon request by the HICOG office or division directly concerned. Recruiting, selection, and clearance of all candidates was the responsibility of the Department of State with IEP acting in consultation with GAI. The appointment of candidates itself, was likewise the responsibility of the Department of State. Candidates were expected to have the necessary qualifications that would enable them to carry out a successful mission. This included, usually, a sufficient knowledge of German to establish contacts and to participate effectively in the activities of German organizations, and especially to cooperate in projects developed with German counterparts. Detailed procedures regulated travel, status of dependents, medical certification, and reporting requirements. At least in the beginning, specialists would undergo a 5-day orientation course before their departure for Germany, arranged by the Foreign Service Institute, and visitors were requested to submit a final report to the Department summarizing his or her activities in Germany and giving an evaluation of the project with specific recommendations.[38] By and large, all appear to have complied with the request, although there is a vast difference in detail and in quality. Many of the evaluation reports written in the earlier days were highly critical of conditions, notably in the educational field. Some contained extremely valuable suggestions for institutional and social reform (see above).

American students who wished to study in Germany were asked to apply directly to the university of their choice. If the university accepted the application, it had to forward it to the Office of the High Commissioner for final approval. After final approval, the latter would recommend authorization of an entry permit to the Allied High Commission Permit Office for Germany. The student then had to submit an application for an entry permit to the Commission accompanied by a valid passport. Students were not entitled to the use of U.S. Army facilities. Instead, the university was to assist them in obtaining billets and ration cards. The universities which first resumed enrollment and were accessible to foreign students were: Erlangen, Frankfurt, Free University of Berlin, Heidelberg, Marburg, Munich, and Wuerzburg.[39]

In the following years, HICOG spent considerable efforts on refining all these procedures, taking account of the change of political conditions, for instance, by permitting a higher degree of German participation and also giving greater attention to followup. In retrospect, the machinery developed to execute the program may seem highly intricate, often bureaucratic and cumbersome, but, by and large, the results achieved vindicated the method. Moreover, procedures were kept flexible and adjustments were made frequently. Most important, however, they were supplemented by the good rapport that existed between field and home base and between Americans and Germans. As with other problems involving public affairs, exchange officers of the Department and HICOG were in nearly daily contact with each other by telecon. Department officers visited HICOG with fair regularity to study programs on all levels and HICOG officials came to Washington for purposes of consultation. Conferences were held in the United States and in Germany to deal with specific problem areas, to enunciate policy, or, with the help of outside experts, to introduce fresh ideas into ongoing programs. Without the strong personal working relations and the close personal ties existing between some of the principal officers on both sides of the Atlantic, the procedures, no matter how carefully drafted, might have remained a dead letter.

Notes

CHAPTER V

1. "Basic Recommendations for the Public Affairs Program in Germany," quoted in Henry P. Pilgert, *The Exchange of Persons Program in Western Germany* (Historical Division, Office of the U.S. High Commissioner for Germany, 1951), p. 15.
2. While the orientation of new arrivals was eventually farmed out to sponsoring agencies, the briefing of political and civic leaders on matters of U.S. policy was carried out by officers of the Bureau of German Public Affairs, mostly by the Director of the Office of German Public Affairs.

ADMINISTRATION OF HICOG PROGRAM 149

3. Pilgert, *op. cit.*, p. 20.
4. *Ibid.*, p. 15.
5. Was in charge of reopening German schools in Land Hessen from the beginning of the occupation.
6. For organizational structure and direction of GER and GAI, see Chapter VI, below.
7. See also Chapter VI, p. 166 and note 26.
8. GOAG budget justification for FY 1950-51; WNRC, RG 59, 63 A 217, Box 313. See also Manual of Regulations and Procedures, Vol. II, Organization U.S. Dept. of State, Jan. 25, 1950. Copy in CU/H.
9. See GOAG budget justification for FY 1950-51, WNRC, RG 59, 63 A 217, Box 313.
10. See Manual, *op. cit.*
11. See pp. 139-140, below.
12. For details, see "Revised Operational Procedures for Foreign Leader Programs," Mar. 6, 1952, and "Guide for Cooperating Agencies for the Foreign Leader Program," Apr. 20, 1954. International Educational Exchange Service, Department of State. Copies in CU/H.
13. Many of these agencies, in turn, used private resources in the planning and execution of projects. The Women's Bureau, for instance, was supported by such organizations as the American Association of University Women, the General Federation of Women's Clubs, the National Board of the YWCA, the National Council of Catholic Women, the National Council of Jewish Women, the National Federation of Business and Professional Women's Clubs, the League of Women Voters, and the National Women's Trade Union League of America.
14. Report of the Staff of COA, by Harold E. Snyder and George E. Beauchamp, *An Experiment in International Cultural Relations*, American Council on Education Studies, Aug. 1951, pp. 20-27.
15. Report of a Team of Inquiry on "The Role of American Voluntary Agencies in Germany and Austria," Commission on the Occupied Areas, American Council on Education, p. 9. See also, Harold E. Snyder and George E. Beauchamp, ed., *Responsibilities of Voluntary Agencies in Occupied Areas*, American Council on Education Studies, Feb. 1951. Copy in CU/H.
16. Report of Team of Inquiry, *op. cit.*, pp. 12-13.
17. Eventually the Institute assumed responsibility for leader exchanges from other countries as well.
18. Guide for Cooperating Agencies for the Foreign Leader Program, Apr. 20, 1954, *op. cit.*
19. See Snyder and Beauchamp, *An Experiment in International Cultural Relations*, *op. cit.*, pp. 26-27.
20. Guide for Cooperating Agencies for the Foreign Leader Program, Apr. 20, 1954, *op. cit.*
21. Report of CIP to the Department of State, 1964. Copy in CU/H. See also Chapter VIII, note 88, below.
22. Fifteenth Semiannual Report on Educational Exchange Activities. Letter from Chairman, U.S. Advisory Commission on Educational Exchange. Copy in CU/H. George Rock, *American Field Service, 1920-1955* (New York: The American Field Service, The Platen Press, 1956), pp. 589-607.
23. Ralph A. Burns, "Catalysts for Democracy," reprinted from the *Dartmouth Alumni Magazine* (April 1953). Copy in CU/H.

150 CULTURAL RELATIONS—INSTRUMENT OF FOREIGN POLICY

24. Quoted by Pilgert, *op. cit.*, p. 13; see also Instruction to the Public Affairs Officer, 1949. Copy in CU/H.
25. By special arrangement, the Exchanges Division jointly with the Office of Economics Affairs coordinated the exchange of persons sponsored by the ECA Technical Assistance Program.
26. For details, see Manual of Organization, Section 5, quoted in HICOG Report on Public Affairs, Vol. IV, May 1953. Copy in CU/H.
27. GOAG budget justification for FY 1951. Copy in CU/H.
28. Technical Instruction 1, Nov. 29, 1949. Copy in CU/H. See also Pilgert, *op. cit.*, pp. 24–27.
29. Instruction to the Public Affairs Officer, 1949, Attachment I, General Principles. Copy in CU/H.
30. See Chapter IV, "Germans to the United States," "The Leader Exchange Program," above; Technical Instruction 4, Nov. 29, 1949; Pilgert, *op. cit.*, pp. 20 ff.
31. Technical Instruction 3, Nov. 29, 1949. Copy in CU/H. In 1949 the review function in the Department of State was divided among the Division of German and Austrian Information and Reorientation Affairs (later Office of German Public Affairs) for area policy, the Public Affairs Program Planning and Evaluation Staff for overall policy, and the Office of Educational Exchange for operating policy.
32. *Ibid.*
33. *Ibid.*, Appendix B.
34. Technical Instruction 1, Nov. 29, 1949. Copy in CU/H.
35. Burns, *op. cit.*
36. Technical Instruction 2, Nov. 29, 1949. Copy in CU/H. See also Pilgert, *op. cit.*, pp. 18–19 ff.
37. Technical Instruction 5, Dec. 29, 1949, *ibid.*, p. 20.
38. *Ibid.*; see also Department of State, Division of Exchange of Persons, General Instructions, 1950. Copy in CU/H.
39. WNRC, RG 59, 66 A 363, Box 752. Copy in CU/H.

Return to Normalcy

CHAPTER VI

Revision of Policy—From Unilateralism to Bilateralism

Political Determinants

The transfer of authority from military to civilian control had been achieved by the establishment of the U.S. High Commission in 1949. The next step was the gradual shift of power from the Allies to a renascent German government, culminating in the termination of the occupation and the restoration of sovereignty to the German Federal Republic. The transition was implicit in the mandate of the Allied Commission. What was not contemplated and indeed not foreseen, however, was the speed with which this process developed. In 1945 no one had the temerity to predict that 10 years after the end of hostilities Germany would obtain not only national independence but full political, economic, and military partnership with the West; yet this is precisely what happened.

The precipitation of events was due, in large part, to circumstances beyond the control of the Allies. They had been set in motion by Soviet unwillingness to accept quadripartite agreement except on their terms, clinched by the Russian walkout of the Allied Control Council, by the breakdown of the quadripartite control machinery and finally by the outbreak of the cold war. On the positive side, spurred by the Marshall Plan, the phenomenal recovery of the German economy and the success of the reconstruction effort on all levels of national life deserved some measure of recognition. They were acknowledged in the form of a series of diplomatic and political initiatives by the U.S. Government which were designed to accord the Federal Republic a status of greater responsibility and equality. They determined the course of U.S. policy under HICOG and left their mark on all aspects of the HICOG program, including cultural exchange.

Among the changes that were made, those that had the most immediate impact were the replacement of the Occupation Statute by contractual arrangements,[1] and the acceptance of the Federal Republic to full and equal membership in the European community and its various institutional bodies. Previously, it had joined such international organizations as the World Health Organization (WHO) and the United Nations Educational, Scientific and Cultural Organization (UNESCO). This trend was climaxed in May 1955 by Germany's admission to the North Atlantic Treaty Organization (NATO).[2] Another factor of considerable weight was the progressive recovery of Germany's economic position as well as the new regulations for currency conversion which eventually permitted financial cosponsorship of exchange programs, at least on a modest scale.

The most significant of these milestones was the agreement reached on September 14, 1951 at Washington by the Foreign Ministers of France, Great Britain, and the United States. The agreement established the basic principles which were to guide the High Commissioners in their future negotiations with the Federal Republic with respect to contractual arrangements. The latter were to supplant the Occupation Statute and prepare the way for final decisions which, it was hoped, would be reached within the following few months. This was no decision taken overnight. Work on a revision of the Occupation Statute had begun as early as May 1950. In September of that year the Foreign Ministers met in New York and instructed the Intergovernmental Study Group to review the 1949 Agreement on Tripartite Controls and the Charter of the Allied High Commission, although no plans were then made for fundamental changes in relationships. As HICOG pointed out correctly,[3] the Washington conference merely epitomized a series of steps toward liberalization of policy adopted at Foreign Ministers conferences at Paris (1949), London (1950), New York (1950), and Brussels (1950).

The Washington conference was followed in November 1951 by a meeting of the three Foreign Ministers in Paris with Chancellor Adenauer. The participants agreed then and there to draft a "General Agreement" which would set forth the main principles that were to determine the future relationship between the three Allies and Germany. The draft agreement, in turn, became part of the Contractual Agreements which were signed at Bonn in May 1952. They consisted of a basic agreement, three conventions and supplementary annexes, and an exchange of notes. The basic agreement restored to the Federal Republic full authority over its internal and external affairs, once the convention had come into effect. Sovereignty was withheld only in matters of security, the stationing of armed forces, and the peace settlement.

The 1951 Policy Paper

The progressive change in overall policy demanded corresponding adaptation in public affairs policy. Fortunately, the existing organizational structure of HICOG which provided for a high degree of managerial integration, both in the United States and in Germany, facilitated greatly a coordinated adjustment of policy between the public affairs office and its counterparts on the political, economic, legal, and other substantive levels.[4]

In March 1951, i.e., half a year before the Washington conference but in anticipation of the events that it was to set in motion, the author prepared a policy paper, which attempted to bring the Public Affairs Program abreast of general developments.[5] The opening paragraph presented the rationale for a change in emphasis, format, and content of the program. It stated:

"The approaching end of the occupation and the impending transfer of United States operations in Germany to Embassy status require an immediate examination of the Public Affairs Program. Any evaluation of the program must be undertaken with a view to determining the need for such adaptations, both in content and volume, as appear indicated in the face of changes in policy. A vital principle of this policy is to remove the major vestiges of the occupation and to restore to Germany the status appropriate to a member of the free association of Western nations and to a potential participant in their common defense effort. While this does not imply immediate or necessarily early return of full sovereignty, it calls for arrangements which reflect recognition of widest possible control over domestic affairs by the responsible German authorities."

The removal of "the major vestiges of the occupation" under the terms of the proposed new policy required, first of all, a change in method and emphasis. So far, the policy paper pointed out, the Public Affairs program of HICOG had been "reformist," that is, designed primarily to eliminate or correct certain deficiencies in German society. Accordingly, "reorientation" or "democratization" had provided the common denominator and the rationale for most of the activities carried on under the label of Public Affairs. True, many of these deficiencies persisted and demanded continuing and vigorous remedial action. However, with the restoration of sovereignty such action could no longer remain the predominant responsibility of third parties. Instead, the task required at an increasing pace the participation of German nationals in all phases of the program. Yet, while the HICOG program, as against that of OMGUS, no longer rested on authority by fiat but on "advice and assistance," even the proffering of advice and assistance appeared inherent in the authority of the occupying power, and with the diminution of such authority could no longer be rendered without prior solicitation by the recipients.

Most importantly, however, not only methods and protocol had to be adapted to the change of pace but, above all, the objectives of the Public Affairs Program had to be attuned to the new priorities of the United States or, for that matter, of tripartite Allied policy, which in the words of the declaration of Foreign Ministers of the United States, Great Britain, and France, issued at Washington on September 14, 1951, aimed "at the inclusion of a democratic Germany on the basis of equality in a continental European community." The Public Affairs Program, the policy paper stated, could make a singular and very specific contribution to this aim. Whereas German membership in the Council of Europe, in the European Coal and Fuel Community, and in the European Defense Community was to achieve integration on the political, economic, and military levels, respectively, the Public Affairs Program would lay the psychological and cultural ground ("create understanding and support") for Germany's association with the West and for a "United Europe." Rather than continuing the reorientation effort through unsolicited advice, the Program would endeavor to support the work of democratic reconstruction by indirection, that is to say, by assisting democratic forces within Germany. As a new objective, in line with new overall policies accentuating the exigencies of the cold war, the Program was to encourage militant rejection of *any* kind of totalitarianism.

In its final recommendations, the Department's 1951 policy paper proposed, therefore, the following overall objectives:

1. to help integrate Germany into Europe and into the community of Western nations;

2. to help establish, stabilize and protect a truly democratic order in Germany and to foster the realization of those principles upon which such an order is based; and

3. to help eliminate, counter, contain and, wherever possible, roll back all totalitarian influences whether from the Right or Left which aim at subverting and destroying the democratic order and at preventing Germany's association with the free nations.[6]

As the normalization of Germany's relations with the United States and the Western European community proceeded apace, the U.S. Government's exchange program with Germany was gradually assimilated to the characteristics of the State Department's worldwide educational and cultural exchange program under the Smith-Mundt and Fulbright Acts. Two years later, the "Guiding Principles" issued by the Chief of the Exchange of Persons Branch [7] no longer referred to reorientation directly. Instead, they defined the purpose of the Exchange of Persons Program as that of "giving (exchangees) an opportunity to experience a democratic environment which contributes to a cooperative way of life and to stimulate the free interchange of ideas between free nations." The tutorial approach had disappeared, but not the underlying political purpose. The "Guiding Principles" made it quite clear that the German program still differed from "normal" exchange programs. "The primary purpose of the Exchange of Persons Program," they stipulated, "is not to increase academic and cultural knowledge or professional and technical skill, or to enable participants to visit a particular area to make business or personal contacts," but to maintain its targeted approach aimed at individuals "who will, upon their return to Germany, contribute the most toward realization of democratic principles."

A series of so-called "transition papers" prepared by working teams under the direction of Albert D. Sims, deputy director of the Office of German Public Affairs in the Department, to prepare the orderly transition from High Commission to Embassy status, defined the general objectives of the program along the lines of the 1951 policy paper. "Joint participation and mutuality" wherever feasible and to the greatest extent possible, were declared to be the predominant features of a trend away from unilateralism and leading eventually toward binationalism.[8] The exchange program, in particular, was to focus more than ever on educational institutions, community life, and the arts, and directed toward leaders, youth, labor, women, and others whose participation would further these U.S. policy objectives.[9]

In order to achieve these objectives, the 1951 policy paper had proposed a series of major modifications for the exchange program, namely, a correction of the existing imbalance of exchange categories with its preponderance of German participants and greater stress on the two-way character of the program; emphasis on the mutuality of national interests in the conduct of the program through the early inauguration of a binational Fulbright exchange agreement; a higher degree of responsible participation by Germans in the administration of the program, notably in the development and financing of projects; greater emphasis on younger age groups and women; intensified followup; and extension of the program through a revival of inter-European exchanges as a means of achieving greater impetus and support for the idea of a "United Europe." In conclusion, the policy paper recommended the incorporation of the total program in a "Cultural Treaty" which would "symbolize and implement a policy which, in the future, will govern the relationship not merely between the U.S. Government and the German Government but between the American people and the German people."

The new departure proposed by the policy paper and the transition papers had unquestionably strong political overtones. It was a concession to growing demands in the United States and elsewhere to accord Germany a place within the Western community appropriate to its newly gained political and economic status. At the same time, Germany's prospective membership within a "community of strength," itself resolved to resist aggression from totalitarian quarters, was clearly a reflection of the exigencies of cold war confrontation. As such it was intended not merely to adjust public affairs policy and programs to the new political realities in Germany, but, beyond that, to assimilate them to the changing postulates of the Department's worldwide policy.

By the fifties, the cold war between East and West had become global. Soviet propaganda attacks on the United States grew more bitter with every passing day. The "Campaign of Truth" was launched by President Truman in 1951. It was a hard-hitting propaganda response to the "hate America" campaign unleashed by Soviet propaganda and, in the words of Secretary of State Dean Acheson, intended "to counteract the vicious lies about this nation and its objectives as perpetrated by the Communists, and to build a positive psychological force around which the free world and freedom-loving people everywhere can rally." [10]

In this atmosphere, the U.S. Government's worldwide educational and cultural exchange program underwent modification "to serve immediate needs more effectively." These considerations, after several years of delay, spurred the passage by Congress of the United States Information and Educational Exchange Act of 1948 (the Smith-Mundt Act), which, as noted earlier, authorized for the first time a worldwide information and educational exchange program under the sponsorship of the Department. Appropriations for the program increased annually in the early fifties, especially for that part of the program concerned with the dissemination of U.S. information overseas. The "Campaign of Truth," injected a decidedly political element into the U.S. information and educational exchange programs, not unlike that introduced prior to and during World War II to counter Nazi propaganda. The purpose of the campaign was to strengthen the unity of the free nations and to emphasize the coincidence of their interests with those of the United States; to build up the image of the United States as an enlightened and strong power; and to develop and maintain psychological resistance to Soviet propaganda against the United States.[11]

The exchange program was considered a suitable vehicle for carrying this message, and within its framework the leaders and specialists program, having the highest potential for molding public opinion, appeared to be the most logical category on which to focus attention. Considering their close exposure to a constant barrage of Soviet pressure and propaganda, German leaders were believed to be particularly sensitive to the need for cooperative counteraction. Moreover, with the end of the occupation and national sovereignty rapidly approaching, closer association of the German exchange program with the U.S. worldwide policy appeared to be a foregone conclusion. The time had come to create a stronger psychological foundation for Germany's impending partnership with the West. Hence the need for an intensified effort to acquaint German leaders with "the basic principles governing American life in the political, economic, social, cultural and educational fields," and a more systematic attempt to familiarize them with American ideas, attitudes, and institutions, and with the objectives of American domestic and foreign policy. The early fifties, thus, saw an increase in the number of invitations to cabinet members, Members of Parliament, government officials, party leaders, and other politicians on various levels of authority. Among them were Walter Scheel, Minister of Foreign Affairs, now Federal President; Gerhard Schroeder, Minister of the Interior, later Minister of Labor; Kurt Georg Kiesinger and Ludwig Erhard, both later Federal Chancellors; Franz Josef Strauss, later Minister of Defense, and many others.[12] The resulting presence of important German personages in Washington necessitated special arrangements for their orientation, in the form of weekly briefing sessions for leaders and specialists in the Department of State as a regular feature of the Washington orientation program. These were generally conducted by the author with the assistance of other Departmental officers.

The cold war was to continue, but after the mid-fifties the worldwide educational and cultural exchange program of the Department moved into an era in which these political requirements subsided, and cooperative educational and cultural relations reemerged as the predominant consideration in the conduct of the educational exchange program worldwide, with which the German program was now closely identified.

The Cultural Agreement

The Cultural Agreement between the United States of America and the Federal Republic of Germany which came into effect in 1953, two years after it had been proposed in the policy paper of 1951, was intended to epitomize and to give formal recognition to the trend toward full bilateralism in the field of cultural exchange. The idea of a cultural treaty or convention appeared to be a logical corollary to the decision of the three Western Foreign Ministers taken in December 1950 at Brussels, to replace the Occupation Statute with a series of contractual agreements. Although the Occupation Statute had retained no special powers in the cultural field that needed to be abandoned or modified, it nevertheless seemed good politics to divest the "reorientation" program not only of its tutorial pretensions but of any residues that smacked of unilateral intervention, even if only by way of moral suasion. Also, whereas U.S. policy remained devoted to the accomplishment of its earlier objectives to assist in the creation of a democratic society in Germany, the accomplishment of these objectives should now become a matter of mutual consent with the United States showing its willingness to move toward a reciprocal type of relationship resting on cooperative undertakings. "A cultural treaty," the policy paper of 1951 had argued, "would demonstrate visibly the changing character of U.S.-German relationships and would lend force and credence to our declared intentions for inviting German consent and contribution in an area of foreign affairs which is normally governed by the principles of mutual acceptance and reciprocity."

The instrument of agreement had been envisaged in the policy paper as a regular treaty, with some of the language of earlier educational and cultural exchange legislation and agreements concluded with other countries serving as a model. It was to consist of a covenant in which the two contracting parties, adopting the language of the UNESCO charter, pledged "to develop and increase the means of communication between their peoples and to employ these means for the purpose of mutual understanding and truer and more perfect knowledge of each other's life." It was furthermore to contain a specific stipulation "to continue, within the limits of available funds, a program of cultural assistance to Germany." It was, finally, to define categories of activities, specifically authorizing "the initiation, conduct, and support of programs concerning the production, distribution, or exhibition of informational and cultural materials, the exchange of ideas and persons, and the inauguration of binational or multinational programs, such programs to be sponsored by either public or private agencies and to be organized and conducted, whenever possible, on a basis of reciprocity."

The details and language of the agreement were worked out in close cooperation with the German Chargé d'Affaires and later the first German Ambassador, Heinz Krekeler, and with the cultural counselor of the Embassy of the Federal Republic, Dr. Bruno Werner, both stout advocates of democratic reform and sincere friends of the United States. They cleared the text with their government in Bonn. The document was then to be signed by President Eisenhower and Chancellor Adenauer at a public ceremony in Washington on the occasion of the forthcoming visit of the Chancellor in April 1953.

The proposal was warmly welcomed, and approved in the Department and transmitted through channels to the White House. The President, on April 7, signed the formal authorization paper directing Secretary Dulles "to negotiate, conclude, and sign a cultural convention between the United States of America and the Federal Republic of Germany, the said convention to be transmitted to the President of the United States of America for his ratification by and with the advice and consent thereto of the Senate of the United States of America." All was in readiness when to the consternation of all parties concerned the formalities were rather dramatically delayed by a last-minute veto of Secretary Dulles who objected to the "paternalism," in fact, what he termed back-door "socialism" implicit in the concept and format of a cultural treaty or convention and specifically in the idea of continued "cultural assistance." The text had to be hastily revised and the legal status of the instrument changed to that of an "Agreement between the United States of America and the Federal Republic of Germany." It was effected by an exchange of notes and signed in a brief ceremony by Secretary Dulles and Chancellor Adenauer on April 9, 1953 in the Department of State.[13]

As stipulated in two identical notes, one in English and one in German, both governments declared their intent to join efforts "in cultural cooperation and to foster mutual understanding of the intellectual, artistic, scientific and social lives of the peoples of the two countries." To this end, they pledged to encourage the extension of mutual knowledge of their history, civilization, institutions, literature, and other cultural accomplishments, to accord favorable treatment to their citizens engaged in activities pursuant to the agreement, with respect to entry, travel, residence, and exit; to promote and facilitate the interchange of prominent citizens, specialists, professors, teachers, students and other youths, and qualified individuals from all walks of life; to favor the establishment of scholarships, travel grants, and other forms of assistance in their academic and cultural institutions; and to endeavor, whenever desirable, to establish binational committees to further the purpose of the agreement.

In deference to the newly-acquired sovereign status of the Federal Republic and specifically to Secretary Dulles' concern about undue interference in the internal affairs of either country, the agreement postulated specifically that the responsibilities assumed by each government under the agreement were to be executed "within the framework of domestic policy and legislation, procedures and practices defining internal jurisdiction of governmental and other agencies within their respective territories."[14] The agreement was made applicable also in the territory of Berlin upon delivery of a conforming declaration by the Government of the United States of America. The declaration was formalized by note of October 2, 1953 from the German Chargé d'Affaires to the Secretary of State. True, the agreement did not change the cutural exchange program in substance nor even alter the modalities of operation, but it gave official sanction and legal status to the *de facto* bilateralism that had characterized U.S.-German cultural cooperation for quite some time, pronouncing the new relationship as one based on equality and consent for mutual benefit.

New Look Towards Europe

With the return to normal relations, the Public Affairs Program and, with it, the exchange program, could have been reduced in size to the level of other country exchange programs. Actually, the reduction was gradual, and did not start before 1953. The 1951 and 1952 fiscal years proved to be peak years in terms of budget expenditures for public affairs and of the total number of persons actually exchanged with the allied countries (3,319 in 1951, and 3,922 in 1952). It was only in 1953 that exchanges began to drop sharply (see statistics in Appendixes I and III, which differ slightly but closely present the approximate figures). In point of fact, exchanges between the United States and Germany had already started to diminish slightly in 1951 and 1952 (from 2,643 to 2,539 in 1951, and to 2,377 in 1952). The decline in German-American exchanges, however, was made up for by the resumption of exchanges between Germany and other European countries (780 in 1951, and 1,545 in 1952) reflecting the new emphasis on European integration.

The extension of the program to European countries required special delegation of authority to the Chief of the Exchange of Persons Branch of HICOG. It was quickly forthcoming. Pursuant to the authority contained in section 4 of Public Law 73, 81st Congress, the Exchange of Persons Branch was empowered by the Department of State "to make, amend or terminate grants, (a) to German students, trainees, teachers, guest instructors, professors and leaders in fields of special knowledge or skills, (b) to teachers, guest instructors, professors and leaders in fields of special knowledge and skill from other European countries, and (c) to German private or governmental agencies or institutions, for the purpose of carrying out exchange of persons programs between Germany and other European countries administered or serviced by the Office of the U.S. HICOG under authority vested in the Department of State." [15]

This extension was terminated in 1953, after Germany's progressive integration into Europe had been consummated through its membership in the European Payments Union, the Council of Europe, and the Coal and Steel Community, and its pledged adherence to the European Defense Community, then in the planning stage. But as long as the European extension program was in effect (during 1951 and 1952), 1,755 Germans went to European countries and 241 European specialists to Germany. An interim analysis of a sample of 476 cases made by HICOG in November 1951 [16] shows that most of the German visitors went to Great Britain (301) and, in descending order of magnitude, to Scandinavian countries—Sweden, Denmark, Finland (79), Switzerland (49), Holland (35), and France (12). They were selected from the fields of education (211), food and agriculture (58), community activities (55), political affairs (36), public health and welfare (28), and legal affairs (18).

The program was organized on a project basis with the visitors either participating in specially organized training courses and conferences or observing institutions and practices related to their professional concern. Projects were sponsored by such authorities as the Educational Interchange Council (EIC) and the German Educational Reconstruction (GER), in Germany; the British Council and the Civil Service Commission in Great Britain; the Ministry of Agriculture in France; and the City of Zurich; or by high level officials of the host government, members of the diplomatic corps, and the like. As a rule, visits were of relatively short duration, shorter in any event than visits to the United States.[17] Prompted, as it were, by considerations of policy that served urgent political objectives, and conceived as a stimulant to spark German initiatives along similar lines, the European exchange program lacked the depth and the complexity of the U.S.-Germany exchange program. It was, nevertheless, far from being a mere series of junkets. Nor was it an academic exchange program in the conventional sense. The subject areas selected for study projects were carefully chosen, again with a view to helping German political leaders, educators, legal experts, and the like, deal more effectively with critical domestic problems. Courses included such themes as the "Liberalization of the German Civil Service," "Political Science and Public Administration," "Western European Integration," "Theory and Operation of Municipal Government," "Observation of Prisons and Parole Systems in Europe," "Medical and Public Health Practices," "Farm Cooperatives," "Home Economics," and various subjects in the field of education.[18]

Despite its declared intention to cede greater responsibility to German authorities and agencies, in the case of the inter-European exchange program HICOG was reluctant to relinquish control and to assign to its German counterparts more than a minimum of functions. Considering the urgent political purpose of the program, HICOG officials felt that the basic philosophy and traditions of German agencies engaged in inter-European exchanges, with their emphasis on academic and recreational programs, would simply not permit rapid enough adjustments to the objectives of U.S. policy.[19] The division of labor between HICOG and its German counterparts was thus heavily weighted in favor of American sponsorship. HICOG's exchanges staff retained responsibility for approval of projects, selections and clearance of exchangees, coordination with local German sponsors, transportation of selected German participants from point of origin to point of departure, and participation in the briefing of exchangees. German agencies, on the other hand, were expected to obtain the necessary visas, to arrange round-trip transportation from the point of departure to the foreign country, to issue grants and instructions, to participate in the briefing of exchangees, to evaluate the effectiveness of each project from the German exchangee's viewpoint, and to render financial and evaluation reports to the exchanges staff of HICOG. As regards financial arrangements, HICOG retained sole fiscal control of the $277,000 set aside for European exchange projects, although grants were made available to selected agencies to cover administrative expenses amounting to ten percent of total project cost.[20]

It was anticipated, however, that by 1953 all project proposals and selections would come from German agencies. Funds for 1953 would be used in the following manner: part would be given as subsidies to German exchange agencies to strengthen their administrative capabilities, including program planning, selection, and evaluation; another part would be made available to these agencies to broaden the exchange programs, notably through the increase of European exchanges; and the balance would be used for financing specific pilot projects deemed desirable and important to the accomplishment of the HICOG mission.[21]

Two German agencies were handling the majority of the projects, the Institute of Public Affairs, Inc. (Institut zur Foerderung Oeffentlicher Angelegenheiten, E.V.), and the International Council for Youth Self-Help (Internationaler Rat fuer Jugendselbsthilfe, E.V.). Other agencies included the German Academic Exchange Service (DAAD), the German-British Exchange Office, the European Exchange Service, the Institute for Social Research, and the Auxiliary Service of the Evangelical Church in Germany. Most of these were concerned with the facilitation of exchanges. The Institute for Social Research in Frankfurt concentrated on public opinion surveys evaluating the result of exchanges, whereas the Auxiliary Service of the Evangelical Church assisted in the screening of candidates.

Revision of Project Approach

In keeping with the trend toward normalization of relations, certain features which had been characteristic of the German exchange program were now found to be increasingly incompatible with the changed situation and gradual downgrading was recommended. One of these features had been the "project approach" which, although not totally abandoned, was largely replaced by a more individualized treatment of exchangees. As the result of extensive discussions within the Department, it was decided that bringing Germans to undergo group training was inconsistent with a policy that placed emphasis on personalized procedures. Participation in "package deals" with tight travel schedules and preplanned programs requiring firm commitments for fixed periods of time seemed no longer in tune with the new relationship and besides in many cases had proved impractical. It had often become rather difficult for program organizers to recruit the most qualified candidates. Many of them, because of their prominent position in public or professional life, could not adjust their schedule sufficiently to avail themselves of the experience. The change to more personalized and shorter leader visits was expected to improve the quality of the participants and thereby of the program. This expectation was confirmed by State Department officials who attested in 1953 to the fact that the elimination of group projects, together with the simplification of selection procedures, had resulted in an average caliber of German leader grantees "substantially above that in any previous year." [22] Actually, though, the group project approach was never fully abandoned and in some special cases proved to be still highly beneficial.[23]

To assure compliance with the new trend the State Department had issued, as early as March 1952, a guidance to primary and local sponsors which emphasized the need for an individualized treatment of foreign leaders and for a tailormade approach.[24] Sponsors were advised that visits should be planned with consideration being given to the leader's "own desires and interests" which, in fact, had to be "the determining factors," even where such interests lay outside his or her professional field. Visits had to provide for extensive opportunities to see American home and community life, with 2 or 3 weeks as a minimum spent in at least one community. Sponsors were particularly alerted that "every American who provided information and assistance to a visiting foreign leader under this program is contributing significantly to United States foreign policy." [25] These guidelines, again, brought the program into closer conformity with the program as it was carried out worldwide.

Organizational Changes

The gradual return to normalcy in the early fifties necessitated organizational changes, both in Washington and in Germany, in the administration of the exchange program. The general pattern was responsive to the worldwide requirements at that time. In the special case of Germany these changes constituted progressive steps leading to the establishment of full diplomatic relations between the two countries. Eventually the Office of the High Commissioner (HICOG) was replaced in May 1955 by an Embassy and James A. Conant, the U.S. High Commissioner, was appointed U.S. Ambassador to Germany.

In the Department of State, the administrative structure for operating the exchange program with Germany remained largely unchanged until 1952, with the Bureau of German Affairs through its Office of German Public Affairs (GAI) discharging policy and planning responsibilities, and the Bureau of Public Affairs, through its Office of Educational Exchange (OEX), and under it its Division of Exchange of Persons (IEP), performing all program functions.

But in 1952, the educational exchange and information elements of the Department's Bureau of Public Affairs were reorganized as the International Information Administration (IIA), a semiautonomous agency within the Department. More stress was placed on overseas information goals, as the title of the agency indicated. IIA continued to handle both the exchange program functions and those of overseas information through its International Information Service (IIS) and International Educational Exchange Service (IES), the latter, an enlarged successor to IEP under Assistant Administrator, and later Director, Russell L. Riley. The German exchange program was only one, but remained by far the largest, of the growing worldwide exchange activities in which IES was engaged. In 1953, the Bureau of German Affairs was integrated with the Bureau of European Affairs and became the Office of German Affairs under Director Cecil B. Lyon. All but the policy and planning functions handled previously by GAI moved to IES. Then, in another major reorganization in the summer of 1953, the overseas information activities of IIA, the fast media and the cultural centers and information libraries programs, were removed from the State Department and established as the U.S. Information Agency (USIA), an independent agency of the executive branch. The staff administering the exchange program at posts overseas, U.S. Information Service (USIS), was also placed under USIA. IES, which administered the exchange of persons programs, and the UNESCO relations staff, remained in the Department, returning to the jurisdiction of the Assistant Secretary for Public Affairs, where they had been prior to the ephemeral IIA appearance.[26]

The organization in Germany underwent corresponding changes. In January 1952 the Education and Cultural Relations Division became the Division of Cultural Affairs. The branches for education, religious affairs, public health and welfare, community activities, etc., were transformed into advisory staffs. Public affairs functions, until then performed by other HICOG offices, e.g., political, labor, and legal, were transferred to the Division of Cultural Affairs. Later that year, the exchange program, previously handled by the Exchanges Division, was incorporated as the Exchange of Persons Branch in the Division of Cultural Affairs. At the end of 1952 the Office of Public Affairs consisted of the Office of the Director, headed eventually by Alfred V. (Mickey) Boerner, the Mutual Security Act Information Staff, the Policy Staff, the Information Division, and the Division of Cultural Affairs which included the Projects Staff that administered grants-in-aid, the Exchange of Persons Branch, the Information Centers Branch, and the Cultural Liaison Staff.[27]

Although certain budgetary and managerial controls for exchanges were handled at the division level, the Exchange of Persons Branch retained most of the administrative and all of the substantive program responsibilities. The major functions of the branch chief were to advise the chief of the Division of Cultural Affairs on policy matters and to control, administer, and evaluate the program. Other duties included the development of procedures and the allocation of exchange opportunities among the various consular districts.[28] Selection of high level government leaders was made by the Division of Cultural Affairs in concert with other offices and divisions. Field exchange of persons officers selected the qualified leaders at the local level in all phases of cultural, political, and social life. These administrative changes did not have any noticeable effect on the field operations. The pattern established under HICOG, especially the infrastructure, prevailed by and large and assured continued interoffice and interdivisional coordination.

Procedural Changes

Procedures underwent a series of modifications which manifested the increasingly binational character of U.S.-German relationships. Selection procedures were brought under the general criteria governing the State Department's worldwide programs. Some criteria previously applied in practice, were now made explicit. Potential emigrants or children of emigrants were barred from participation, as were persons with dual citizenship, persons convicted of a felony, and members of the Communist Party or of any organization affiliated with or controlled by it. Categories of eligible candidates were even more carefully defined.[29]

The new instructions listed, aside from leader categories, urban youth, farm and rural youth, and trainees. Grants were directly administered by the Division of Cultural Affairs through the Exchange of Persons Branch. Leaders, in particular, were still to be selected with a view to their capability by virtue of their position to "insure positive impact upon the German community."[30] If circumstances so recommended, English language knowledge could be dispensed with. Urban and rural youth were to be given preference, if they had demonstrated "an active interest in extracurricular and community activities." [31] In their case as well as in that of trainees a basic or adequate knowledge of English was held "essential."

Students and other academic exchangees now became the responsibility of the binational Fulbright Commission, under the Fulbright program officially established by the two governments in 1952 (see Chapter VII). The Exchange of Persons Branch thereafter assumed only such duties as were delegated to it by the Commission. While special objectives and supplementary eligibility requirements were established for each category, perhaps the most significant change in procedure was the increase in the extent of German participation in the selection of German candidates in the academic categories, under the Fulbright program, which was now declared to be of "paramount importance." Under the Fulbright program, candidates applied in open competition, and preselection of candidates was delegated to screening committees that included representatives of the competent ministries and organizations in the individual Laender. One of the immediate benefits was that grantees whose applications were thus processed by German authorities, found it easier to obtain leave of absence and reemployment guarantees.

German participation in the exchange program was no longer to be limited to proposals of projects, nomination of candidates, and administration and evaluation of the program, but was to include "the assumption of financial responsibility through voluntary contributions." [32] The economic recovery in Germany and the new currency conversion now permitted stronger German participation in the financing of exchange projects. German funds, through private contributions, were used mainly to defray the costs of visits by Americans to Germany. By the end of 1953 HICOG reported that both German governmental and private agencies had activated projects to bring U.S. citizens to Germany on planned itineraries wholly at German expense—eg., 48 experts in local government, welfare, religion, and architecture, and 200 teenagers. Informal talks with labor leaders had disclosed the possibility of organizing exchange programs financed by trade unions.[33] The latter prospects were developed in addition to private projects sponsored directly by American and German private organizations, such as the American Field Service and the Experiment in International Living.

Notes

CHAPTER VI

1. Through contracts entered into by the U.S. Government either with the German Federal Government, in the form of implementary agreements or with the competent authorities or private owners, on the Land, or local level, replacing the Tripartite Occupation policies. See O/FADRC, 58 D 372, Box 3000.
2. For further details see Harold Zink, *The United States in Germany, 1944–1955* (Princeton: D. Van Nostrand Company, 1957); Roger Morgan, *The United States and West Germany, 1945–1973; A Study in Alliance Politics* (London: Oxford University Press, 1974).
3. *Report on Germany*, 8th Quarterly, Office of the U.S. High Commissioner for Germany (July 1–Sept. 30, 1951), p. 13, copy in CU/H.
4. For details see: Report by Guy A. Lee, *The Organization of the Office of the U.S. High Commissioner for Germany, 1949–1952* (Historical Division, Office of the U.S. High Commissioner for Germany, 1953).
5. Policy paper of Mar. 13, 1951, O/FADRC, 52 D 432, Box 2. Copy in CU/H.
6. Reflecting the political change of pace as expressed in the new policy, the highlight statement of the 1951 budget presentation prepared for Congress on the public affairs program focused even more sharply on political aspirations of U.S. policy. To be sure, it reaffirmed the positive aspects of democratization but it also emphasized more strongly than ever the need for tying Germany more closely to the United States and for encouraging resistance to totalitarianism, specifically to Soviet encroachment. In language adapted to the climate of the cold war, it redefined the purpose of the public affairs program as follows:

1. To provide Germans with practical knowledge of the concepts and institutions of democracy, confidence in their effectiveness, and experience in exercising as individuals and in groups the responsibility of democratic citizenship;

2. To develop in Germans, through information about the United States and its institutions, a confidence in American purposes which will prove of lasting benefit in international relations;

3. To gain German understanding and support of U.S. policies in the occupation and in world affairs; [and]

4. To expose and counter Soviet and Communist propaganda, and assist Germans who are resisting Communist threats and promises.

In 1952 the language of the budget justification had become even more specific and more strictly oriented on U.S. political objectives. The latter were now declared to be:

1. Germany's military participation in the defense of Western Europe and economic support of the common defense;

2. The replacement of occupation controls with contractual arrangements between the occupying powers and Germany by which Germany can be given substantial freedom . . .

3. The maintenance of effective occupation government until contractual arrangements are effected, and the completion of specific Allied programs by that time;

4. After completion of contractual arrangements the subsequent performance of U.S. responsibilities in Germany and the establishment of diplomatic relations with the Federal Republic;

5. The further strengthening of the Federal Republic as an effective responsible, and democratic government, and continued assistance to the Federal Republic in its efforts toward political and economic integration with the democratic West; and

6. Protection of German and Allied purposes against Communist interference and continual frustration of Communist efforts to gain strength in Germany, (O/FADRC, 58 D 372, Box 3000, and WNRC, 63 A 217, Boxes 212, 213.

7. Technical Instruction 11 (Revised) issued by the Chief of Exchange of Persons Branch, HICOG, Feb. 3, 1953, actually still continued to categorize exchangees in the form of projects and assigns the development of project proposals to headquarters and field program area staffs; copy in CU/H.

8. Public Affairs Transition Papers, 4/3, O/FADRC, 56 D 12 and 57 D 221; NARS, RG 306, 63 A 190, Boxes 652–653; Lee report, *op. cit.*, pp. 412–419.

9. *Ibid.*

10. "Statement of Objectives for Programs for Foreign Leaders in the United States," issued by the Educational Exchange Service, International Information Administration, Mar. 6, 1952, copy in CU/H.

11. *Ibid.*

12. "Leader Grantees—Germany," CU/H.

13. "Agreement between the United States of America and the Federal Republic of Germany. Effected by Exchange of Notes, April 9, 1953; Entered into Force April 9, 1953." (Washington, D.C.: Treaties and Other International Acts Series 2798, U.S. Government Printing Office); see Appendix IV. On the basis of records of President Eisenhower's and Secretary Dulles' activities on Thursday, Apr. 9, 1953 contained in the Dwight D. Eisenhower Library, Abilene, Kansas, it is difficult to determine exactly what transpired immediately preceding the signing of the "Cultural Agreement," and what caused Secretary Dulles to modify his position. At the time it was understood that Chancellor Adenauer expected a formal cultural treaty or convention between the two countries, to be signed by President Eisenhower and himself.

The pertinent official records from the Eisenhower Library indicate that the President's appointments from 12:15–12:20 p.m. on that day were as follows:

Thursday, April 9, 1953

12:15 p.m. Dr. James B. Conant, High Commissioner for Germany. (Dr. Conant asked if he might see the President a few minutes alone before the German-American conversations.)

12:20 p.m. (Honorable John Foster Dulles, Secretary of State)
(H. E. Konrad Adenauer, Chancellor of the West German Federal Republic)
(Professor Doctor Walter Hallstein)
(Dr. James B. Conant)
(The above met with the President for a brief talk before the conversations began in the Cabinet Room. This was arranged at request of Secretary Dulles' office, who advised that Chancellor Adenauer had expressed a wish to do this.)

The records in the Eisenhower Library show that the document giving Secretary Dulles full power and authority to negotiate and sign a Cultural Convention between the United States and the Federal Republic of Germany, was marked "VOID, D.E.," in President Eisenhower's own writing, and his signature is scratched out. The latter action may have been the result of memoranda and phone calls between Secretary Dulles and the President on Apr. 9, recorded on Apr. 10, in which Secretary Dulles explained his position and in which it was agreed to sign a "Cultural Agreement" instead of a more formal Cultural Convention. (Based on records of phone calls in the files of the Eisenhower Library.)

14. See Appendix IV, p. 269.
15. Delegation order signed by Carlisle H. Humelsine, Deputy Under Secretary for Administration of Dec. 1, 1952, superseding Delegation of Authority 42 of Aug. 23, 1951, and 21 of May 22, 1950, quoted in HICOG's report of May 1953, copy in CU/H.
16. HICOG report on "European Integration Program, Germans to European Countries," Nov. 23, 1951, WNRC, RG 59, 66 A 363, Box 752, copy in CU/H.

Pilgert points out that at a much earlier date the Education Branch of the British Element of the Control Commission had arranged for an extensive exchange between Germany and Great Britain. It included, by the end of 1950, 1,121 Germans going to Great Britain, and 450 British subjects going to Germany. Most of these exchanges were in the field of education, some in women's affairs, some in cultural and some in religious affairs. Henry P. Pilgert, *The Exchange of Persons Program in Western Germany* (Historical Division, Office of the U.S. High Commissioner for Germany, 1951), pp. 46–47.

17. In addition, U.S. authorities organized inter-European conferences and camps for youth, the most spectacular of which was that organized on the Lorelei Rock, on the Rhine River.
18. HICOG report on "European Integration Program," *op. cit.*
19. See notes on "Conference on Western European Exchange," June 1951. WNRC, RG 59, 66 A 363, Box 752; copy in CU/H.
20. *Ibid.;* HICOG report on "European Integration Program," *op. cit.*
21. *Ibid.*
22. IES, Leader Division, Semi-Annual Exchange Report, July–Dec. 1953, WNRC, RG 59, 64 A 200, Box 154.
23. Technical Instruction 11 (Revised), Feb. 3, 1953, *op. cit.*
24. "Statement of Objectives for Programs for Foreign Leaders in the United States," *op. cit.*
25. *Ibid.*
26. See also p. 135, above. The Bureau of Public Affairs in the Department performed all major program functions from 1948–1952 through its Office of Educational Exchange (OEX) and its Division of Exchange of Persons (IEP). Within IEP, the day-to-day responsibilities for carrying out German exchange activities, which it assumed in the fall of 1949, were under Oliver J. Caldwell, Chief of the Federal Programs Branch. When IIA was established in 1952, the exchange program functions in the Department were administered through it International Educational Exchange Service (IES), as indicated. Within IES, program operations were coordinated by Howard H. Russell and divided among five divisions: leaders (under Douglas N. Batson), professional activities (under J. Manuel Espinosa), specialists (under Joseph M. Roland), special services

(under John N. Hayes, later under Ivan Nelson), and youth activities (under Donald B. Cook). The organizational structure of IES remained essentially the same until 1958. Up until that time IES remained under the direction of Russell L. Riley.

During the brief IIA interlude referred to on page 166, Wilson S. Compton served as IIA's Administrator in 1952, and Robert L. Johnson in 1953.

27. Report on HICOG Public Affairs—Policy, Organization, Program, 1949–1950, O/FADRC, RG 59, 58 D 372, Box 3000.
28. Technical Instruction 11 (Revised), Feb. 3, 1953, *op. cit.*
29. *Ibid.* In general, previous criteria of eligibility were maintained.
30. *Ibid.*
31. *Ibid.*
32. *Ibid.*
33. HICOG, Semi-Annual Exchange Report, July–Dec. 1953. WNRC, RG 59, 64 A 200, Box 154.

CHAPTER VII

The Fulbright Program

The 1952 Agreement

Since 1951, preliminary discussions had been held by HICOG officials and representatives of the German Foreign Office and the Ministry of the Interior concerning "a coordinated binational exchange program." The actual inauguration of such a program under the Fulbright Act, following the Bonn Convention which replaced the Occupation Statute, can be rightfully considered as the first implemental act symbolizing the advent of full normalization of relations between the United States and Germany.

The Fulbright agreement with Germany, or, as it is known by its official title, the "Agreement between the Governments of the United States of America and the Federal Republic of Germany for Financing Certain Educational Exchange Programs," was signed on July 18, 1952 by U.S. High Commissioner John J. McCloy for the Government of the United States of America and by Chancellor Konrad Adenauer for the Government of the Federal Republic of Germany.[1] It preceded the restoration of Germany to the status of sovereignty. There was no reference, implied or otherwise, to reorientation or democratization. It restored binationalism in the fullest sense in the field of educational and cultural relations between the two countries.

The worldwide binational Fulbright program had originated with the passage of Public Law 584 by the U.S. Congress in 1946, introduced by Senator J. William Fulbright. The purpose of the Act was to strengthen mutual knowledge and understanding between countries, prerequisites for a peaceful world, through the financing of studies, research, instruction, and other educational activities between the United States and participating countries. By 1952, the major countries of Western Europe had signed Fulbright agreements and were engaged in such exchange activities. The program, by bringing the wartorn countries back into the mainstream of international educational and scientific life, had established itself as a symbol of mutual cooperation. Educational exchanges under the Fulbright Act were in operation between the United States and 24 other countries of the world, including 10 countries in Western Europe. The terms of the various Fulbright agreements, and the policies and procedures established to carry them out, were essentially the same for all programs of binational Commissions wherever they were established.

As was the case with earlier binational Fulbright agreements, the agreement with Germany permitted the U.S. Government to draw on foreign currencies or credits acquired as a payment for surplus property disposals, to finance the program. Its purpose, as specifically enunciated in its preamble, was "to promote further mutual understanding between the peoples of the United States of America and the Federal Republic of Germany by a wider exchange of knowledge and professional talents through educational contacts." Citizens of the United States were eligible for full funding of transportation, tuition, maintenance, and other expenses related to scholastic activities in schools and institutions of higher learning located in the territory of the Federal Republic of Germany, as were Germans having their permanent residence in the Federal Republic of Germany and/or the Western Sectors of Berlin who chose to engage in educational activities in U.S. schools or institutions of higher learning. German nationals having their permanent residence in the Federal Republic of Germany and/or the Western Sectors of Berlin who desired to attend U.S. schools and institutions of higher learning in the continental United States, Hawaii, Alaska (including the Aleutian Islands), Puerto Rico, and the Virgin Islands, were provided with transportation only, as long as their attendance did not deprive U.S. citizens of an opportunity to attend such schools and institutions. Since only foreign currencies were available under the program, the dollar expenses in the United States were to be provided from U.S. Government and private sources.

The principle of binationalism was inherent also in the administration of the Fulbright program. A binational commission in Germany, known as "United States Educational Commission in the the Federal Republic of Germany," henceforth referred to as the USEC/G or the "Commission," was given the responsibility "to facilitate the administration" of the program in Germany. The Commission was composed of ten members, five of whom were U.S. citizens and five German nationals having their permanent residence in the Federal Republic of Germany and/or in the Western Sectors of Berlin.[2]

THE FULBRIGHT PROGRAM

In common with all of the Fulbright agreements, the principal officer in charge of the U.S. Diplomatic Mission to the Federal Republic of Germany, i.e., at first the High Commissioner and subsequently the Ambassador, was the Honorary Chairman of the Commission in Germany. He had the right to cast the deciding vote in the event of a tie and also to appoint the regular Chairman of the Commission. The Commission was responsible for engaging an Executive Secretary to carry out its administrative responsibilities. Both the regular Chairman and the Executive Secretary, at the beginning, were American citizens. Among the principal responsibilities of the Commission was the preparation of the annual program and its submission to the Department, the nomination of German candidates for grants, and the placement and the rendering of other related services for U.S. recipients of grants to Germany.

In the United States, a Presidentially-appointed Board of Foreign Scholarships, composed of 10 (now 12) distinguished representatives of cultural and educational life, had been created by the Fulbright Act to supervise the program and to make the final selection of individuals and institutions to be assisted. It also had the responsibility for approving the annual program submitted by the Commission. The Board was assisted by three principal cooperating agencies, financed by the Department, for announcing opportunities and screening applications in the United States and for arranging placement of foreign recipients of grants in U.S. institutions, and related services: the Conference Board of Associated Research Councils, representing the four national research councils in the United States (American Council of Learned Societies, National Research Council, Social Science Research Council, and the American Council on Education) for advanced scholars and professors; the Institute of International Education for students; and the U.S. Office of Education for school teachers. The Department of State through its International Educational Exchange Service served as the Secretariat for the Board.

The Secretary of State was responsible for administering the overall program to assure compliance with the terms of the Act as authorized by Congress, with responsibility for approval of the annual budget "pursuant to such regulations as he may prescribe." The United States funded the annual program by requesting the Federal Republic of Germany to make available payments against its dollar indebtedness. Sums of German currency equivalent to $5 million were to be made available. An amount not to exceed $1 million could be placed at the disposal of the Commission for any single calendar year. This sum was to be supplemented by dollar amounts (in 1953: $507,000) taken from the regular appropriation for the exchange program of HICOG to defray expenses incurred by German Fulbright grantees in the United States.[3] At first the U.S. Government bore the brunt of the cost—a characteristic of the Fulbright program worldwide. With the rapid recovery of their economy, German authorities began to view the imbalance in funding as a drawback that deprived the agreement of full binationalism. Yet, it was only in 1962, when the agreement was renewed, that the financial contributions of both parties were equalized. After that Germany recognized the Fulbright program as a "truly binational undertaking."[4]

Although by definition Fulbright agreements were cultural undertakings whose binationalism was based on the principle of full reciprocity,[5] the climate of the early fifties introduced a mildly political note in the deliberation of the new German Fulbright Commission. Binationalism and reciprocity notwithstanding, the new U.S. High Commissioner, Walter W. Donnelly, reminded the Commission at its first session on September 29, 1952 that the Fulbright program in Germany had a mandate over and above that carried by other programs of its kind. Being a most effective means of promoting international understanding and cooperation, he hoped that, as the executor of the Fulbright program, the Commission would succeed in helping "remove many misunderstandings which may still exist between Germany and America."[6] His German counterpart, State Secretary Walter Hallstein, struck a similar but somewhat less guarded note. He classified the initiative associated with the name Fulbright as "only one stage" in the larger effort of the American Government and the American people "to achieve a closer rapprochement between our two peoples."[7] Hallstein and his colleagues placed the accent on youth. Giving full credit to American generosity in opening their country to thousands of young Germans, Hallstein saw the great merit of the Fulbright program in the corresponding effort to acquaint young Americans with the conditions, the culture, and the people of Germany. "Cultural exchange," Hallstein concluded, "is quite simply not a one-way street."[8]

Another factor that German officials were quick to realize was that the Fulbright program offered German authorities and citizens, sooner than in the case of other exchanges, a higher degree of participation in various stages of planning and execution. They accepted this new responsibility eagerly. Their enthusiasm did not wane in the coming years but kept on growing as did their financial contributions.

Today the German contribution to the financing of the binational Fulbright program exceeds by far that of the United States.[9]

The Fulbright program started as a supplementary effort. As Sam H. Linch, Cultural Attaché of HICOG and the Commission's first chairman, pointed out at the first session of the Commission, "the program will augment and be in addition to the regular exchange of persons program carried out by the U.S. High Commissioner," which he noted would, in fact, send about 2,000 German leaders, trainees, and teenagers to the United States in the coming year (1953).[10]

The Program's Structure and Scope

The Fulbright program absorbed the essentially academic categories of exchange previously handled under the auspices of the regular exchange program of HICOG; namely, university and college professors, lecturers, research scholars, school teachers, and graduate students.[11] German and American participants were about equal in number, a major and significant change from the character of the regular HICOG administered program, giving an added accent to the two-way character of the program.

During 1953, the first year of the operation of the program, for instance, the total number of German exchangees was 235, that of American exchangees 239. Of the German groups the largest single category was graduate students (178), followed by professors and lecturers (33), and teachers (8). In addition, 16 Germans participated in special study projects, along with participants from other European countries, such as the annual Salzburg Seminar in American Studies in Austria, administered by a private group in the United States in close cooperation with Harvard; and the program at the Bologna Center, in Italy, a school of advanced political study administered jointly by Johns Hopkins University and the University of Bologna. Each of these centers received financial support through grants-in-aid from the U.S. Department of State. The participants were financed by the respective Fulbright Commissions.

The corresponding figures within the total American group were 192 students, 19 professors and lecturers, 16 research scholars (a category that in the German listings of grants was frequently combined with professors and lecturers), and 12 teachers. In the following year totals showed slight increases in most categories, notably among American students, but after 1954 remained by and large on the same level. By 1955 the number of German participants had reached an annual total of 732 (351 students, 108 professors and lecturers, and 66 teachers and 29 participants in special study projects), and that of their American counterparts 827, including renewal grants (594 students, 71 professors, 56 research scholars, and 76 teachers), (see Appendix III). Thus the program as planned by the Commission included a larger number of grants to Americans than to Germans. However, as noted earlier, the imbalance was more than amply compensated for by the regular HICOG exchange program with its preponderance of German participants, mostly in the category of German leaders.

Innovations

The Fulbright agreement introduced subtle but significant changes in the exchange program in general—that is, in approach, emphasis, and administration. With students, scholars, teachers and professors removed from the regular HICOG exchange program, these groups were no longer committed to engage, individually or collectively, in studies serving "reorientation" purposes. True to the program's objective "to promote further mutual understanding . . . by a wider exchange of knowledge and professional talents," the goals pursued by each participant were scholastic and on the whole highly individualized, which applied to German no less than to American participants. Except in the most general terms and contrary to the reorientation exchange program, the Fulbright program was wholly nonpolitical as regards selection of candidates and fields of study. According to a report submitted in 1952 to USEC/G by the "Committee to Survey Educationally Needed Facilities in Germany,"[12] the "entire exchange of knowledge" was to be furthered through the Fulbright program. The Committee acknowledged that German students and scholars going to the United States for purposes of training were to represent "all recognized areas of advanced study and research." However, the special relationship between the United States and the Federal Republic of Germany which in 1952 was still an occupied country, could not be entirely overlooked. With a view to the special needs and deficiencies prevailing in postwar Germany, the Committee recommended that special emphasis be placed on the following fields: social sciences, including political science with emphasis on empirical research methods rather than pure theory; problems of human relations as reflected in such fields as education; psychology and psychiatry; community planning; medicine and public health; architecture; humanities; natural sciences; engineering in all its facets; labor and management problems; American studies; and economics.[13] Nearly every one of these subjects was related to problem areas critical to the German national reconstruction effort. Expertise in these fields was at a premium, with German facilities for training still recovering from traditional weaknesses and the effects of political indoctrination.

When the binational Fulbright exchanges began in 1947, the Board of Foreign Scholarships placed total emphasis on open competition as the method for securing grantees. This was partly the result of the American belief in an equal chance for all, and partly reflected the wish of the Board to gain wider experience before focusing the program on projects. In 1950 and 1951 the Board began to place stronger emphasis on projects, and on the direct recruitment of high quality U.S. professors and lecturers to implement such projects. Part of the new emphasis stressed the development of American studies. Thus, when the Fulbright program with Germany was activated in January of 1953, exchange opportunities were organized under several projects, each project representing a cluster of grants to Germans and Americans in a specific field of activity. Contrary to the earlier projects developed by OMGUS and HICOG, the Fulbright projects constituted broad academic areas, encompassing a number of disciplines where demands and interests were most pronounced and where the resources of one country could effectively supplement those of the other. Six major project areas were identified: (I) University Exchanges in the Humanities; (II) University Exchanges in the Social Sciences; (III) American Studies in German Universities; (IV) University Exchanges in Mathematics and the Natural Sciences; (V) University Exchanges in Music and Art; and (VI) Teacher Exchange Program. There were two additional categories: Special Projects (such as the German Youth Specialist Program) and the Inter-Foundation Lectureship Program.[14] The order in which the projects were listed seems to have been intended to reflect a scale of priority for meeting needs and interests in order of urgency. The "consequences," as the Fulbright Commission later pointed out in its first 10-year report,[15] were "reciprocal appreciation of the achievements of German and American academic endeavor and enrichment of scholarship on both sides of the Atlantic."

As regards their importance and beneficial effect for either country, the 10-year report of the Commission suggested that Project I: "Humanities" had proved a most timely response to a growing interest in the United States in "Germanics" or German literature. Curiously, no reference was made to the impact, if any, on the development of liberal arts studies (studium generale) at German universities. Project II: "Social Sciences," on the other hand, was described as a real boon to German efforts to broaden the scope of university disciplinary curriculum and professional horizons, particularly through empiric research and through the study of political science and international relations. For obvious reasons, the beneficiaries of Project III: "American Studies" were German students and scholars, especially those who intended to use later their newly acquired knowledge of American history and literature for teaching purposes. Project IV: "Mathematics and the Natural Sciences" appears to have been the most reciprocal one as regards participation and benefit. Because of Germany's rich tradition in "Music and Art," Project V was very popular, although by no means exclusively so, with American students. Project VI: "Teacher Exchange" was conceived almost from the beginning as largely a 50–50 reciprocal proposition with German and American school teachers replacing each other, principally in language teaching but occasionally in literature and social studies classes.[16]

American Studies

"Amerika Studien" or American Studies deserve special mention because they constituted perhaps the most important and most truly innovative feature of the Fulbright program. Their purpose, in support of U.S. overall policy, and in response to a widespread interest in the United States, was to afford German students an opportunity to learn more about American culture and civilization and thus to strengthen cultural ties between the two countries.[17] The reasons for U.S. interest in fostering indepth study of America were obvious and compelling. The American image in Germany was riddled with clichés. Never quite free of controversy, it had been viciously distorted by Nazi (and later Communist) propaganda and vestiges were abundant. In contrast thereto, Hollywood had glamorized the American scene to a degree that was often suspect. The presence of occupation authorities and of military personnel had done little to correct the picture or to improve relations. Cultural contacts had remained minimal. At the same time, there was considerable and growing curiosity among Germans in nearly all social strata about America and things American. There was, in fact, a keenly felt need to learn about the United States in a more systematic fashion. German educational institutions, from high schools to universities, partly in response to U.S. suggestions, partly on their own initiative, began to introduce American studies in their curricula.[18] "America Institutes" sprang up at various universities, although in most cases "Amerikanistik" was not recognized as a major obligatory subject but merely as a so-called "Zusatzfach," i.e., an optional subject.[19] The time for an American initiative thus seemed propitious. Implicitly, in the immediate post-Nazi period, emphasis on American studies was another way of teaching democracy by live example, thereby reinforcing the reorientation thrust of the regular exchange program.

American studies, broadly defined, received probably more attention and support from the Commission than any other single Fulbright project. Special seminars were planned in 1954 to afford German students, teachers, and research scholars an opportunity to become acquainted with American literature, history, sociology, education, fine arts, political and social sciences, and the teaching of English as a second language, by means of a series of lectures and discussions. Moreover, to a degree of sophistication not previously attempted in Germany, American studies were now being adapted to the scholastic preferences and needs of German universities. The first Fulbright program proposal, for 1953–1954, stipulated, for instance, that American visiting lecturers in American studies should be specialists in modern American history. The role of the United States in world affairs, no less than its dominant position in international relations, was considered to be of particular interest to German students.

American sociology as taught in American universities was generally unknown in Germany. And although prewar Germany had a rich tradition in sociology, there was now a critical lag compared with other disciplines. This suggested an acute need for stimulating modern methods of sociological research and the use of statistics.

With due respect to German accomplishments in pedagogics and psychology, the traditional stress on theory in these disciplines seemed to require some balance by greater emphasis on empirical methods and modern trends of research in both fields. Lectures were, for example, to highlight the child-centered curriculum as opposed to traditional subject centered concepts. An approach of this nature was expected to meet the interest of German teachers who were eager to exchange ideas and experiences with their American colleagues in an effort to develop new goals in German education.

Social sciences, and in particular political science, as developed in the United States, were regarded as academic disciplines most pertinent as vehicles for demonstrating democracy in action and training new cadres of leadership.

In the field of architecture, the Commission felt that modern American achievements might serve as models to German architects in replacing and restoring public buildings and private dwellings. American influence in this regard had only recently begun to assert itself in Germany. Courses in the design of schools, hospitals, and theaters were especially welcome. So were courses on the use of new building materials permitting greater efficiency and economy with emphasis on low-cost housing and more functional design.

Finally, the teaching of English emerged as a subject of surpassing significance, principally for three reasons: first, although some American lecturers taught in German, knowledge of English was vital to full comprehension of the variety of subject matters included in the American studies program; second, while German teachers were quite proficient in English grammar, phonetics, and literature, their speaking knowledge was often deficient; and third, in the Federal Republic at least, English was fast replacing French as the most popular foreign language. Thus English became an obligatory subject in all secondary schools, including the classical gymnasium.

The program proposal for 1953–1954 as approved by the Commission with its heavy emphasis on American studies responded in part to the policy of the Board of Foreign Scholarships to focus the Fulbright programs around project concepts. The promotion of American studies in German universities, attracting the interest of the German academician in the form of scholarly study projects, raised reorientation to a more sophisticated level. This undoubtedly was the intent of the Commission. Yet, wishing to avoid charges that it was focusing the major part of the program on American studies, the Commission pointed out that the rest of the program was reserved for studies in any recognized academic field for which adequate facilities existed.[20] Special reference was made to the fine arts, science, and mathematics. The Commission, in fact, expressed certain reservations concerning the degree of emphasis placed on American studies in the program. It averred that it had by no means been its purpose to insist that universities and other educational institutions in Germany accept American studies as a part of their regular program—although some (e.g., Munich) had done so. It was merely responding to the expressed interest of German and American educators who were voluntarily engaged in such studies.[21] Yet, actually, the Commission made every conceivable effort to encourage German universities to develop programs in American literature, history, education, economics, and sociology. It gave priority to the applications of those who had chosen American studies as their field of participation and who, as it happened, constituted the largest single group among American senior grantees. American interest proved a welcome boost to the project, but German support was sometimes lacking. In 1955, for example, the Commission saw itself compelled to abandon plans of a seminar for American studies because of what it described to be "administrative difficulties and lack of financial support from German sources."[22] The American studies program as such, however, continued on an undiminished scale.

Problems of Adjustment

The "Fulbrighters" introduced a new kind of Americans to Germany. Germans had come to know the American "expert," the American artist and, above all, the American GI. The American image produced by them was, if not distorted, at least controversial. Personal contact, moreover, had remained limited. The Fulbright program now brought forth the American scholar and the American student, both of whom were to become part of the German academic scene. Conversely, German scholars and students were to be introduced to the American academic system and campus life. American high school teachers were to take the place of their German counterparts and, vice versa, German high school teachers would substitute for their colleagues.

The basic assumption was that academic standards and practices in both countries were sufficiently equivalent or at least similar to permit such exchanges without major complications. The assumption proved to be fallacious, particularly in the case of students. The Commission soon discovered that, in general, German students were slightly older and had a stronger academic background than American students in the same age group. German members of the Commission pointed out that German and American curricula simply did not correspond in level and that an American high school graduate with 4 years of college training had just about reached the level of a German high school graduate (Abiturient) with 2 years of university training, "since American students," as German experts pointed out, "go to college two years before the Germans go." [23] Furthermore, study methods varied. Many German students accustomed to the independent pursuit of their studies, found the discipline of American colleges, such as compulsory attendance of classes, stifling. American students, on the other hand, used to the stricter routine of their colleges, felt lost on German campuses and often strayed away from their studies with the result that their performance was difficult to evaluate.[24]

The problems faced by university faculty and school teachers were more technical. School vacation and work schedules in the two countries did not coincide and hence led to troublesome delays in the selection of participants. German scholars in responsible admininstrative positions found it difficult to be absent for a period of 9 months in face of the acute shortage of teaching personnel. The younger teachers were reluctant to commit themselves for fear of losing their prospects for employment or their place on faculties—an understandable but not wholly realistic apprehension in view of the urgent need for well-trained teachers. Some of the more prominent German scholars found the small stipend of $9 per day inadequate. American teachers had similar complaints. German salaries and stipends which in the beginning were paid in nonconvertible German Marks were below the level of American remunerations. All of the American participants, especially students, felt the pinch of an extremely tight housing situation and of living conditions which in the early fifties were still far from normal and often substandard by comparison with conditions in the United States.

There were other problems, especially at the beginning. Exchange candidates complained about delays in the selection process. Some American professors were disappointed to find that the subjects they taught were not compulsory (no "Examensfach") and that class attendance was therefore neither required nor indeed observed by students. Some, not in adequate command of German, came up hard against the language barrier. Social contact with German colleagues or fellow students was rare. The tendency on the part of American students to stick together complicated the situation, which may have been in part a reaction to the traditional reserve and status consciousness of German faculty members and of their habit of keeping students at a distance.

In the case of American professors, similar difficulties of adjustment were sometimes compounded by the inability on the part of the Commission to obtain advance approval of the American candidate by the German dean or "Ordinarius." In such cases the American "Fulbrighter" found himself snubbed by his German colleagues. Complications of this nature, combined with the low rates of compensation noted earlier, may have been the cause for German suspicions that the program was not attracting high caliber scholars from the United States. A few American Fulbright professors apparently joined the critics. But most of the American professors seldom had such problems. In fact, the majority of the participants not only profited from their personal and professional experience, but enhanced the prestige of the program.[25] By and large, the reports from and about "Fulbrighters" in the United States attested to the valuable contribution the program was making in building closer ties between the educational communities of the two countries.[26]

Both American and German authorities did their utmost to reduce or eliminate the problems of grant recipients. An extensive orientation program for both Americans and Germans, before and after arrival in the host country, including shipboard orientation conferences, introduced participants, notably students and teachers, to conditions in the respective host countries. The Institute of International Education and the Committee on Friendly Relations among Foreign Students (now the International Student Service) assisted German students upon their arrival in the United States by arranging for reception, social contacts, and sightseeing. Universities organized orientation centers. Students were provided with helpful literature, and with lists of fellow grantees.

American students in Germany participated in systematic orientation courses lasting 3 weeks (later reduced to 2). Introductory language instruction was provided on board ship. With the help of the Experiment in International Living, many were placed with German families for 1-month periods; some decided to board with their hosts for the rest of their study period. During their stay in Germany the Commission endeavored to remain in touch with the American students by way of correspondence and personal visits, organizing regional conferences, and meeting with grantees at individual universities. In order to break the ice and to facilitate contact with German faculty members and students, the Commission financed a series of social meetings.

Since the Commission's contacts with American students were intended, as the Commission took pains to point out, to assist rather than supervise them, evaluation of their academic pursuits remained a difficult problem and the Commission was unable to reach a satisfactory solution. Responsibility for evaluation was first left with the so-called "foreign bureau" (Auslandsamt) of each university which by and large was not equipped to handle the job. Eventually the "Conference of German University Presidents" (Rektorenkonferenze) agreed to cooperate. A number of adjustments were gradually made to meet some of the most critical problems experienced by American grantees. Universities helped in providing housing for individuals, but facilities for those with families proved well nigh impossible to find. Grantees were therefore discouraged from bringing dependents to Germany. On the other hand, special allowance was made for the need of music students to supplement their university courses by refunding the costs of private instruction on an average of 2 hours per week. Further, in a few instances, the Commission approved supplementary funds for grantees to compensate for travel costs, microfilming and stenographic expenses when they appeared necessary to the completion of a given project.[27]

The German "Fulbrighters"

As indicated above, the vast majority of German grantees were university students at various stages of their academic training. With this emphasis on youth, the Fulbright program reinforced a policy started by HICOG. But there were certain differences in approach which permitted more individualized treatment with respect to selection of candidates and program development.

During the first years of its operation the Commission refined its criteria and procedures extensively. At its first session on September 29, 1952,[28] it divided the German students according to sources of funding and proposed a few rough criteria, not essentially different from those used by HICOG. Grants given to students were of three types: those whose transportation was furnished out of Fulbright funds and whose maintenance was paid out of the HICOG exchange budget; those whose transportation was provided from Fulbright funds and who received scholarships from an American university; and those whose transportation was guaranteed by Fulbright funds but who were able to obtain a private scholarship or had private means to take care of their dollar expenditures.

Personal criteria for eligibility were fairly simple, namely: German citizenship (or nationality), proficiency in English, and age below 35. There appears to have been some difference of opinion with respect to academic requirements. Some German members of the Commission argued in favor of selection of advanced over first semester students, i.e. graduates or postgraduates, others preferred recent high school graduates (Abiturienten). For the first year the Commission accepted a compromise proposal. Screening agencies were instructed to submit recommendations of candidates by using the following categories and percentages: (a) high school graduates (Abiturienten) who had not yet entered a university—15 percent; (b) first to sixth semester university students (provided that they had completed two semesters at a German university at the time of their departure)—25 percent; and (c) upperclassmen, graduate, and postgraduate students—50 percent. A flexible margin of 10 percent was left for categories (a), (b), and (c).[29]

The candidacy of early semester students might have been hard to justify if admission had been based on academic standards alone, a practice followed frequently by German universities. In observance of the general guidelines of the Fulbright agreement, however, the Fulbright Scholarship Committees which made the final recommendations, did not consider academic excellence as the sole criterion, but placed great emphasis on such intangibles as personality, character, extracurricular interests, and social and political awareness.[30] On the basis of experience up to that point, a policy guide issued by the Commission to Fulbright Scholarship Committees for the 1955–1956 student program was quite explicit in this regard. Students, it was pointed out, would be judged in the United States not only on the basis of their scholarly achievements but also "on the impression they make as representatives of the Federal Republic." Therefore, due consideration should be given to personality traits, attitudes, and appearance. Hobbies, recreational activities, as well as social, political, and community interests were declared important criteria. Leadership, either demonstrated or potential, was a factor to be carefully weighed. The wish to visit the United States to learn about American life was not to be regarded as a valid reason for favorable consideration. Instead, the policy demanded that students show proof of a definite "goal" which the student's stay in the United States could substantially achieve. Choice of academic studies which could be just as successfully pursued in Germany would not justify participation in the program. Political and religious beliefs which in principle were stated to be of no concern to the screening bodies, could become relevant and legitimate criteria if they helped to "ascertain the applicant's openmindedness, tolerance, and understanding of the social and cultural climate of both the United States and Germany."[31] Emphasis on such intangibles seems to have led in some cases to neglect of academic standards, for the Commission found it necessary to admonish Fulbright Scholarship Committees to give more careful consideration to the academic achievements of candidates.[32] Moreover, the Commission stipulated that those with a questionable political background, in order to qualify for consideration, had to support their application "by unusually strong recommendations on academic qualifications."[33]

Further requirements had to be added when in the course of the following years the student group was expanded or, more correctly, supplemented with the addition of so-called "Jungakademiker" (young academicians),[34] young teachers, young lawyers, and youth specialists, underlining increased emphasis on those young professionals who, upon their return to Germany, could apply immediately their newly gained knowledge within their fields.[35] The modified criteria were publicized in all German universities, ministries of education, and U.S. consular offices by special announcement.[36] The new category of young professionals included six groups: (a) students in their third, fourth, and fifth semesters at a university or technical university as of July 1955 (students from so-called pedagogical institutes of higher learning were not eligible unless they had completed their first examen); (b) students at a university or technical university who had completed six semesters or more of academic training as of July 1955; (c) students of "Sonstige [specialized] Hochschulen" (e.g., academies of music, arts, and the like) who qualified under "(a)" above; and (d) "Jungakademiker," or persons who had completed their formal university education, no matter what their profession, provided that they were under 35 years of age and desired to engage in specialized graduate studies in the United States.

The category of young lawyers, or so-called legal trainees, was adopted from the HICOG exchange program as an especially critical group of recruits for future managerial and executive positions.[37] The requirements for these young lawyers (not to be confused with "Referendare," see Chapter II) were especially strict. Not only were they expected to have passed the second bar ("Assessor") examen but also to have spent 3 years in government service. Other young academicians included chemists, physicists, engineers, physicians, university assistants, and "Habilitanten" (i.e., candidates preparing themselves for an academic career). Physicians, however, were advised that they could not be placed in American medical schools but could study in other fields or be recommended for travel grants to accept internships in American hospitals. In all cases, the scholastic record of candidates in the young professionals category had to be better than average. They had to have sufficient command of English to read with comprehension and to participate effectively in group discussions. Beyond this they had to show awareness of current affairs and proof of community activities. Finally, each candidate had to present evidence that he would continue his present work upon his return, and agree in writing that he would return to Germany upon completion of his studies.[38]

At its 22d session (in February 1955), the Commission decided to include in its 1956 Annual Program proposal a "Youth Specialists" project [39] which was sponsored by the Neighborhood Settlement Association of Cleveland, Ohio, Inc., under the direction of Dr. Henry Ollendorff.[40] The latter had agreed to defray all expenses of the participants while in the United States, i.e., for maintenance, transportation, and administration, with only tuition for enrollment at Western Reserve University paid for with dollars provided by the U.S. Government, appropriated under Public Law 402 (the Smith-Mundt Act). The Department of State, with approval from the Board of Foreign Scholarships, strongly recommended acceptance of the proposal, but it created a lively controversy within the Commission. In deference to the academic character of the Fulbright program and perhaps also to German policy which in those days denied full academic standing to social work schools and institutions from which the young candidates were to be recruited, Chairman Chester Y. Easum, the American cultural officer, dissented from the majority of the Commission, stating that the project did not meet the established academic requirements of the Fulbright program which was intended for longer study than provided for youth specialists. The Commission, though recognizing that the project deviated from the normal standards of the Fulbright program, overruled the Chairman declaring that the encouragement of continuing education for the leaders in this field was desirable.[41] The Commission, however, stipulated that applicants under this project must meet the Commission's standards, i.e., graduation from an approved German high school, selection through competitive procedures, and payment of travel costs within the United States by the sponsor or participants.[42]

To what extent German student grantees availed themselves of the variety of courses offered them at American universities is not fully ascertainable from available records. Fulbright program proposals established certain ceilings in such broad fields as American studies and social sciences, leaving all other fields unspecified, but neither they nor the annual reports of the Commission shed much light on actual student preferences. A sample of 166 students contained in the Annual Report for Program Year 1955 lists the following subjects in order of size of enrollment: humanities (54), law (45), mathematics and science (25), medicine (13), fine arts (12), theology (9), agriculture (5), and economics (3). Whether these examples were typical is hard to verify. The *Appraisal of the German Fulbright Program*, which summarized the findings of a study of the experiences of German senior scholars and students between 1953 and 1959, conducted from December 1959 to February 1960,[43] listed the following fields in order of preference: humanities (39 percent students, 47 percent senior scholars); mathematics and natural science technology (27 percent students, 41 percent seniors); law (14 percent students, 3 percent seniors); political and social sciences, journalism (17 percent students, 8 percent seniors); economics (11 percent students, 2 percent seniors); and others, e.g., general education and physical education (2 percent students, 6 percent seniors). The fields of study correspond roughly, but not exactly, to the subjects chosen by the respondents in Germany. There was a substantial increase, more than triple, of students electing political and social sciences and journalism as their discipline in the United States. Their preference, no doubt, reflected a gap in the German academic system which only gradually, and partly under American influence, was beginning to build up its departments and institutes of social and political sciences.[44]

Between 40 and 50 American universities and colleges participated nearly from the very outset as sponsors. These included 11 American institutions which had established so-called head-for-head or one-way exchange programs with a German university, e.g., California with Cologne; Chicago with Frankfurt; Colorado with Erlangen; Georgia Tech with the Technical University of Stuttgart; Harvard, Michigan, and Minnesota with the Free University of Berlin; Indiana with Kiel; North Carolina with Goettingen; Ohio with Muenster; Skidmore with Freiburg; Stanford with Hamburg; and Yale with Heidelberg. These arrangements were not exclusive and did not prevent students from other universities from attending any of the above-mentioned institutions or students from the latter to enroll at other institutions. By and large, the record of academic achievements, as far as available, appears to have been relatively high.[45]

German university lecturers and research scholars, and school teachers, constituted only a modest fraction of the total number of grantees, as noted earlier. Although requirements for eligibility in each case were different from those for students, completion of academic training, good knowledge of English, and, in the case of research scholars, a specific advanced research plan were obligatory. Preference was given to applicants who were willing to commit themselves to a stay of 9 to 10 months.[46] As in the case of students, capacity to convey their experience in the United States to audiences in Germany and to apply it in their work upon their return was considered a vital criterion for selection.[47]

There appears to have been a wide variety in the academic affiliation at home, status, and interests of German lecturers and research scholars. A review conducted by the binational screening committees in Germany in 1954 [48] shows that most of the applicants who came from universities and institutions of higher learning throughout West Germany and West Berlin, were from Berlin, Bonn, Detmold, Giessen, Goettingen, Heidelberg, Karlsruhe, Cologne, Mainz, Munich, and Wuerzburg, with the largest single group coming from the University of Goettingen. They ranked from full professors and lecturers (Dozenten) to assistants and high level professionals, with the Dozenten constituting the bulk. Their subjects of research and teaching included natural sciences (physics, biophysics, chemistry), mathematics, medicine, social sciences (political science and geography), forestry, music, and arts, with the comparatively largest aggregate in the natural sciences and medicine. Annual Commission reports make special reference to academic accomplishments of German grantees in the fields of architecture, biology, and epidemiology.

The annual reports contain evidence that the activities of German scholars were greatly appreciated by the American host institutions, and that, in a number of instances, their achievements led to special professional appointments and promotions after their return to Germany.[49]

The American "Fulbrighters"

A real breakthrough occurred on the American side, with Americans assuming the role of equal partners both in a contributory and beneficiary capacity. The element that established parity, at least in numbers, was the large number of American students. The Department's annual report for fiscal year 1954, covering exchanges from January 1953 to June 1954, lists 208 American students.[50] Except for France (241) and the United Kingdom (189), no other country had anywhere near this number of students. All of the students were expected to have "at least a fair knowledge of German," a stipulation that was generally met, but most satisfactorily in the case of students who were given assistant teaching assignments at high schools. Other than that, the same requirements applied to them as did to other students in the worldwide Fulbright program. They had to pursue academic study and research projects at the predoctoral level. A majority had to be graduate students who, in most cases, would conduct research for Ph.D dissertations, or advanced qualified students not working for a degree who had other good reasons to study abroad. Holders of the B.A., or equivalent, and M.A. candidates presenting academically sound study projects were considered eligible.

As far as scholastic background was concerned, students had to have received most of their school education and their undergraduate training at high schools and colleges in the United States. Excellence in their academic performance and other meritorious academic or professional experience were considered significant factors for selection, as were the standards of the host institution and the feasibility of the proposed study or research project. Special requirements were established for certain fields, such as 4 years of professional study and/or performance in the creative and performing arts, an M.S. degree with 2 years of professional experience after receipt of the degree for students of social work, and an M.D. degree at the time of application for students of medicine. Of course, all had to be acceptable to the host country and to the institutions at which they proposed to pursue their projects.[51]

As far as personal qualifications were concerned, applicants had to be U.S. citizens. Race, color, or sex were not to be considered as criteria for selection. Their age had to be between 20 and 35. Adaptability to living conditions overseas and academic requirements were to be established by faculty verification or by interview. An important factor was their representation potential, that is, their capacity to contribute to a better understanding of the culture and civilization of the United States and thereby to contribute to better "understanding and friendship between the people of the United States and those of the host country." American students for the first Fulbright year (1953) were from more than 100 universities nationwide.

At least in the beginning, American students showed distinct preferences in the choice of their German host institution. The majority wished to enroll at either the University of Heidelberg or Munich. When this proved neither desirable nor practical, students accepted fairly wide distribution among the various universities in West Germany and West Berlin. The bilateral relationship that had been established between a number of American and German universities which provided sponsorship for German students, also proved useful in the case of American students. Eventually nearly all German universities and institutions of higher learning participated, including the various state academies for music and the arts.

An examination of the fields selected by American students during the first Fulbright year reveals an interesting but understandable imbalance of subject matter in favor of the arts and languages as against sciences, notably the social sciences, and against such professional categories as law (one student) and medicine (none). More than a third studied various fields of music (46) and the arts (20), fields with traditional standards of excellence in Germany.[52] A fifth (34) chose literature, especially Germanistics, and linguistics where German competence was obvious. Twenty-five elected the natural sciences, e.g., chemistry, physics and mathematics, and engineering, and 22 the social sciences. The remainder studied history (14), philosophy and the humanities (8), and theology (7). One student chose horticulture. The placement of students by the Commission reflected an intelligent judgment of institutions with respect to those whose integrity of reputation and academic standards had, by and large, been preserved and which had not been destroyed or compromised by the Nazis.

Computations made by USEC/G of American students' preferences in the following years showed remarkable shifts. The annual reports for 1954 and 1955 revealed the largest aggregates in Germanistics and comparative literature (40), in various fields of the (natural) sciences (35), and history and political science (35). Music and art dropped to 30. Theology, philosophy and the other humanities remained the same (15). Social sciences (without political science) now hit bottom (10).[53] With the recovery of German academic life, with the increase of the number of universities, and with full academic accreditation gradually being accorded to a number of professional schools, student preferences underwent further changes in the following years.

Those graduate students who were given assignments in English language teaching at secondary schools found their work pretty much cut out for them. They were assigned as assistants to German teachers of English. Instead of giving formal instruction, they helped the teachers conduct discussion groups and afforded pupils an opportunity to engage in English conversation.[54]

Lecturers and research scholars as well as teachers, notably the former, supplemented and eventually replaced the specialists first used by OMGUS and later HICOG as consultants to assist and advise American officials and German authorities, agencies, and institutions. By comparison with American students, the number of lecturers and research scholars remained modest, rarely exceeding more than a fourth of the students, which was actually a larger percentage than in most other Fulbright programs. The level of their academic standing was remarkably high and included prominent members of the faculties of leading universities such as California, Chicago, Columbia, Duke, Georgetown, Harvard, Illinois, Indiana, Michigan, Minnesota, Princeton, Stanford, Wisconsin, and Yale. Among them were a number of outstanding scientists and scholars of German origin who had left Germany or Austria during the Nazi regime, such as Karl Brandt, John A. Herz, Heinrich Kronstein, and Sigmund Neumann. The list is too large to be reproduced in full. It included during the first 3 years of the program such scholars as Raymond W. Albright, Professor of Church History, Episcopal Theological School, Cambridge, Massachusetts; Howard K. Beale, Professor of American History, University of Wisconsin; Milton Burton, Professor of Chemistry, University of Notre Dame; Mabel A. Elliot, Professor of Sociology, Pennsylvania College for Women; Joseph H. Fichter, Department of Sociology, Loyola University (New Orleans); Hermann Frankel, Emeritus Professor of Classics, Stanford University; Harold Grimm, Professor of American History, Ohio State University; John H. Hallowell, Professor of Political Science, Duke University; Arthur D. Hastler, Professor of Zoology, University of Wisconsin; Einar Hille, Professor of Mathematics, Yale; Morris Janowitz, Professor of Sociology, University of Michigan; Joseph Kwiat, Professor of American Literature, University of Minnesota; Richard A. Musgrave, Professor of Economics, University of Michigan; Ralph Dornfield Owen, Professor of Education, Temple University; Burke Shartel, Professor of Law, University of Michigan; S. D. Shirley Spragg, Professor of Psychology, University of Rochester; Reynold M. Wik, Professor of American History, Mills College; Harvey Wish, Professor of American History, Western Reserve University, Cleveland; Charles C. Fries, Director, English Language Institute, University of Michigan; and many others of equal distinction in their respective fields.[55]

Most German universities were included in the arrangements. Again, as in the case of students, the special university-to-university relationships between certain American and German universities proved most useful. Requirements for eligibility were the same as those set by the Board of Foreign Scholarships for scholars sent to other countries. By definition, lecturers were considered persons at a Ph.D. or equivalent level who would teach or consult on a full-time basis at a university. Research scholars were expected to engage in full-time advanced research. Achievement in professional or scholarly fields at the post-doctoral level was a major criterion, as was competence in teaching or other academic experience. Research scholars were divided into two groups: mature, professionally established scholars, and recent recipients of Ph.D. or equivalent degrees in early stages of their career.[56] Although opportunities were generally announced in open competition, a number of the lecturers were selected upon specific request by German institutions.[57]

As a rule, the recipients of these grants had to be U.S. citizens. Consideration was given to the educational background of the applicant, that is, whether higher education had been received at American colleges or universities. Age, race, religion, and sex were not regarded as relevant. However, suitability, adaptability, and emotional stability were considered important criteria to be determined through interviews and special screening procedures. Candidates were expected to be "representative and responsible citizens" giving promise of furthering cooperative intellectual inquiry and protecting the nonpolitical character of the program.

Subjects for teaching and research by American grantees varied widely. A majority concentrated, at least in the beginning, as noted earlier, on American studies, especially in the fields of history, literature, sociology, psychology, education, political science, architecture, and English language.[58] But subjects ranged far beyond these fields and included mathematics and sciences (biology), medicine, psychiatry, law, economics, geography, and others. Research scholars engaged in studies of German literature, history, theology, and science in that order of preference.[59]

The professors and lecturers were augmented by participants in the "Inter-Foundation Lectureship Program" carried out with neighboring countries under the auspices of Fulbright programs. Under this program German universities were furnished with lists of Fulbright lecturers and research scholars who were teaching or lecturing in neighboring countries but who were available for lectures in Germany, provided that the German universities agreed to defray their expenses in Germany. The proposal proved to be extraordinarily popular. A number of outstanding American scholars gave lectures in Germany on a series of topics, most of them dealing with specific facets of American politics, economics, social conditions (minority problems), business management, history, literature, and the sciences.[60]

By all accounts American scholars acquitted themselves of their assignments with considerable success; and while quite naturally the degree of impact differed according to personality and project, the net result from the beginning appears to have been positive.[61]

Under the established program policies,[62] American school teachers were considered for full-time teaching or consultation in elementary, secondary, technical, or vocational schools. Included were teachers substituting for their German counterparts under the program for interchange of teachers. Personal eligibility requirements were not much different from those established for lecturers, research scholars, or students except that preference was to be given to school teachers under 50 years of age. As concerns professional experience, applicants for full-time teaching grants had to have at least a bachelor's degree and a minimum of 3 years of professional experience in the U.S. school system. However, in the case of candidates for short-term seminars the requirement was 2 years of previous full-time teaching at the time of the application, or related professional employment in the U.S. school system in the subject treated in the seminar. Acceptability to the host country and institution of affiliation were prerequisites. As indicated earlier, the program occasionally ran into technical difficulties, due to differences in academic year schedules and differing teaching methods and conditions, situations which were usually adjusted satisfactorily.

Administering the Program in the United States and in Germany

The binational administration of the Fulbright program in Germany demanded a type of support structure that was different and separate from the regular HICOG exchange program, which operated directly under the auspices of the Department of State and HICOG, under its own budget. New criteria for selection and administrative procedures had to be introduced following the terms of the Fulbright Act and the operational policies as formulated by the Board of Foreign Scholarships for the Fulbright program worldwide.

With regard to the administration of the program in the United States, the responsibilities of the Board of Foreign Scholarships (BFS), the Department, and the major cooperating educational agencies have been described in the early pages of this chapter. The Chairman of the Board from 1950 to 1953 was Walter Johnson, Professor of History, University of Chicago, and from 1953 to 1955 Frederick Hovde, President of Purdue University. Other members during the period 1950 to 1954 were leading representatives of university faculties, university administrators, and educators active in international affairs.

The Board's Secretariat consisted of a small staff headed by an Executive Secretary appointed by the Department and approved by the Board. Executive Secretaries serving during the first 10 years were Kenneth Holland (1947–1948) and Francis J. Colligan (1948–1956). Chiefs of the Operations Staff were Joseph M. Roland (1948–1949), George T. Moody (1949–1950), John Lund (1950–1952), and Robert S. Black (1952–1955). When the Fulbright program began, the task of organizing a whole new program required a separate unit exclusively concerned with the Fulbright program, which operated from 1948 to 1951 as the Fulbright Program Branch of the Division of Exchange of Persons. Chiefs of the Branch were Frederic O. Bundy (1948–1949) and Howard P. Backus (1949–1951). Subsequently, all operational functions in the Department for academic exchanges were integrated into the regular program units of the exchange-of-persons office of the Department.[63]

Through these channels the Department provided staff services to the Board. It reviewed the budgets submitted by the Commission for approval by the Board; financed the various principal cooperating agencies; supervised the administration of the program by the principal cooperating agencies, which in turn relied on scores of voluntary committees throughout the United States; secured dollar funds from universities and other private donors to assist foreign students who received travel grants only; and discharged responsibility for the expenditure of all Department funds made available for orientation, counseling of foreign and American grantees, and for the screening and recommending of foreign applicants. To perform these functions the Department leaned heavily on the supportive services of outside organizations other than the principal cooperating agencies referred to earlier. Cooperation was required in numerous ways, and board policies were frequently revised to meet new educational developments.[64]

The development of the support structure in Germany, as in all countries participating in a binational Fulbright program, was equally complex. It was of necessity so, inasmuch as the program called for a higher degree of direct participation by German elements than heretofore in the management of exchange programs in Germany. The Commission was able to benefit from the experience of other countries with programs already in operation. At the top of the structure, as in all other countries, stood the Binational Commission, as described earlier. Article 2 of the German Fulbright agreement defined the functions of the Commission in detail: namely (1) to plan, adopt, and carry out exchange programs, including the preparation of annual program proposals; (2) to recommend to the Board of Foreign Scholarships students, professors, research scholars, teachers, resident in the Federal Republic of Germany, and institutions of the Federal Republic qualified to participate in the program; (3) to recommend to the Board such qualifications for the selection of participants as it deemed necessary for achieving the purpose and objectives of the agreement; (4) to authorize the Treasurer of the Commission to receive funds to be deposited in bank accounts; (5) to authorize the disbursement of funds and the making of grants and advancement of funds; (6) to provide for periodic audits; and (7) to engage an executive director or officer and administrative and clerical staff, and fix and pay their salaries and wages. An additional function of the Commission not listed in the agreement, but of major importance, was the cooperative placement of Americans in German educational institutions.

The Commission, which met for the first time on September 29, 1952, convened thereafter several times each year at irregular intervals. Appointments of both the U.S. and German members were made annually, although some appointments were annually renewed for several years. The honorary chairmanship was reserved to the U.S. High Commissioner and later to the U.S. Ambassador, who appointed an Embassy officer to act for him as the active Chairman. High Commissioner Walter W. Donnelly, the first honorary chairman, retired soon after his appointment and his place was taken by the High Commissioner, subsequently Ambassador, the late James B. Conant. During the first 3 years the active chairmen, designated by the honorary chairman of the Commission, were: the Cultural Attaché of the American Embassy, Sam H. Linch; thereafter in acting capacity Treasurer George A. Selke, Chief of the Division of Cultural Affairs; who was followed by the Senior Science Adviser, William Greulich; and eventually the Cultural Attachés Chester V. Easum and E. Wilder Spaulding. Treasurers, during the same period, also appointed by the Embassy, were George A. Selke; Everett G. Chapman, Chief of the Exchange of Persons Division; Henry B. Cox; and Dean Chamberlin. The nongovernmental American members of the Commission, selected from prominent American residents in Germany, representing industry and various civic organizations and institutions, as a rule, showed more constancy of tenure than their governmental colleagues.

Professor Dr. Walter Hallstein, State Secretary of the Foreign Office, headed the group of German members which consisted of high-level dignitaries of the German bureaucracy and academic life. Among them, during the years under review, were Ministerial Counselor Dr. August Fehling, representing the Permanent Conference of the Ministries of Culture; Professor Dr. Egon Huebinger, Ministerial Director in the Ministry of Interior; Professor Dr. Hermann Heimpel, President, and Professors Dr. Erwin Fuess and Dr. Walter Kolb, members of the West German Conference of University Presidents; Professor Dr. Werner Richter, President, and Professor Dr. Theodor Clausen, Chairman, of the German Academic Exchange Service; and others. The Commission appointed Dr. John Mead as Executive Secretary, Heinrich H. Pfeiffer, Chief of the German Program Unit, and Karl Roeloffs, Chief of the American Program Unit in the secretariat.

The German Program Unit of the Commission staff was responsible for drawing up the panels of candidates for grants to be awarded to German professors, teachers, and students, with final selection made by the Board of Foreign Scholarships. It handled their processing from the moment of application to the point of departure and it maintained contact with the grant recipients during their stay in the United States and after their return to Germany.[65] The American Program Unit administered the sector of the program which was concerned with American grantees and acted "as guardian over the well-being of American grantees during their year in the host country." [66] For the placement of interchange teachers and teaching assistants, the American Unit availed itself of the cooperation of the German Academic Exchange Service (Deutscher Akademischer Austauschdienst—DAAD) and later of the German Teacher Exchange Service.

The Commission established contacts with German universities, particularly with those that had arranged direct head-for-head exchanges to secure placements for professors, lecturers, and research scholars. Other cooperating agencies, some of which were represented on the membership of the Commission were the Permanent Conference of Ministers of Culture (Staendige Konferenz der Kultusminister), the West German Conference of German University Presidents (West-deutsche Rektoren Konferenz), the DAAD, the German Research Society (Deutsche Forschungsgemeinschaft), the Max Planck Institutes, the Association for American Studies (Gesellschaft fuer Amerika-Studien), and Inter-Nationes which provided a series of highly useful briefing materials for exchangees. Naturally, the Commission maintained close liaison, partly guaranteed by an overlap of personnel, with the Exchange of Persons Division of HICOG.

The Commission required a substructure of its own in marshalling the cooperation of the educational community in Germany. With the help of the Exchange of Persons Division and the American consulates, "Fulbright Scholarship Committees" (FSC) were organized in each consular district. Each committee consisted of five Americans and five Germans. The five Americans were appointed by the Consul General. He also served as Honorary Chairman and appointed the regular chairman of the Committee. One of the American members had to be the exchange officer attached to each consulate who, however, was not to be designated as chairman. The rest of the American members were to be, if possible, prominent citizens residing in the district. The Executive Secretary of the Commission was an ex officio member of each committee and consequently was invited to attend each meeting.

The German membership of the committees seems to have varied over time with representatives of various organizations and groups alternating. Members were appointed by the competent (Land) Ministry of Culture in a given state upon nomination by the Permanent Conference of Ministers of Culture. At one time or another membership had to include a German university professor, a professor from another institute of higher learning, a German student who had studied in the United States under the auspices of the exchange program and was active in student affairs, a representative of the student organization (Allgemeine Studentenausschuss—ASTA), and a distinguished German professor or research scholar.[67] In addition to their professional and personal qualifications, members of the committees were expected to represent such organizations as the Ministries of Culture, the West German Conference of University Presidents, and the German Academic Exchange Service.[68]

The functions of the Fulbright Scholarship Committees were, in the main, to interview student applicants and to make appropriate recommendations to the Commission. At least in the beginning, the committees were instructed to submit twice the number of candidates, that is, alternative recommendations for each opening allotted to the districts. Numbers were adjusted to university enrollment and population in each district.[69] Each student appearing before the committee had to undergo a prescreening interview at his university which, in turn, transmitted applications to the appropriate committee.[70] The Commission established special subcommittees for the screening of student applicants for travel grants only, composed of a university professor, a representative of DAAD, a representative of ASTA, a German student returnee, a representative of the Commission's secretariat, and two representatives from HICOG's Office of Public Affairs (an exchange-of-persons official and a cultural officer.)[71]

So-called "Jungakademiker" (young academicians—see above) at first applied directly to the Commission. However, obviously in face of the heavy load carried by it, the Commission eventually began to refer their applications, with the exception of those of young teachers and young lawyers, back to the committees within the districts from which they applied.[72] For the first time, these candidates were interviewed by the committees themselves as well as by the aforementioned special committees. Young teachers and young lawyers were interviewed by the committees after a prescreening by the Land Ministries of Education or Justice.[73]

Teachers who applied for participation in the interchange program were prescreened by the various Ministries of Culture with the cooperation of the DAAD.[74]

Professors and research scholars, on the other hand, by-passed the committees altogether. Nor were they required to appear for personal interviews. Instead, a binational committee consisting of members of the Commission and representatives of the Permanent Conference of Ministers of Culture, the West German Conference of University Presidents, the German Research Society, and the Association of Universities directly examined their applications.[75]

The German Fulbright program, which followed by only a few years the period of American military occupation, was influenced during its first years of operation by certain objectives and operational features different from those of other countries. The selection of projects, geared to subject matters relating to specific German needs and deficiencies, perpetuated in a more sophisticated way HICOG reorientation policy. At the same time, the Fulbright program had to be coordinated with a large exchange program in Germany that had been initiated with different objectives, funds, machinery, and procedures.

The nationwide support system, on balance, proved adequate to carry out a program which was substantial and diversified. The minutes of the Fulbright Commission reveal, not altogether surprisingly, at least during the first 3 years, a high degree of preoccupation with technical and procedural detail with less attention paid to matters of substance. On balance, the Commission worked as efficiently as could be expected under the circumstances. Its work represented a notable step forward in building closer ties of friendship and cooperation between the United States and Germany.

Senator Fulbright himself acknowledged the positive role of the Commission in a message sent on the occasion of the 10th anniversary of the program, in which he said:

"In marking this significant anniversary we owe special gratitude to the services of the United States Educational Commission in Germany, whose membership is drawn from both German and American citizens.

"Here is truly a leading example of how effectively the binational commission can function in the exchange field. Without the conscientious and devoted service of Commission members and staff over this beginning decade, the Commission could not now enjoy the record of accomplishment it has achieved, nor look ahead so assuredly to the program's increasing influence in the decade to come." [76]

Notes

CHAPTER VII

1. "United States Educational Commission in the Federal Republic of Germany. Agreement between the United States of America and the Federal Republic of Germany, signed at Bonn July 18, 1952, entered into force July 18, 1952." Treaties and Other International Acts Series 2553 (Washington, D.C.: U.S. Government Printing Office). See Appendix V for full text of the Agreement.
2. Minutes of the First Meeting of USEC/G, Sept. 29, 1952; copy in CU/H.
3. Memorandum for Fulbright Secretariat to U.S. Minister, Dr. Martin Hillenbrand, Jan. 1964. Files of German Fulbright Commission, Bonn; copy in CU/H.
4. Quote from Howard H. Russell, Chairman of the U.S. Educational Commission for Germany, in the summer edition of "Amerikanischer Kulturbrief," 1962. Files of German Fulbright Commission, Bonn; copy in CU/H.

The agreement signed in Nov. 1962 assured the financing for a 5-year period of the educational exchange program between the United States and the Federal Republic of Germany carried out through the binational Fulbright Commission in Bad Godesberg. It provided for continuation of the program which had been developed and carried out under the Fulbright Act (superseded in 1961 by the Fulbright-Hays Act). During the first 10 years of its operation the program had been financed exclusively by the U.S. Government out of German payments on surplus property obligations to the United States.

The 1962 agreement called for the annual transfer to the Commission of the DM equivalent of $800,000 by the Federal Republic of Germany and $200,000 by the U.S. Government. In the first year the United States was further required to transfer $900,000 which remained available under the terms of the original agreement. This amount, which was transferred in 1964, was actually surplus to the current program needs of the Commission and was added to its reserve fund.

Besides the German currency transferred to the Commission, the U.S. Government annually provided dollar funds for the administrative and operational costs of the program in the United States and for the support of a few German travel grantees. This contribution amounted to $200,000 in 1964 and $210,000 in 1965. In addition, the value of scholarships, fellowships, stipends, and salaries provided from nongovernmental sources to some 240 German grantees in the United States was conservatively estimated at $400,000 yearly. This made a total annual contribution from the U.S. side of $800,000.

Discussions regarding the joint financing of the program were initiated in 1960. At that time it was contemplated that the program would be financed on an equal-shares basis, with each side contributing $4 million over an 8-year period. The original proposal was for the German contribution to be provided out of counterpart funds as part of an over-all counterpart settlement agreement. However, after it was determined that all available counterpart funds were needed for other purposes, the German side committed itself to contribute $4 million from other sources, with the first German contribution to be made in 1964. Since the United States would contribute an additional $3 million to support the program in 1961, 1962, and 1963, it was agreed that the contributions would be equalized over the 8-year period from 1961 through 1968, as originally proposed. Therefore the agreement stipulated that $4 million should be transferred by the Federal Republic and an additional $1 million by the United States, both in yearly installments from 1964 through 1968.

The rationale of the respective contributions and the agreement in principle of the two governments were clearly set forth in the Note Verbale 147, dated Jan. 16, 1961, from the American Embassy to the Foreign Office of the Federal Republic, and the Note Verbale from the Foreign Office to the Embassy dated Apr. 24, 1961. The latter communication stated that the respective contributions of the two governments could be regarded as representing parity.

The agreement of 1962 covered only those contributions made directly to the binational commission and not the additional dollar support from the U.S. side mentioned above. There were also additional contributions from the German side, notably the subsidized tuition for American students at German universities and certain stipends and fellowships awarded to senior American scholars. (Department of State Memorandum in the files of CU/H, dated Apr. 29, 1965.)

5. Minutes of the First Meeting of USEC/G, Sept. 29, 1952, *op. cit.*
6. *Ibid.*
7. *Ibid.*
8. *Ibid.*
9. *A Report of the Board of Foreign Scholarships—A Quarter Century— The American Adventure in Academic Exchange* (Washington, D.C.: Board of Foreign Scholarships, 1971), pp. 17, 22.
10. Minutes of First Meeting of USEC/G, Sept. 29, 1952, *op. cit.*
11. In 1955 USEC/G established a "youth specialists" category which included youth leaders and young social group workers. See below, pp. 190–191.)
12. Appendix to Minutes of Third Meeting of USEC/G, Dec. 15–16, 1952; copy in CU/H.
13. Subsequently, the same subjects were recommended for inclusion in study programs on American culture and civilization to be given at German universities. Annual Program Proposal of USEC/G for 1954. Copy in CU/H.
14. *The Funnel*, Special edition of the USEC/G newsletter, on the tenth anniversary of the German-American Fulbright program, Bad Godesberg, Germany, 1962, p. 25. Copy in CU/H.
15. *Ibid.*
16. *Ibid.*, pp. 26 ff.
17. Annual Program Proposal of USEC/G for 1954, Sept. 21, 1953, WNRC, RG 59, 63 A 389, Box 285.

18. For details, see Sigmund Skard, *American Studies in Europe—Their History and Present Organization*, 2 vols. (Philadelphia: Univ. of Pennsylvania Press, 1958), I, p. 40, pp. 291 ff.
19. *Ibid.*, p. 305.
20. *Ibid.*
21. In the case of the seminars on American studies planned to be held at Marburg Univ., the responsibility for programming and planning the project had been left exclusively with two German sponsors, namely, the Univ. of Marburg and the Society for American Studies (Gesellschaft fuer Amerika Studien). The Commission explicitly refrained from assuming any control over the curriculum or the policies.
22. Minutes of Twenty-Second Meeting of USEC/G, Mar. 31, 1955; copy in CU/H.
23. Minutes of First Meeting of USEC/G, Sept. 29, 1952, *op. cit.*
24. See also Chap. VIII, pp. 226–231.
25. See "Comments of former American Fulbright Grantees in Germany," USEC/G, n.d., excerpts from annual reports of American grantees submitted to USEC/G; copy in CU/H.
26. See *A German Appraisal of the Fulbright Program* (Frankfurt am Main: DIVO-Institut, 1961); copy in CU/H.
27. See Annual Reports of USEC/G, Program Years 1954 and 1955; copies in CU/H.
28. Minutes of First Meeting of USEC/G, Sept. 29, 1952, *op. cit.*
29. Minutes of Sixth Meeting of USEC/G, May 11, 1953; copy in CU/H.
30. Minutes of Eleventh Meeting of USEC/G, Nov. 9, 1953; copy in CU/H.
31. Policy Guide Outlining Implementation Plan for 1955–1956, Fulbright Student Program, USEC/G. WNRC, RG 59, 63 A 389, Box 285; copy in CU/H.
32. Minutes of Twenty-Seventh Meeting of USEC/G, Nov. 14, 1955; copy in CU/H.
33. Minutes of Nineteenth Meeting of USEC/G, Dec. 20, 1954; copy in CU/H.
34. Corresponds roughly to "trainees."
35. Minutes of Twenty-Second Meeting of USEC/G, Mar. 31, 1955, and addendum; copy in CU/H.
36. Policy Guide Outlining Implementation Plan for 1955–1956, Fulbright Student Program, *op. cit.*
37. A special group of young lawyers who were members of the civil service or prepared themselves for a career in public administration seems to have remained the responsibility of the regular HICOG exchange program.
38. WNRC, RG 59, 65 A 389, Box 601 and 56 D 492.
39. Minutes of Twentieth Meeting of USEC/G, Feb. 8, 1955; copy in CU/H.
40. See Chap. VIII, note 89.
41. Minutes of Twentieth Meeting of USEC/G, *op. cit.*
42. Minutes of Twenty-Second Meeting of USEC/G, Mar. 31, 1955, *op. cit.*
43. *A German Appraisal of the Fulbright Program, op. cit.*, p. 21.
44. The samples do not necessarily reflect the motivations and preferences expressed by a sample of 229 students, cited in HICOG's Report on Public Affairs, Vol. IV, May 1953, O/FADRC, 58 D 372, Box 3000. Only a minority gave as their reason for participation the pursuit of specific academic studies in history, literature, natural sciences, and medicine. The majority listed nonacademic areas, that is, various aspects of American life, governmental institutions, political parties, "U.S. democracy in action," school systems, economic problems, social conditions, etc. A canvass of so-called

trainees produced similar results. The DIVO study (notes 29 and 46), on the other hand, shows a strong discrepancy in the motivations of "juniors" and "seniors," the terminology used in the study to distinguish between students and senior scholars. Of 437 juniors 59 percent gave as reasons for their application for a Fulbright grant their intentions to study, whereas 56 percent of the seniors, in keeping with their more advanced status, stated that they wished to become acquainted with special scientific methods and institutions. Twenty percent of the juniors and only 13 percent of the seniors said that they wanted to learn about "the American way of life."

45. See note 24, above.
46. Annex to Minutes of the Seventeenth Meeting of USEC/G, Sept. 20, 1954; copy in CU/H.
47. *Ibid.*
48. Appendix to the Nineteenth Meeting of USEC/G, Dec. 20, 1954, *op. cit.*
49. See note 24, above.
50. "Partners in International Understanding—International Educational Exchange Service," Dept. of State (U.S. Government Printing Office: Washington, D.C., 1955), p. 41.
51. For further details, see "The Policy Statements of the Board of Foreign Scholarships," revised periodically. Copies in CU/BFS.
52. A contributing factor to the high percentage of students choosing the arts and music appears to have been a tendency on the part of the Institute of International Education, as the agent for the Board of Foreign Scholarships, to emphasize and recommend these fields to prospective American student grantees.
53. Annual reports of USEC/G for program years 1954 and 1955; copies in CU/H.
54. Twenty-five graduates were given such assignments in 1953. Minutes of Eighth Meeting of USEC/G, July 13, 1952; copy in CU/H.
55. For full account, see lists of "American Lecturers and Research Scholars Receiving United States Fulbright Awards for 1953-54, 1954-55, 1955-56, Academic Years." Copy in CU/H.
56. "The Policy Statements of the Board of Foreign Scholarships," *op. cit.*
57. Minutes of Fifth Meeting of USEC/G, Apr. 13, 1953; copy in CU/H.
58. Annual Report of USEC/G for 1954; copy in CU/H.
59. *Ibid.* See also, as noted on p. 183 above, Commission preference for visiting lecturers in American studies to teach *modern* American literature, history (i.e., the role of the United States in world affairs since 1900), research methods in sociology and in educational psychology, architecture, and political science, including the role of public opinion.
60. See *The Funnel, op. cit.*, p. 35.
61. See Annual reports of USEC/G, *passim.*
62. "The Policy Statements of the Board of Foreign Scholarships," *op. cit.*
63. Walter Johnson and Francis J. Colligan, *The Fulbright Program: A History* (Chicago: The University of Chicago Press, 1965), Appendix IV, pp. 347-348.
64. Statement by Francis J. Colligan before the Second Meeting of USEC/G, Oct. 24, 1952. Minutes of Meeting; copy in CU/H.
65. *The Funnel, op. cit.*, p. 22.
66. *Ibid.*, p. 23.
67. Minutes of Sixth and Seventh Meetings of USEC/G, May 11, and June 8, 1953; copies in CU/H.

68. Annual Report of USEC/G for Program Year 1953 ; copy in CU/H.
69. *Ibid.*; also Annual Report for Program Year 1954, *op. cit.*
70. Minutes of Fourteenth Meeting of USEC/G, Apr. 5, 1954; copy in CU/H.
71. Minutes of Twentieth Meeting of USEC/G, Feb. 8, 1955, *op. cit.*
72. Minutes of Fifteenth Meeting of USEC/G, June 2, 1954 ; copy in CU/H.
73. Policy Guide Outlining Implementation Plan for 1955–56, Fulbright Student Program, *op. cit.*
74. Minutes of the Fourteenth Meeting of USEC/G, Apr. 5, 1954, *op. cit.*
75. *Ibid.*
76. *The Funnel, op. cit.*, p. 42.

The Impact

CHAPTER VIII

Measuring the Results of the Program

The question that needs to be answered, is whether and to what extent the investment made by the United States in American-German exchanges during the postwar period benefited both countries, indeed whether there was any tangible, lasting, and traceable effect. This was, of course, the principal question which representatives of the Department of State were asked time and time again when justifying the program budget at the annual hearings before Congress in the early fifties. In those days effectiveness could be measured only in terms of instant visible results, such as direct personal actions taken or opinions voiced by participants upon their return home. Much of the evidence available then was spotty and inconclusive. Moreover, long-range effects were hard to predict with any degree of assurance. In the absence of a systematic year-by-year followup record, it has now become difficult to establish with any degree of certainty the causal connection between the exchange experience and institutional or attitudinal changes in Germany.

Nevertheless, in the case of the U.S.-German exchange program of the post-World War II period, evidence documenting the effectiveness of the program is more substantial than that accumulated for other country programs. It exists in the form of testimonials by high public officials in Germany and in the United States; of institutional evaluations; of reports and letters written by sponsors and participants; and quite especially of government-sponsored evaluation studies and opinion surveys conducted by HICOG's special survey staff under the able direction of Leo Crespi. In fact, it may be said that no other exchange program of the U.S. Government has been the subject of such intensive efforts to collect systematic evidence to measure and evaluate its results in terms of the goals it set out to accomplish.

209

The U.S. Government-sponsored surveys, in particular, were of major value not merely in assessing the effectiveness of the program, but also in administering and occasionally, when the evidence so indicated, in modifying it. The surveys and evaluation studies were made during the short span of time when the program was at its peak, in the late forties and early fifties. They reflect changes which were observed during that period, but they do not provide firm conclusions about the lasting effect.

There are other factors to be kept in mind. In the case of institutional changes, such as political, social, and educational reforms, any attempt to identify specific change agents is compounded by a variety of intangible, often elusive, factors.* Many of the institutional innovations in postwar Germany adapted from American models have by now become an integral part of German life, to the extent that a search for causes and effects would be a difficult and problematical task. Personal as well as national pride in their accomplishments may keep German reformers from sharing the credit with outsiders. To be sure, many institutional changes that may have been stimulated by external influence were not simple copies of foreign models but required major adaptations based on extensive research and development, with the result that the new model could claim as much originality as the one on which it was patterned.

Current German literature dealing with the problem of educational reform (Bildungsreform), for instance, practically ignores the immediate post-World War II influence of American or, for that matter, British and French reorientation and exchange programs. There is a distinct tendency on the part of German educators to date the current reform movement back to the creation of the German Educational Council (Deutscher Bildungsrat) in 1965, or even later.[1] The mid-sixties indeed witnessed the beginning of a systematic overhaul of the structure of the educational system under wholly German auspices. A report issued in 1974 by Inter-Nationes, the government-financed information agency,[2] contains not a single reference to earlier reforms stimulated by the U.S. reorientation program. In fact, it stresses the absence of any such initiatives prior to 1960, pointing out that the first 10 or 15 years after 1945 were devoted to repairing the war damage, to restoring school buildings, and to remedying the teacher shortage. Only after physical reconstruction had been completed, the article says, "could thought be

---

*A factor not considered in this study, for instance, is the influence of German prisoners of war who during their internment applied themselves systematically to the study of American ideas and institutions. A notable example was Walter Hallstein, who later became Secretary of State in the Ministry of Foreign Affairs.

given to further development and internal reforms." Substantive reform, according to other sources, was patterned on German experience, namely, the democratic model of the Weimar Republic.[3] Only occasionally can a reference be found to the "accelerating" influence of the exchange experience with "Anglo-Saxon" countries upon certain innovations such as the development of "comprehensive schools."[4] Yet, in private conversation, German educators as well as others, including important government officials now in office, who remember the American effort in the late forties and early fifties, acknowledge the influence of American experts, of their own experience in the United States or that of others, on the emergence of new ideas and new programs, indeed, on the movement toward educational reforms that now preoccupies the Federal Republic and its Laender.

The relationship between the exchange experience and institutional reform then is, for reasons indicated above, a delicate question. To answer it satisfactorily would require an investigation far beyond the scope of this study. The random samples of evaluation surveys and studies used in this chapter have been selected to illustrate short- and long-term effectiveness. They do not tell the whole story. For measuring attitudinal changes among German participants in the program, the evaluator had to deal with the problems of predictability and constancy. He was dealing with the factor of constant change.[5] To be more specific, the exchange program was based on the following assumptions: first, that exposure to a different environment would produce changes in the views and attitudes of the visitors, enrich their knowledge and skills, and, with it, raise prospects for personal improvement; second, that these changes might cause them to share their (favorable, one hoped) impressions with others, thus contributing to better understanding and improvement of relations between host and home country; and, third, that the German participants would apply the benefits of their experience by initiating or stimulating actions upon their return which, in turn, would generate political, social, and educational changes. The last assumption was, of course, a major one in the rationale of the postwar German reorientation program, and one which made the exchange program an important instrument of U.S. policy.

The surveys conducted under the auspices of the Department of State and HICOG in the early fifties indicate that these assumptions were basically correct. Substantial numbers of Germans changed their views of the United States and some of them took specific actions that confirmed this change upon their return to Germany. Criteria used to verify such changes were growth of political concern, appreciation of democratic concepts, understanding of the United States and its foreign policy, awareness of the educational, scientific, and cultural achievements of other countries, sense of international cooperation, contribution to the common (Western) defense effort, and the like. That the changes in attitudes were caused by the exchange experience was tested in two ways: by comparing the views of Germans who came to the United States and returned home with those of so-called "eligibles," that is, persons who were qualified but were not selected for participation in exchange visits;[6] and by examining the views of participants at the beginning and after completion of their visit.[7] The first type of study established clearly that those who participated in exchange visits, most of whom had by then been back in Germany for 2 or 3 years—some more than 5—exhibited more favorable views of the United States than "eligibles." The questionnaires used in the second case ("before" and "after" the exchange experience) showed distinct shifts in the direction of more democratic and more pro-American attitudes.

There were exceptions. In a few cases the exchanges produced effects that were not intended and others that were wholly undesired, such as unqualified criticism. But these instances were rare, as were those of exchangees who returned to Germany with, on balance, unfavorable impressions. True in some cases visits to the United States, far from changing attitudes, simply reinforced prejudices held previously. But conversely, some young exchangees, greatly attracted by conditions in the United States, refused to return to their homeland or, upon their return, emigrated to America or to other countries. While all these cases were relatively insignificant in number, they demonstrate the unpredictability of personal reactions to the exchange experience.

Even more important in assessing attitudinal changes are factors that subsequently modify the intensity and the nature of the impact achieved. How high, indeed, is the probability that impressions gained during a relatively short period of exposure will not fade over time, be altered or altogether erased by new, possibly conflicting experiences? A survey made in 1955 of students and information specialists who returned from exchange visits [8] showed that approximately 25 percent of the students and a smaller percentage of the specialists after short visits had revised their judgment about the United States downward (from favorable to unfavorable) or upward. While "relapses" or other changes of mind do not invalidate the overall effectiveness of the exchange experience, they indicate an element of instability that must be taken into consideration in determining long-range effects. Followup programs instituted by HICOG in the form of conferences, workshops, "alumni clubs," bulletins, organized correspondence with overseas contacts and hosts, and the use of returnees on screening committees for the selection of new candidates and in public media—all did a great deal in prolonging the impact, in extending the benefits of the exchange experience and in improving the quality of the overall effort. But the effectiveness of this sort of postprogram activity, unless actively pursued over a long period of time, was bound to wane.

There were other factors, apart from time lapse, which precluded facile generalizations and which made for considerable variety in both the durability and nature of changes produced. Most of those modifiers, as the surveys show, were age, professional and social status, and background of the individual exchangee. High school students, as expected, were the most impressionable group. Studies made of teenagers' reactions [9] showed that their visits had a profound personal effect upon nearly all of them. Largely uninformed and in some cases strongly biased concerning things American when they started their visit, they returned to Germany with a universally favorable view of the United States, so much so in fact, that some of them began to draw invidious comparisons between the United States and their home country, unfavorable to the latter, which resulted in serious problems of readjustment. Shifts to more positive attitudes toward the United States during their visits were far more pronounced among teenagers than among any other group. Unquestionably, the malleability of this age group that was more intimately and more consistently exposed to American community and family life than any other, was chiefly responsible for the close and friendly relations engendered by the teenage program, but it was also the very factor which raised doubts about the longevity of the impact. Evaluators cautioned that the volatility of this age group, the controls of their home environment where steadily improving conditions gradually began to match the magnetism of America, and the growing distance from the exchange experience, in some cases may have combined to dim the memory of the American impressions.

With respect to age, a study conducted by the National Social Welfare Assembly [10] which grouped the degree of acceptance of democratic values by persons between the ages of 18 and 69 on a plus or minus scale, found the highest aggregate of pluses in the oldest age group, i.e., 51 to 69 years of age (87 percent), and the highest minus aggregate in the youngest age group, i.e., 18 to 23 (38.1 percent). The majority of the critical 24 to 31 year age group were in the plus category but mostly on the lowest "average plus" level. When applied to social and professional groups, the scale gave the highest plus rating to journalists, artists, and architects (83.3 percent). Industrialists, civil service employees, white-collar workers and laborers ranked next, and the majority of teachers and ministers represented an average plus in the evaluation scale.

The minus showing of the lower age group (18 to 23) in the study is largely borne out by other surveys which examined the attitudes of university students. In many instances, involving judgments of democratic concepts, American institutions and practices, students emerged, at least in the beginning, as critics and skeptics and occasionally as outright rejectionists. Their criticism was leveled at American "materialism," certain personal characteristics of Americans, the "mechanization" of human relations, racial and religious discrimination, the predominance of technology over culture, and standards of education on all levels. These, however, were the opinions of only a few.[11] The majority of students were positive in their evaluations and became even more so during the time of their stay. Curiously, some of the aspects of American life that received the strongest criticism by some were the very same that were singled out by others for highest praise, such as American social life and human relations, the American "way of life," and the American educational system. Group solidarity on the part of the Germans—"sticking together"—seems to have produced occasional tendencies to maintain and reinforce rejection and criticism. Those who after a period of self-imposed segregation broke ranks and went out on their own to study and observe frequently turned into ardent enthusiasts.[12]

Student criticism, no less than evident contradictions in judgment, must be attributed in part to the heterogeneous character of a group of young adults, most of whom had spent their formative years under the Nazi regime, had been exposed to Nazi propaganda aimed at the United States and other democracies, and, above all, had been left totally without choice of alternatives to National Socialist indoctrination. Their concept of democracy rarely went beyond theoretical definitions and scarcely ever included notions of a way of life. Their visit to the United States was the first encounter with a free, democratic society. Prepared to embrace the virtues of democracy, their criticism of conditions in the United States was often directed not so much at the United States or its political system as at its failure to live up to its promises and to their own expectations, e.g., social justice, nondiscrimination, and the like. At the same time, conscious of the recent past, they were highly defensive, i.e., determined to disclaim any association with nazism, and eager to extol what they considered Germany's best traditions and cultural achievements against American "materialism," anti-intellectualism, and egalitarianism. They were suspicious of programs that smacked of reorientation. In part, their criticism reflected disillusionment with the old and distrust of new "systems." In part, this reaction was the result of misunderstanding or sheer ignorance of the broad spectrum of American life because of relative isolation on the campus.

Unlike teenagers who were integrated into the American community, and specialists and leaders who were continuously on the road, students were by and large confined to a controlled environment. Despite occasional trips outside the campus, their exposure to the American community was more circumscribed and their impressions therefore more limited, that is, conditioned by their immediate surroundings.

Leaders, on the other hand, by virtue of their status at home, emerged as the group with the highest potential for applying American models to their home environment but with a relatively low showing of attitudinal changes. This was not altogether surprising. Being an older and more mature group, their views, some of which had been formed by experiences predating the Nazi period, were on the whole more balanced and more impervious to external influence. Their predisposition toward the United States was mostly positive from the outset, needed less adjustment, and therefore underwent only marginal changes. Resolved to demonstrate their democratic convictions, leaders, however, assumed a more critical stance with respect to such issues as racial discrimination. On the positive side, American patterns of social conduct impressed them most favorably and prompted nearly half of the leaders to revise original preconceptions. A special study examining the views expressed by leaders [13] confirmed them as the relatively most stable group. Changes in attitude occurred, mostly in a positive direction, but on the whole were slight and limited to a minority.

Geographic background appears to have been a factor of relatively minor weight, except in the case of Berlin. Exchange visitors from Berlin, more militantly pro-American and anti-Soviet from the start than the rest of their fellow countrymen, showed a definite tendency to adopt more favorable attitudes toward the United States and its policy.[14] The reasons are understandable. A strong democratic tradition dating back to pre-Nazi days, a frontline position in the cold war, and military protection guaranteed by the American presence, e.g., the airlift, had created especially close ties between the United States and the people of Berlin.

Making due allowance for modifications of effects caused by all of the above factors, the following comments on the analyses and conclusions of evaluation studies and reports, which attempted to measure the effectiveness of the exchange program up to 1955, summarize evidence of changes in the light of desired objectives. Questions which these studies attempted to answer were: In what way did the program contribute to the reorientation effort? Did it contribute to institutional changes? How did it assist in projecting the American image? Did it lead to a better understanding and support of U.S.

policy toward Germany? Did this understanding and support extend to the population at large? Did the program benefit the individual German participant, for instance, by enhancing his prospects for personal advancement? Finally, was the program appreciated on its own merits as a means of improving relations between the United States and Germany?

Reorientation Impact

To what extent the exchange program contributed to the growth of democratic attitudes and democratic institutions in post-Nazi Germany is the question that is hardest to answer. Germans, as we noted, take justified pride in having created, out of the ashes left by nazism and World War II, a viable political system which is economically sound, firmly allied with Western democracies, and well respected by the international community. German leadership, to an overwhelming extent, recognizes the role that American assistance has played in accomplishing these results, but it would reject, quite understandably, any suggestions that "the German miracle" of postwar reconstruction had been the achievement of outsiders. Assertions to that effect would, indeed, be offensive inasmuch as they would be considered to deny to German democracy the title to a self-chosen and self-made system of government and way of life. The fate of the Weimar Republic that fell victim to charges of external interference and of being a carbon copy of alien models is still alive in the memory of many members of the older generation.

Institutional Changes

Yet, evidence of American contributions is equally undeniable. Traces can be detected everywhere, in the governmental system, in national legislation, in administrative procedures, in academic life, in educational institutions, in social welfare, in women's affairs, in the new architecture, in business, in advertising techniques, and so on. Some of these innovations are attributable, directly or indirectly, to OMGUS and later to HICOG initiatives, specifically to the influence of American experts and specialists who visited Germany during the early years of the occupation. Examples of those set in motion by American experts are the promotion of civil liberties and of citizen participation in public affairs, notably of women; the creation of new institutions of learning, such as the Free University and the American Memorial Library, both in Berlin; the emergence of the so-called "comprehensive school" (Gesamtschule), an experimental new school type that broke with the two-track or multitrack system in German education; the "studium generale" which made the study of the liberal arts and humanities a prerequisite to professional training; the introduction of "Politologie" (political science) as a legitimate and fully recognized subject for serious study in the curriculum of universities; the emphasis on social studies in elementary and secondary school curricula; the trend toward the elevation of "other" (sonstige) institutes of higher learning, e.g., for pedagogics, social work, arts and music, to the status of full academic accreditation; the increase of the student population to about twice its former size; and the introduction of the open-shelf library system. This list is by no means complete, but may suffice to illustrate the wide range and the fundamental nature of reforms that can be ascribed to external, especially American, influence.

Reflecting on the long-range effects of the educational program, James M. Read, who served as chief of HICOG's Education and Cultural Relations Division during the early years of the program, later offered a cautious and perhaps unduly modest appraisal. "I do think," Read states,[15] "[that] the educational effort made a dent." As to institutional changes, Read felt that university reform in his days made great strides forward, an opinion shared by many observers. Granted certain exceptions, the "two-track" system was not abolished, but then, Read points out, it is a system practiced in other European countries and notably in Great Britain. While Read is right in saying that some of the most fundamental objectives were not achieved under HICOG, it is an undeniable fact that the efforts of Read and his colleagues began trends toward reform which gripped the educational community in Germany and have not come to rest to this day.

An even larger series of innovations was initiated by Germans who visited the United States under the program after their return to Germany—a point also made by Read. For example, one of the first groups of Bundestag members to visit the United States studied the Legislative Reference Service[16] of the Library of Congress with a view to its possible adoption by the Bundestag (see Chapter IV). The group was convinced that the establishment of an institution of this kind would insure greater independence of the legislature vis a vis the executive branch. As pointed out earlier, German legislators had to rely on the resources and cooperation of the executive branch even in the exercise of their constitutional prerogatives, such as the preparation of bills. The visit gave fresh impetus to frequent demands "to restructure and expand the Research Division" of the Bundestag on the model of the U.S. Congress. It was argued that the Bundestag could only hope to exercise its constitutional prerogatives as "the" legislator and supreme organ of control of the Federation, if it were to perform its functions in complete independence of the executive branch. Pending approval of a more fundamental revision of the existing system, the "Research Division" was to concentrate on the buildup of the library, the archives, the service for "legislative materials," and the press and information office.[17]

An even more important project was the visit of the Bundestag Security Committee which in 1954–1955 was drafting new defense legislation (see Chapter IV). The author developed the proposal to invite members of the Committee to study the American defense system, not so much from the military point of view but rather from the angle of its constitutional requirements, such as civilian control, service regulations, judicial provisions, and the like.* The group, consisting of eight members of the Bundestag Committee and three officials of the Federal Defense Ministry, was given a thorough briefing by high-level civilian and military authorities in Washington, and thereafter inspected a number of military installations across the country. It ended its tour with a full-day discussion with American political leaders and experts under the auspices of the Council on Foreign Relations. The Chairman of the Committee, Vice-President of the Bundestag, Richard Jaeger, declared that the group had come to the United States to find out by studying the American model how to build a democratic army. He said: "We Germans had a good army in the past. We hope to have a good democracy. Our tragedy has been that we have never been able to have both simultaneously. You Americans have both. We are here to find out how to work it." [18] Upon their return to Germany, members of the group set out to defeat the so-called "Blitz" bill for the creation of a new army then pending before the Bundestag, which, they pointed out, did not guarantee sufficient civilian control of the armed forces as they had observed it in the United States. Largely on the strength of their testimony, the Bundestag rejected the proposed bill. Alternative legislation was prepared which finally emerged in the form of two laws, the Defense Service Law (Wehrpflichtgesetz) and a law concerning the Legal Status of Soldiers (Soldatengesetz). The laws regulated the duties and rights of the members of the German defense forces in a manner that was exemplary in terms of the protection of individual rights and democratic procedures. Neither law was an exact replica of American policies or regulations. Yet the drafters would have been the last to deny that they had benefited substantially from their American experience.

For reasons indicated above, institutional changes in such fields as public administration, education, and social welfare introduced by German exchange visitors are more difficult to trace. In the early fifties German authorities and, in particular, returning visitors were far less reticent, often eager to point to changes which they had initiated

---

*The project was co-initiated in HICOG by Foreign Service officer Jonathan Dean, who served as HICOG liaison officer with the Bundestag.

as a result of observations made during their stay in the United States. We noted earlier the enthusiastic endorsement of the "Basic Principles for Democratization of Education in Germany," enunciated in Control Council Directive 54, by a leading German educator. HICOG's reports during these years record a substantial number of innovations introduced by leaders, specialists, and students, based on their own testimony on observations made in the United States.

Franz Meyers, Minister of the Interior for North Rhine-Westphalia in 1952, for instance, initiated upon his return a far-reaching administrative reform program in his own jurisdiction reflecting his appreciation of the American system.[19] Police officials remodeled traffic systems and improved training for traffic control.

Examples of changes in the field of education are more numerous. Professor Hellmut Becker, Director of the Max Planck Institute for Educational Research at Berlin, points out that the whole idea for his institute was developed as a result of his first visit to the United States after the war.[20] As a member of the National Educational Planning Association of the Federal Republic, Professor Becker recommended: (1) the introduction of comprehensive school systems on an experimental basis, (2) increased autonomy of schools, and (3) greater participation of teachers, students and parents in the administration of schools.[21]

Other educational leaders returning from their visits introduced significant innovations in their immediate sphere of competence. Eva Richter, teacher at Ruedesheim, introduced courses in political science over the protest of faculty members. The President of the Free University of Berlin, Freiherr von Kress, instituted night school extension courses to provide academic training and the obtainment of degrees for daytime workers. Dr. Anton Fingerle, inspector of the Munich school system, established a school test institute, a home economics institute, and a social studies institute patterned after models he had studied during his 3-month visit to the United States. Other innovations promoted by exchange participants included courses in civics and women's education, and extension courses for the rural population.[22]

In the field of law and law enforcement, high officials from different states (Laender) who had studied American prison, parole, and correction practices, launched a series of reforms tending toward a liberalization and improvement of the German system, including new investigative, supervisory, parole planning and probation methods, and the use of new psychometric techniques in prison welfare work.[23]

Labor leaders established training courses for workers in industry, first on the state and later on the federal level.

Women exchange visitors founded nonpartisan women's organizations along the lines of the League of Women Voters preparing and disseminating information to educate women in civic affairs.

Health and welfare officials, greatly impressed with American physical and mental hygiene practices, introduced corresponding methods within their respective areas of jurisdiction, e.g., medical examinations for school children and for grocery store and meat market personnel, using physical, visual, and oral tests observed in the United States, and team methodology.

Journalists and other media specialists instituted new programs in citizen education—discussions of public issues aimed specifically at youth audiences. Newspaper publishers and editors established compulsory training courses for editorial staffs to improve journalistic techniques, as stated by one editor, "on the basis of the knowledge I gained in American schools of journalism and of discussions with American newspapermen in 1951." [24]

A social worker from Munich arranged courses for coworkers in which she introduced them to the techniques of the American "casework" method. Later she was selected to organize child guidance programs in Bavaria.

Upon his return the city architect of Bremerhaven built a new playground with distinctive American features.

Students, inspired by American examples, wrote new constitutions for their student bodies, formed advisory groups to orient foreign students, and established workshops on "democracy in action."

U.S. attempts to stimulate citizen initiative and cooperation in community affairs through so-called "Cooperative Action Teams" deserve special mention. The composition of their membership emphasized the cooperative nature of community work in the public and private sector. They met with varying degrees of success. Some of the returnees, inspired by what they had observed in the United States, instituted a series of innovations on the local level, such as traffic safety councils, parent-teacher organizations, state-wide teachers' organizations, civics courses for young and old, associations for civic participation, groups concerned with special interests of women, and the like. City councils opened their sessions to the public.

Some members of the teams were more successful than others in getting community reforms under way. The teams which studied community conditions and institutions in American cities gave special attention to schools, welfare institutions, family life, housing, and the like. The impressions they gained were predominantly positive and, although in general favorably disposed to the United States before their departure, there was a measurable increase of affirmative attitudes at the time of their return. Moreover, the results of a survey of 135 such team members showed clearly that they were more inclined to believe on the basis of their American experience that Germany could learn from America in matters relating to labor-management relations, government and municipal administration, and education.

Yet, not all teams were equally successful in introducing significant changes on their return. While their impressions were positive, some remained unconvinced that their experiences were applicable to conditions at home. Also, quite often, there was little evidence of a concerted effort to recommend or initiate democratic reforms as a means of solving community problems. This failure to transfer their new knowledge and to convert it into constructive action may have been the result of lack of individual initiative or of community resistance. But it may also have been due to defective selection and organization of the team itself. In an effort to achieve a broad range of representation, teams had been composed in many instances of persons who had never formed a closely-knit group before their departure, never achieved a team spirit during their visit, and never cooperated as a team upon their return.[25] Except for the teams from Krefeld and Giessen, who carried out some of the above-mentioned reforms, most changes that were accomplished on the community level were attributable to the initiative of individual team members rather than to a cooperative effort by all.

Attitudinal Changes

The aforementioned examples of institutional reforms, it should be emphasized once again, do not give more than a fragmentary picture of the efforts made by German participants, least of all of the long-range and fundamental effects of the program. On the other hand, more comprehensive evidence of the psychological impact on the participants is available in the form of a series of studies conducted in the early fifties under the auspices of the Department of State and HICOG. The studies provide occasional glimpses of changes of attitude toward the concepts and merits of democracy, but they focus mainly on impressions about the exchange program and its purposes, American policy in Germany, and American institutions and attitudes.

A survey conducted in 1950 and 1951, by the Institute for Research in Human Relations, through the use of two questionnaires, checked the attitudes of 49 leaders, 258 university students, and 85 secondary school students (teenagers), before and after their visit to the United States. This survey probed into the prevalence of elitist-authoritarian versus democratic-equalitarian attitudes. It established marked shifts from the authoritarian to the equalitarian pattern in all three groups. The changes were most pronounced among high school and university students with one-third of the former and one-half of the latter switching from "slightly authoritarian" to "slightly equalitarian" or "equalitarian" views. Changes among leaders were less drastic with most of them exhibiting equalitarian attitudes from the outset. Nearly 90 percent ended up in the "equalitarian" (45 percent) or "slightly equalitarian" category (42 percent).[26] These observations tally with reports quoted earlier in this chapter that found the older age groups (32 to 69 years) far more ready to accept democratic values than the younger ones.

Changes toward more democratic attitudes became apparent in response to deliberately provocative statements such as "leaders are born, not made;" "it is wasteful to make secondary education available to everybody, because some cannot benefit from it;" "if important decisions for an organization can be made quickly by one person, it is unnecessary to put up with the delay involved in committee deliberation and voting;" and "the government should have the right to ban newspapers which consistently distort and attack government policy." When they arrived in the United States, the majority of respondents in all three groups disagreed with the views expressed in the statements (except that a majority of teenagers felt at the beginning of their visit to the United States that leaders were "born, not made"). After the visit, the number of those who had originally agreed with the statements declined substantially. The total of those who disagreed increased. Most of those who had pleaded ignorance or had failed to give an answer in the first questionnaire committed themselves to a definite position in the second. (In the case of teenagers, the ratio of dissidents and consenters to the first question was reversed.) The change of basic beliefs had an interesting practical implication. A majority of teenagers (81 percent) and students (68 percent) felt that the exchange experience would change their future role as German citizens.[27]

While the influence of the exchange program on attitudes is undeniable, the evidence is not always conclusive.[28] On balance though, subsequent events have demonstrated that exchangees returned with new knowledge, that in the light of new insights gained many revised their attitudes, and moved by their experience, applied the benefits they had reaped in the pursuit of their political, professional, or personal goals. Therefore, quite often institutional changes did occur as a result of attitudinal changes. In other cases they may have been the result of a combination of factors.

Impact of the American Scene

The presentation of American democracy and the American "way of life" stimulated, at least during the period covered in this study, domestic innovations. It had, in fact, been hoped that independent

RESULTS OF THE PROGRAM

on-the-spot observations by German exchangees might lead to a greater appreciation of, and the voluntary adoption or adaptation of certain features of American democracy and life. There is good reason to believe, as indicated above, that this occurred. Documentary films recently produced by Germans to picture the "Americanization of Germany" are impressive but not always favorable and in some instances quite critical. None of them, however, attempts to relate these changes to any aspect of the exchange program.

The studies made under State Department and HICOG auspices which examine the impressions gained by German exchangees during their stay in the United States were more conclusive. By no means were all of them positive and some too were highly critical, but on balance favorable views seem to have prevailed. A study, conducted in 1959–1960, upon the request of the United States Educational Commission in Germany, and based on a sample of 647 Fulbright grantees, both students and senior scholars,[29] showed that nearly two-thirds had changed their opinion about the United States to a more positive one. An earlier 1951 study, in which grantees of all categories, academic and nonacademic, were queried, had tried to refine similar findings by focusing the views of the German participants on specific aspects of American democracy and life.[30] They were asked to sort out favorable and unfavorable impressions of such features as American democratic concepts and practices (especially with respect to everyday conduct), governmental structure, exercise of individual rights and freedoms, American institutions, and above all the qualities of Americans as hard-working and friendly people of good will ("not so much different from Germans"). Their reactions were largely favorable, although never quite reaching 50 percent in all cases.

Some of the subjects covered in these two studies, made 10 years apart, namely, government, democracy in actual practice, institutions, and stereotypes about personal qualities of Americans (superficiality, naiveté vis-a-vis Germany, materialism, lack of culture, and zest for fun) evoked also the highest percentage of stereotyped negative judgments from German participants. Racial and other types of discrimination were cited prominently among the unfavorable impressions.[31] On the whole, differences of opinion among the three groups—leaders, students, and teenagers—were rather slight except that leaders, as noted earlier, were more outspokenly critical of the treatment of minorities, notably the black population. Surveys conducted in and since 1955 revealed a higher percentage of favorable impressions among students and information specialists with respect to such aspects as American social life and human relations. Favorable views of outlook on life and way of living far outweighed negative judgments.[32] Fulbright grantees listed those areas in which they developed more positive opinions about the United States, as "character and behavior of Americans," "characteristics of Americans as individuals," "educational system," "Americans as citizens," "the American way of life," "cultural life," "family life," and "open-mindedness of Americans toward Germany and other countries." [33]

The years between 1951 and 1960 were years of progressive rapprochement in German-American relations. More Germans had seen more of the United States and, on balance, liked what they saw. Increasingly, returning Germans were ready to concede that Germany could learn from America in such matters as democratic concepts, "melting pot" philosophy, and personal freedom. Early surveys conducted in 1951 showed a slow growth of such opinions, eventually exceeding 50 percent.[34] A survey made in 1953 revealed that more than two-thirds of those interviewed responded that their country had "a lot" to learn from the United States in fields such as government, municipal administration, and other features of political life, and labor-management relations.[35] Yet another survey showed that the enthusiasm of many appears to have faded upon their return when they came once more face to face with traditional German apathy and suspicion toward civic cooperation ("groupism") as a threat to individual initiative. Some concluded that the application of American methods to German civic life was simply not practical.[36]

It had been the hope of those who had fashioned the U.S. program that the projection of the American image would generate reactions that went beyond mere acknowledgment of the merits of a democratic system. They were not disappointed. "My way of thinking which at the beginning was still nationalistic," wrote a student, "has now changed to an international or universal one." He added that this was "due to the study of the political pattern of the U.S.A., effected by contact with many Americans . . ." [37] Internationalism, according to one evaluation study,[38] became indeed an issue of increasingly personal importance to the visitors who reported that they had become more cosmopolitan. So did democracy, in the sense that they felt that they had become more independent in forming their opinions, more tolerant, and more flexible. Also, their attempts to bring about democratic reforms at the national level reflected a stronger commitment to democratic values, although they did not necessarily use ideological labels in introducing political and administrative innovations.

The emergence of a more positive and, at the same time, more realistic view of the United States is evident when impressions are related to specific facets of American democracy. As far as concepts of the government's functions were concerned, the various surveys indicated that students and leaders changed their views from a more idealistic or extreme to a more moderate position. For instance, few, if any, expressed the view that Americans saw the role of government primarily as that of protecting life and property. But while they conceded that Americans accepted some governmental control in the economic sphere, they also preferred to see such powers limited. By the same token, the number of those who at the beginning thought that the American economy was operating under an unrestricted "laissez-faire" system decreased in favor of a substantial majority who concluded on the basis of their observations, that there was some regulation of business, although basically the "laissez-faire" principle prevailed.

Education

Education was the most highly admired but also the most severely criticized feature of American life. As indicated in the findings of a study made in the mid-fifties, German students and leaders seemed especially impressed with the goals of a system in which "the development of the total personality" and "the development of an inquisitive mind" appeared to be the highest, and the "teaching of discipline and obedience" one of the lowest goals. "Acquisition of factual information and of special skills," the ability "to earn money," and "preparation for good citizenship" ranked somewhere in the middle.[39] A later study indicated that nearly one-third of the Fulbright grantees found that conditions in the field of American education exceeded their expectations, with the highest percentage (52) among postgraduate students. Among the most positive aspects cited were "relationships between professors and students," "academic level of universities and schools," "industry, seriousness of purpose and discipline of American students," "scientific and educational standards of Americans," "university facilities and scientific equipment," "training and working methods," and "social and civic education."[40]

Members of the German cooperative action teams, as evident in studies made in 1953 and 1954, expressed themselves favorably about such matters as training for citizenship, the flexibility of high school curricula, the quality of school buildings, the quantity and diversity of teaching equipment, the informality of relationships between teachers and students, and the cooperation among parents and teachers.[41] At the same time they felt that these very advantages in the U.S. school system were obtained at a price. American school children, they concluded, learned less than their German counterparts—a fact stressed also by German teenagers enrolled in public schools.[42] Opinions were mixed, though, with respect to the applicability of features of the American system to German education, even of those that were much admired.

A relatively small percentage of Fulbright students thought that certain features of American education lent themselves to suitable adaptation in Germany. Among those most frequently mentioned were: teaching methods, research equipment, group and team work, and ratio of students to professors.[43] While many exchangees, especially teenagers and specialists, stated their estimates of transferability in more generalized terms by saying that Germany had "a lot" to learn from the United States in the field of education, and a substantial additional number thought that "something" could be learned, university students maintained a more reserved posture.[44]

It was the democratic structure of American education that elicited some of the highest praise. In the mid-fifties a teacher trainee at Southwest Texas State Teachers College put it this way:[45] "I got a feeling for two things which were new to me, two things I will never lose in my life: the idea of equal education for everybody, regardless of class or his parents' position; secondly the idea of real freedom . . . I confess that I got another point of view about the education we are so proud of in Germany . . . The world of the Twentieth Century in which we live requires more than a small well-trained and educated group of people who may work for the benefit of their nation—but who can also misuse their intelligence by authoritative means . . . I found the key to American democratic life. We teach democracy today—your children live democracy. I recognized the entire American way of life reflected in American education, and I think from that Germany has a lot to learn."

The Special Case of College and University Students—Clash of Standards

Exposure to the American system of education, specifically higher education, however, also produced controversy and, in some cases, negative results. The most articulate critics of American standards, particularly in higher education, proved to be a minority of German university students who, for reasons of their own, were critical and least cooperative. Their reactions to American institutions, national characteristics, and political attitudes, often ranged from negative to hostile.[46]

The special university-student leader projects on student government of the early and mid-fifties evoked some of the most critical comments. German students argued that there were fundamental and seemingly unbridgeable differences between American and German standards. (It should be noted that some of these were short-term observation visits.) In some instances the German students were careful to limit their critique to the host university, but often it was sweeping and uncompromising, aimed at the American university campus system in its totality. In essence, objections of visiting teams of German students could be epitomized as an indictment of American acceptance of college discipline as against German espousal of "academic freedom" as they conceived it.

"The [American] student," in the words of a member of the German student team observing student government at the University of Minnesota, "is deprived of very specific freedoms: the freedom of having a responsibility; the freedom of thinking and acting independently; the freedom of thinking critically; the freedom of cooperating in the solution of his real problems; the freedom of learning from his own mistakes. The student is denied the opportunity of expressing himself critically on the needs of his education . . . He is educated to be a subject instead of a citizen. He is forced into a system that . . . offers all characteristics . . . usually found in a police state [sic] . . . "[47] This statement was, of course, extreme, but it tallied with the views of other students, if not in tone, at least in substance. To a degree, it reflected once again the high level of sensitivity of a generation which had suffered the trauma of authoritarianism at its worst and which, now moving in the opposite direction, had begun to suspect and reject any kind of control, even guided teamwork, as a manifestation of political or social coercion. As a student put it, "They were jealous of their democratic rights." More fundamentally, though, the criticism revealed a clash of philosophies and traditions which predated the Nazi period and contrasted the German elitist with the American democratic system of education.

"The German-European university," argued a woman member of the same team,[48] "is a school for a selected group and there is no desire to change this situation, because it is appropriate to the function of the university and of university trained people within European society." Coupled with this concept of elitism was that of the German student concept of "academic freedom" which entrusted to the German student the choice of subject matter and left him in sole control of his studies, without external supervision and guidance. The twin concepts of elitism and freedom, the student added, make "the atmosphere at a [German] European university much more 'academic' and . . . , as a rule, an intellectualism is prevalent which would very likely be considered snobbism at an American institution." [49] The American university, on the other hand, was expected "to train masses," as one student put it. It was, as another phrased it more positively, a "university of the people" which "everybody or almost everybody can and does attend" and where emphasis was placed on "training for citizenship, the development of an all-round personality, and responsible attitude toward the community." In the German view neither definition was meant to be wholly commendatory. Both were meant to suggest an American tendency toward "anti-intellectualism." The same tendency was believed to be the cause for greater emphasis on the utilitarian purpose of university training, that is, a high degree of specialization and preference for applied sciences rather than for the humanities. Yet, emphasis on the "pragmatic and the palpable" and on technical expertise seemed to some students to contradict, if not undercut, the declared purpose of citizenship training. According to one student, the system actually made it impossible for the American student to become, like his European colleague, "a factor in the public, cultural and political life" of the nation.[50] "The German team and the American university," the student concluded, "were speaking within two entirely different frames of reference which could hardly ever be reconciled to a common denominator."

The summary report prepared by the faculty of the University of Minnesota did not enter into a discussion of the fundamental issue here, namely a real conflict of values underlying the German and American systems. Instead it treated the problem as a disciplinary one. In its view, as stated in their report, "some regulation is required in order to have freedom." [51]

Views expressed by the German student team observing student government and the role of the American student on the University of Minnesota campus were mixed. Some of the critics seemed to regard student government as a sham and a farce. They pointed out that only a minority were active in campus politics, the rest seemed apathetic; that few were elected to representative bodies, most were appointed; and that the so-called student congress had merely marginal, mostly organizational, responsibilities. In short, it was their view that there was no self-government and no democracy. What was more, the American student appeared to be constantly administered, advised, counseled, and pampered by an over-solicitous administration that kept him in a steady state of dependency. In contrast to his German counterpart who represented his country's "future elite," was more respected, and who might take a stand as a citizen of his university on major controversial issues, the American student and student government were "not an equal partner of the administration and faculty." The students could not make their own policy in administering student government because ultimate responsibility for student activities resided with the administration.[52]

Notwithstanding the negative reactions of this group, it should be recorded that a large body of German students was genuinely impressed with some of the principal features of the American university and with some of the campus institutions. The larger number of students who spent a full academic year in the United States spoke more often of the benefits they had gained from their stay. The accent on citizenship education, personality development, human relations featuring strong anti-elitism, equalitarianism, and extracurricular pursuits, was viewed as a challenge to the German system and produced many positive comments and reluctant recognition of its validity for American society. Student government was recognized as a training ground for democracy and was credited with considerable success in preparing students for their future career in public and professional life.[53] There were favorable comments on the informality and frequency of relations between faculty and students, as exemplified by the office of the Dean of Students, on the value of extracurricular activities, and on the institution of the faculty or student adviser (although to some it seemed to represent an encroachment on student independence). Other aspects of the American university that came in for commendation by German students were the student union, the student loan fund, and the foreign student adviser. The Coffman Memorial Union at the University of Minnesota inspired the German team to address a memorandum to the University of Frankfurt recommending it as a model for the new Student House in that city.[54] The use of committees by student governments evoked both negative and positive reactions; some denounced them as inefficient tools of operation, while others were impressed with their very effectiveness and proposed that here was something that "we can and should adapt to our own situation."

The Minnesota student project from which most of the above illustrations were gleaned may have been an extreme case with both sides stubbornly clinging to their prejudgments. Conceivably, the university administration and faculty, in sponsoring the project, took their responsibilities as "trustee of the American Government" too seriously and refused to play the part of a "passive host" in preference to that of a strict supervisor and guide. The German team, on the other hand, insisting on their rights as "free observers," refused to recognize that some measure of control and regulation was required to have freedom and, in a mood of fighting resistance, accused the university of rank authoritarianism.[55]

Reports by German students in other universities, such as Antioch, Colorado, Florida, Indiana, Michigan, and Syracuse, where teams were engaged in the same type of project, were, on balance, less critical, although occasional references were made to American proclivity for emphasis on social activities at the expense of academic pursuits, a practice disdained by German students who admittedly were fated to become "brilliant scholars" but to miss out on human relations.[56] Some students discovered that generalizations were of dubious value, when they discovered that there were completely different types of student governments at various campuses.

The Minnesota experiment, incidentally, was not a total failure. Both Americans and Germans acknowledged that they had profited from the visit, citing the academic aspects of the program, the social functions and contacts on and off campus and, in the case of the Germans, knowledge of the country acquired through travel.

It should be recalled in this connection that the experience of American students on German campuses presented the other side of the coin—it was the exact reverse of their German counterparts. While the latter resented being "trapped" in a net of rules and regulations, the American student, accustomed to the advisory services of the American college or university, found himself hopelessly adrift in a system that left the initiative to each individual student and provided few, if any, controls to measure scholastic performance. In the absence of any form of supervision or evaluation, American students often left the campuses for varying periods of time spending more time on sightseeing trips than at the institutions with which they were formally registered. American Fulbright professors, who looked into the situation to ascertain how well the students were doing, reported that few had established contact with their professors and that most of them could not be located.[57]

Here, too, the results were not altogether negative. A number of reports submitted by American students prior to their return to the United States show that those who applied themselves seriously to their studies profited from their work. Their outstanding performance netted some Fulbright students awards and prizes and even faculty appointments. Many participated actively in the extensive programs of the America Houses, as the USIS-sponsored cultural centers were called in Germany. Some attended international conferences. Music students gave concerts and others led or attended discussion groups—once they realized, as one of the students put it, that university study in Germany posed demands similar to those in an American graduate school rather than in a college.[58] The discovery came as a surprise to many who complained that this type of information had not been provided in briefings prior to their visit.[59] Failure to furnish data on the host institution in advance, in particular, referred to at the time as one of the failings of the early years of the Fulbright Commission, was evidence of the continuing need for more timely and accurate information about each other's educational system.

The student exchange experience has been described in some detail, because it seems to epitomize the limitations of exchange programs initiated without full appreciation by the participants of the character of national systems which are fundamentally different in philosophy and structure and whose continued validity is vigorously defended by the advocates of each. If the tone of the German students at times sounded defensive and even shrill, it was not simply because they felt challenged by the American model but also because they were under attack from within the German academic community. Reform-minded educators in Germany and some of their returning colleagues had begun to question the merits of their own system, the latter in the light of their new experience on American campuses, and were comparing a different educational system with their own, often to the latter's disadvantage. The exchange program offered them a chance to test their national values and institutions against certain alternatives. The minimum result that could be expected and, in fact, did come about, was a better understanding of each system by the other party. As experience showed, this minimum was exceeded by those who, in the words of one of the spokesmen, "won new conceptions of the principles of education." [60]

"Kultur" and Professional Achievements

Impressions of other aspects of American life varied. Given traditional German emphasis on cultural achievements ("Kultur") and a deep-rooted bias against a civilization often denounced and more often suspected of serving primarily the cause of material growth, the odds appeared to have been against any significant changes in attitude. In actual fact, a number of German visitors under the program indicated at their departure that they had been impressed by the musical and other artistic presentations they had witnessed, and especially by the museums they had visited.[61] Students and media specialists admitted that what they had observed by way of cultural activities had not only exceeded their expectations but actually had ranked among the most favorable impressions they had gathered in the United States.[62] "Cultural life" was also singled out by a majority of librarians, museum experts, lawyers, and by a substantial number of women leaders and political leaders as an impressive aspect of American civilization. According to one of the earlier surveys,[63] teenagers, students, and leaders, when asked to evaluate impressions some of their compatriots had at home of American propensity for monetary gain, excessive materialism and lack of culture, stated that these were unjustifiable criticisms.

Professional fields that came in for special commendation were those in which Germany lagged behind the United States in professional experience. American social work methods, especially casework and group work, drew the admiration of many German experts who decided then and there to put their experience into practice at home. Information specialists appear to have been reasonably well-impressed with the American press but substantially less with film, radio, and television. Here, too, it was not merely the methods and techniques of professional performance in the United States, but rather the underlying philosophy that exerted the strongest influence on German visitors. A young social worker who later became a member of the Bundestag expressed his feelings in the following rather revealing way:

"I got a totally new conception about the aims and implications of group work ... The conscious use of group work will ... give us in Germany a real chance to help our young generation out of the present mood of apathy and distrust ... In Germany there exists a dire need for experience in practical democracy. Especially the youth should have many opportunities to experience a democratic group life to have them overcome the feeling of being a lost generation." [64]

In trying to strike a balance of the net effect of a large scale, first-hand view of the American scene as a result of the exchange experience, it may be said that the program was successful in furnishing the German visitors with a fair and realistic picture of the United States and in causing many of them to revise faulty preconceptions. As we noted in a number of cases, impressions gained during the visit changed views and attitudes in a decidedly favorable direction. Some of the visitors, no doubt, were moved to adopt American models and to apply them to German conditions.

German visitors in all categories, as noted earlier, admitted that they had learned a great deal and that they felt, on the strength of their own experience, that Germany could learn "a lot" or at least "something" from the United States. Areas named for transfer of experience included democratic concepts, features of the governmental system, and structure and functions of public and private institutions. Unquestionably, experiences of this kind provided the impulse for many of the aforementioned institutional innovations set in motion by returning exchangees. In any event, they served as a corrective not only of their own misconceptions but conceivably of those of many thousands of their fellow countrymen to whom they communicated their impressions upon their return, thereby contributing further to better understanding and cooperation.

In contrast, changes of view formed by American exchangees about Germany were less pronounced. On the whole, cliché images prevailed. Among the most positive impressions gained by Americans during the early phases of the exchange program were those produced upon their American hosts by German teenagers who proved to be exceptional ambassadors of good will.

The Impact of American Foreign Policy

A remarkable development of the postwar period in U.S. relations with the Federal Republic of Germany has been the close cooperation of both nations in the area of foreign policy. Several factors must be considered in evaluating this phenomenon. Cooperation during the early stage of relationships was involuntary. Germany had no policy of its own and in the words of the late Kurt Schumacher, leader of the Social Democratic Party in the early postwar period, could have no foreign policy for a long time to come. The Occupation Statute of 1949 reserved powers for the conduct of foreign affairs for the occupation authorities. However, largely under the pressure of external developments, notably the cold war, the Federal Republic was given, in an ever-accelerated measure, greater latitude in determining the conduct of affairs, foreign and domestic, leading eventually to the restoration of full sovereignty and to Germany's alliance in political, economic, and defense matters with the Western nations. The pace of events overtook and invalidated the earlier predictions of Schumacher and public expectations everywhere, including in Germany.

The German Government under the leadership of Chancellor Konrad Adenauer was quick to realize the opportunity and fell readily in line with Allied and especially U.S. policy. Public opinion in Germany, on the other hand, was slower to grasp and to adjust to the change of pace. After a phase of rigorous demilitarization, which they had heartily welcomed—perhaps more generally than any other aspect of the occupation policy—Germans, notably the young, found themselves once again in 1950, to wit, 5 years after ultimate military defeat, faced with a call to arms. Not surprisingly, the Western Allies were charged with inconsistency and duplicity. "This is not what you taught us before," young Germans said. Ironically, their resistance, in a way, proved the effectiveness of the postwar reorientation effort.

Studies made of the attitudes of exchangees confirmed a noticeable lag between official policy and public opinion, particularly in military matters. The study of youth and community leaders conducted in 1951 by the National Social Welfare Assembly [65] showed that respondents fell into five major categories. Less than half (47 percent) favored remilitarization, and of those who did two-thirds thought that Germany "owed" it morally to the Western world, whereas one-third believed that circumstances would force Germany into it. The rest was neither for nor strongly against it. But even those who were not outrightly opposed feared that remilitarization was highly problematical not to say dangerous, because it could bring reactionaries and militarists back into power. Others were unconditionally against it, stating that they had "had enough" of war. Only one-fifth expressed no opinion. Very few respondents were prepared to strike a bargain: they were in favor, but on condition that Germany be given full independence.

Opposition or qualified support of American defense policy was paralleled by a marked tendency on the part of some to question the stated purpose of U.S. foreign policy and to impute selfish and material reasons or still other ulterior motives to American intentions in world affairs. In 1950 a substantial minority of respondents (notably high school and university students; less so, leaders) declared upon arrival in the United States that one of the principal aims of U.S. foreign policy was to develop markets for U.S. exports. Even the Marshall Plan was suspected by a small number of serving such purposes.[66] In the course of their visits these groups changed their opinions by considerable margins, adopting less critical attitudes.

In the following years, with the escalation of the cold war and the growing success of the Marshall Plan, German opposition to defense softened. Now a substantial majority (72 percent) favored a German contribution to European defense, although more than one-half expressed the view that Germany should do everything in her power to avoid getting involved in war in Western Europe. Simultaneously, German conceptions of U.S. foreign policy had become somewhat more sophisticated. In 1950 and 1951 most German visitors under the program (more than 90 percent) had said that the principal objective of U.S. foreign policy was "to encourage the democratic forces in other parts of the world." [67] Objectives such as peace, foreign aid, and anticommunism received only marginal recognition. Two years later, however, 84 percent said that anticommunism was one of the chief aims of the U.S. foreign policy, and 46 percent responded that "to help improve living conditions all over the world" and "to attain peace" were also priority U.S. objectives.[68]

There was also a growing appreciation of the improvement of German-American relations manifest in what was thought to be genuine American concern with Germany's welfare and security. Up to three-fourths of all respondents (81 percent of leaders and specialists) declared that the United States was "very much" concerned with Germany's welfare, and nearly 90 percent were convinced that the United States would go all out to aid Germany in the case of a Soviet invasion. Yet, only 50 percent believed that the United States was doing all she could or should to prevent war. On the question of right or wrong, German exchangees sided overwhelmingly with the United States as against the Soviet Union.[69]

An almost inevitable corollary of the acceptance of American foreign policy by German exchangees was a critical review of Germany and German politics, especially Germany's role in international affairs. A majority of students (61 percent high school and 52 percent university students) declared that, as a result of their experience in the United States, they had changed their opinion about the image and role of Germany. A third of the students and a fourth of the leaders saw their homeland now in a more favorable light, but about a fourth of the students and a tenth of the leaders had changed their rating to unfavorable. Critical judgments were made specifically in regard to politics. In many instances, the critique took the form of suggestions of changes that needed to be made. With respect to international affairs, membership in a United Europe and in the United Nations was named by a plurality of students as an important goal. Leaders among the visitors to the United States recommended closer political ties with the United States and other Western powers and a larger role for Germany in international affairs.[70] Others mentioned a contributory effort by Germany to world peace, unification of East and West Germany, and education for democracy.

To sum up, although the impact of U.S. foreign policy appears to be undeniable, a word of caution is in order. In contrast to impressions of American institutions, American life, and the American people that were gained as a result of direct exposure and first-hand observation, the impact of American policy must be considered to be the result of a multitude of cumulative influences of which the exchange program was only one, although perhaps a crucial one. OMGUS' and HICOG's communication media activities, from press and radio to America Houses, supported by German media and by a German Government wholly committed to a pro-Western and pro-American posture and, above all, the omnipresence of the cold war combined to produce strongly pro-American reactions in the early fifties. By that time the vast majority of the German visitors who came to the United States were familiar with the basic tenets of U.S. policy and disposed to find positive corroboration. Their visit may have provided opportunities to check, reaffirm, and strengthen rather than to form new or correct existing assumptions. It is therefore not surprising that studies comparing the views of returning exchangees, all of whom had been exposed to the influence of the media, with that of their fellow nationals who had not visited the United States showed relatively little differences when it came to acceptance or rejection of U.S. foreign policy.

Dissemination of Information to Fellow Countrymen at Home

Of critical importance was the spread of the exchange experience through communication of the newly gained knowledge to fellow citizens at home, beyond the circle of the participants. This multiplier effect of personal communication has often been regarded as a "crucial criterion" with which to measure the value of the exchange program, as long as mutual understanding remained the basic goal.[71] As stated by HICOG, it considered the dissemination of favorable attitudes as the "primary condition of effectiveness."[72] A common assumption particularly popular with members of Congressional appropriation committees, has always been that the measure for "effectiveness" should be the degree to which favorable foreign attitudes toward official U.S. foreign policy are multiplied. Over-emphasis on short range program benefits, however, tends to overlook other equally important policy objectives, including that of using exchange experiences as stimulants for emulation upon return.

There is, in fact, ample evidence that upon their return home the German visitors lectured, spoke publicly, and wrote extensively about their impressions, using public media, including the Voice of America, in trying to reach a variety of audiences. To solidify and perpetuate the impact, they organized their audiences frequently in the form of discussion groups or committees, in order to provide a continuing focus of attention on problems observed in the United States. Surveys conducted by HICOG disclosed that by 1953 slightly over 60 percent of the returnees were reported to have discussed some significant areas of American life with their fellow countrymen.[73] Each of them was believed to have talked personally to anywhere from 150 to 300 people,[74] which meant that about 2.7 percent of the population (590,000 to 1,200,000 people) had talked to returnees.[75] By 1955, estimates of the number of persons contacted by adult exchangees had risen to 3 million, or 8 percent of the population.[76] These figures do not include audiences reached by mass media nor those reached by news stories that were submitted regularly by journalists in the course of their visits to the United States for publication in newspapers and magazines in Germany.

Subjects discussed by returning Germans covered nearly every important aspect of American life. Education, religion, culture, "way of life," and family living appear to have been among the most popular topics. Leaders devoted a great deal of their presentations to economic problems and politics, and understandably to discussions of subjects falling within their special field of concern. Comments were mostly favorable, particularly on "way of life,"

American personal characteristics, education, employer-employee relations, and family life. Significantly, leaders and experts were nearly always highly complimentary in their evaluation of conditions within their own areas of interest, e.g., church leaders on religious life, educators on education, labor leaders on employer-employee relations, librarians and museum experts on cultural life, and so on. This was important because their judgment had greater credibility due to their expertise and more intensive exposure to problems in their fields through first-hand observation. In contrast, unfavorable judgments passed on some of the same aspects, e.g., family life, social conditions (racial discrimination), cultural standards, television, and a few more, represented a small minority opinion.[77]

What, then, was the effect of a dissemination effort so massive and, on balance, so favorable in its results? Did the message get across to the German population? A study made in 1955 [78] suggests that with all due reservations the impact on the German public was wide and positive. On the basis of a control sample of 1,269 exchangees who returned to Germany and of 315 who returned to West Berlin, and of interviews with 462 persons with whom the returnees came in contact, the study found that the "contacts" were far more pro-American than any other group in the population. Although the study conceded that this might not be due entirely to their exposure to exchangees, the latter were believed to have constituted a vital element in promoting attitudes that were pro-American to the point of being "highly opinionated." The study concluded that there was substantial evidence that the exchange-of-persons program was indeed successful in creating a pro-American orientation among those exposed to dissemination efforts, and that dissemination in turn was creating an ever-widening circle of sympathizers among the general population. The study showed, furthermore, that 54 percent of those who had personal contacts with exchangees claimed that they had been favorably influenced in their attitude toward the United States. Of the 54 percent, three out of five contacts, which approximated 5 percent of all West Germans, said that they had received new ideas with respect to problems of education, "way of life," and technology, and admitted that "it would be a good thing to adopt quite a few of their practices over here." A comparison of strengths of impressions gained by exchangees with those conveyed to their contacts revealed marked evidence of positive contagion. In other words, exchangees succeeded in presenting to their friends, families, and contacts a positive picture of the United States and found a substantial number ready to accept it.

Again, while shifts in attitudes were less pronounced in the case of persons contacted by returned visitors than in that of the returnees themselves, responses by contacts revealed a markedly more favorable attitude after exposure to the views of exchangees than before. They were also strikingly more positive than those found to be shared by a cross section of the population in the returnee's home community. This was true with respect to views on the American scene as well as on American foreign policy. For instance, favorable opinions on American hospitality, charity, and lack of class consciousness nearly doubled. Also, respect for American family life rose among local contacts, whereas there was little evidence of change in regard to education and press affairs. There was a noticeable increase of favorable views among such contacts with respect to certain aspects of U.S. foreign policy, particularly American intentions to promote cooperation with other nations to encourage democracy and peace.

An earlier study made in 1954, based on interviews with members of Cooperative Action Teams, had produced similar evidence.[79] The strong dissemination impact is not too surprising in the case of the Teams, whose members occupied key positions and commanded wide contacts within their home communities. Their effectiveness could doubtless have been even greater, had they continued to operate as a team after their return to Germany.

Personal Benefits From Observation and Study in the United States

The acquisition of new knowledge and skills, as previously noted, has never been considered the overriding objective of official exchange programs. However, it proved to be a prerequisite to the attainment of the ultimate goal of the individual visitor—that is, application of such knowledge and skills in the mutual interest of the countries involved. The probability of this outcome naturally increased when a satisfactory exchange experience led to improvement of career prospects or to promotion to positions carrying higher responsibilities and, with them, greater influence potential. Although a complete record of the German returnees has not been kept, there is ample evidence that their stay in the United States benefited most exchangees, although in varying degrees and in different ways. There are further indications that a substantial number moved to positions which enabled them to break new ground in their fields of specialization.

As far as scholastic improvement was concerned, university students and young academicians were the chief beneficiaries. Instructions from the Department of State to the universities had placed emphasis on "extensive experience and the acquisition of general knowledge rather than a thorough formal education."[80] Accordingly, German students were given a special status. Yet many universities arranged for a regular academic program as part of the total plan and even graded performances. The results showed appreciable degrees of progress. Reports submitted to the Institute of International Education for the academic year 1954–1955 by American universities showed that of 75 students, 37 were rated as "excellent," 33 as "good," 5 as "fair," and none as "poor." One straight "A" student received his A.B. degree *cum laude* and was awarded the "Class of 1875 Prize in American History." Ten other students completed work for a Master's degree. A number of these grantees were successful upon their return in obtaining important positions in academic and political life.[81] The record of German Fulbright students in the following year was even more impressive. Of those graded, 57 percent were rated "excellent," 37 percent "good," 6 percent "fair," and less than 1 percent "poor." One student graduated *summa cum laude*, another received his B.A. *magna cum laude*, and a third completed his Master of Comparative Law at Columbia University Law School with almost a straight "A" average.[82] A number of them were given special recognition by American universities in the form of extensions of their study period or of faculty appointments.

Beyond academic achievements, many reports indicate that the totality of impressions gathered on and away from the campus changed the outlook of the visitors with respect to their professional goals and in some instances deepened their conceptions of their field of specialization. "It seems almost unbelievable to me," wrote a teacher trainee at Bryn Mawr College, "how much my capacity has increased . . . Key interest in education is greater than it ever was and I feel now much more prepared to work in this field . . ."[83] An economist studying at Harvard had this to say: "While I cannot put the finger on any individual aspect, I feel that the past year of study in the United States has been of a value that can hardly be exaggerated. I learned more than I could have learned anywhere in Germany, and this I mean with reference to my special field of study. The many possibilities for first-hand views of America have opened up new intellectual and emotional vistas. I am more mature and balanced than before. The recognition at Harvard has boosted my professional recognition at home. In fact, nothing has helped my career as an economist in Germany more than my work here . . . I must repeat: my career in Germany is made here."[84]

Making due allowance for the fact that exchangees may not always be able to assess accurately the effect, in particular the long-range impact, of their visit and study, it is worth noting that by 1960 nearly three-fourths of German "Fulbrighters" interviewed (73 percent) stated that they received professional or personal advantages from their stay in the United States, with the highest percentage (76 percent) among senior research scholars.[85] Characteristically, a majority of the respondents named personal and intangible benefits as against those that had any immediate consequences for their professional careers. Twenty-seven percent indicated that their professional knowledge had been enlarged; 20 percent stated that their career prospects had been improved or that they had actually launched upon a promising career or had been promoted to higher positions. Other more personal advantages mentioned included increase of general knowledge, greater proficiency in English, enlargement of contacts with Americans, better knowledge of Americans, and the like.[86]

Inquiries into the plans of trainees upon their return, made in 1953 and 1954,[87] showed the group fairly evenly divided between those who planned to use their experience for their personal and professional benefit, i.e., to improve their position or to finish their training, and those who wished to share it with others and use it to ameliorate conditions in Germany or to work toward better understanding. There appeared to be a slight decline of social motivation in favor of self-serving intentions. There were also, as we noted above, a number of "turn arounds," in this case, of participants who after their return decided to emigrate, mostly to the United States, and a few to other countries. The total percentage was low (3.2 percent of the total; 6.6 percent of the teenagers).[88]

Available information on individual status changes of returned German exchangees is exceedingly scarce and, on the whole, inconclusive. Studies show that within a relatively short period after their return about two-thirds of the students had moved into influential positions on varying levels. Many social workers and social work students assumed positions of considerable importance as high level public servants, presidents and professors of social work schools, directors of public or private agencies, even members of the Bundestag.[89]

Most impressive is the number of German participants in the program who over the years were appointed to high office, e.g., to key positions in federal, state or local administrations, or who were elected to the federal or state legislatures. To give a few examples: Walter Scheel, President of the Federal Republic of Germany was one of the political leaders who came to the United States in 1951 under the auspices of the exchange program. So were former Chancellor Willi Brandt, and the present Chancellor Helmut Schmidt, and at one time 7 of his 16 Cabinet members. Other former visitors under the program include, in recent years, one of the leading members of the Christian Democratic Union (CDU), the current opposition party, Minister President of Schleswig-Holstein, Gerhard Stoltenberg; the former National Secretary of the CDU, Kurt Biedenkopf; the National Chairman of the Federation of German Trade Unions, Heinz Vetter; the National Chairman of the Union of Civil Service Transport and Traffic Employees, Heinz Kluncker; and the National Chairman of the German Metal Workers Union, Eugen Loderer. Seven of the State Secretaries, the ranking civil servants in each ministry, were participants, as were four of the so-called Parliamentary Secretaries in various ministries. The Minister Presidents (Governors) of five states, the future Governing Mayor of Berlin, and the Presidents of the Senate and Mayors of Hamburg and Bremen were also exchange visitors to the United States. This list could be expanded to include a large number of ranking officials in the Office of the Federal Chancellor, the Federal Press and Information Office, the Ministries of Foreign Affairs, Defense, Finance, Economics, Food, Agriculture and Forestry, Education, and Science, as well as state government officials and a very substantial number of Bundestag members from all parties, including a President and two Vice Presidents of the Bundestag and others who at one time or another had been Chancellors or Ministers of the Federal Republic, such as Kurt Georg Kiesinger, Ludwig Erhard, Franz Josef Strauss. The presiding judge of the Constitutional Court was an early visitor. Equally impressive is the number of top academicians, i.e., presidents of universities and institutes, scientists, representatives of public bodies, publishers and editors of key newspapers, correspondents, and directors of radio and television who participated in the program.[90] Most of their visits took place during the period covered by this report, but the process has continued to this day.

Tempting as it is, the claim cannot be made that the attainment of high office was always the result of the exchange experience, although the latter was often undoubtedly a contributing factor. In holding positions of influence which involved the responsibility of breaking new ground in public and professional fields, a number of the participants stated that they had drawn on their American experience as visitors to the United States under the program. Far more significant, however, is the fact that by occupying high offices in public life, many were able to translate their personal experience into policies and programs which benefited both countries and over the years contributed to the good relations existing today between the United States and the Federal Republic of Germany.

Americans and Germans alike have criticized and praised the immediate postwar exchange program on innumerable occasions. Criticism has been leveled at specifics, but appreciation has been general, attesting to the value of the program as a whole. U.S.

officials in Washington and in Germany, as we noted earlier, considered it a most important instrument of policy. The Congress appropriated year after year without strictures the funds requested by the executive branch. Support by the private sector was generous and enthusiastic. The leader program, in particular, was singled out by observers as especially effective.

Tributes paid by German officialdom and the public were unstinting. During a Bundestag debate in 1952 speakers from all major parties rose to praise the exchange program as a most constructive and progressive undertaking and as "an effective way gradually to transform the unproductive relationship of victor and vanquished into a partnership of equality." Prominent German leaders wished to see the program continued and, if possible, expanded.[91]

In 1953, as a token of appreciation the President of the Bundestag, Eugen Gerstenmaier, introduced a motion to invite 100 American civic leaders to visit Germany for a month. The Bundestag passed unanimously (except for the Communist members) the legislative authorization, and 100 public servants, educators, journalists, and representatives of other fields, toured Germany for a month as guests of the Federal Republic.[92] Dr. Alois Hundhammer, Minister of Education and Culture in Bavaria, who had been a severe critic and opponent of educational reform, after visiting the United States established scholarships for ten American students at the University of Munich.[93] Returning Germans attested time and again to the contribution the exchange program had made not only to their own professional growth but to the welfare of their communities. "I am convinced," a student wrote, "that this student exchange does more good to Germany's future than any other help which has been given to Germany."[94]

Rather significantly, there was no misunderstanding on the purpose of the program. The vast majority of German participants appreciated it precisely for the reasons for which it had been devised. Neither leaders, students, nor teenagers saw as its prime purpose professional or scholastic benefit. They knew that its purpose was the promotion of international understanding and peace, better understanding of the United States, and of democracy.[95] Very few believed that its objective was to "propagandize Germans".[96] Nearly all thought that the aims of the program were achievable and a high majority thought that they had been achieved.[97]

The least-contested fact was the popularity of the program. Its scope and content may have been obscure to some and controversial to others, but the program as such was widely known and generally appreciated as HICOG studies revealed.[98] By 1955 no less than 55 percent of the German population had heard of the program (in West Berlin 70 percent stated that they were aware of it). An overwhelming majority considered the program beneficial for the participants and for Germany as well (75 percent in West Germany, 93 percent in West Berlin). Moreover, in the eyes of nearly half of the German public, returned participants were accepted as the most reliable interpreters of the United States, exceeding all other channels and media such as the Voice of America, press, radio, film, and resident or visiting U.S. citizens.[99]

The program indeed had become a success. It had provided an impulse for democratic reform. It had helped correct the American image in Germany although to a lesser degree the German image in America. It had gained understanding and support of American foreign policy. It had influenced not only the participants themselves but, beyond this, a large circle of persons with whom the exchangee had come in contact. It had helped individuals to achieve higher scholastic and professional standing and to increase their impact as intercultural interpreters. It had found general recognition as an effective medium of mutual understanding and binational cooperation, and it had served as a model for exchange programs launched with other countries.

In testimony before the Subcommittee of the Committee on Appropriations of the House of Representatives, on February 15, 1955, James A. Conant, the U.S. High Commissioner, made the following comments on the educational exchange program with Germany:

"As you know . . . the Educational Exchange Program with Germany . . . has been removed from the GOA appropriation and will hereafter be included in the worldwide exchange budget . . . This program remains one of my vital concerns as Chief of Mission in Germany . . .

"During the 2 years that I have been in Germany, I have had a chance to assess to some degree the effectiveness of our work in various fields of public relations, as we might call it, and I am convinced that the money which has been spent on the exchange program is some of the most effective money we have ever spent in a foreign country . . .

"We have sent approximately 10,000 Germans to the United States since the inception of the program in late 1947. Of this number some 5,400 fall into what might be termed the 'leader' category, that is, individuals holding influential positions in the political, economic, social, and other fields. As an example, former participants in the German exchange program comprise about 25 percent of the membership of the Bundestag, or lower House of the Federal Republic, and 17 percent of the membership of the Bundesrat, or upper House. In every significant area of German life I have encountered individuals in key positions who have participated in the exchange experience, and whose knowledge and understanding of United States objectives has greatly benefited thereby . . .

"We have had an assessment in the past of the attitudes of various members of this group, but with particular reference to the 5,400 in the leader category, I could almost speak from personal experience I have had what might be called a fair sampling of them, because I have run into them as I have gone around the country in the period of the past 2 years, which involves people running all the way from the governors of the separate States, labor leaders, as well as members of the Bundestag...

"With the coming of sovereignty, the task of communicating clearly the objectives of our foreign policy vis-a-vis Germany will, if anything, increase in importance. The role of the exchange program in this continuing effort to convince the German people of the honesty of our purpose and the mutuality of our interests will be a large one . . .

"The exchange program has shown itself to be an important factor in building German understanding and support of our purposes and policies." [100]

The U.S.-German exchange program of the immediate postwar period was unique because the policies governing its objectives, its scope, and its content were unique. But it was not rigid. As has been shown, within 10 years it went through a series of remarkable adaptations, faithfully reflecting changes in U.S. policy toward Germany and the rest of the world. The experiment will probably never be repeated. Yet, out of it emerged certain features which set a benchmark for other exchange programs. The focus on critical public opinion forming groups, the merger of public and private resources, the integration of program objectives with country policy on all appropriate levels—these were innovations that have proved their merit beyond the confines of time and place. In all of these aspects the massive size of the program provided an unusual opportunity for creative experimentation and innovation.

Notes

CHAPTER VIII

1. Actually the Council published the first result of its deliberations only in June 1970. It proposed a "Structural Plan for the German Educational System."
2. "The School System in the Federal Republic of Germany," in *Bildung und Wissenschaft*, 3-74(e), Inter-Nationes, Bonn-Bad Godesberg, 1974, p. 39.
3. Ulrich Littmann, "An Introduction to the Confusion of German Education," background paper for Conference on German-American Academic Exchange, June 10-28, 1972, printed by Deutscher Akademischer Austauschdienst, Bonn-Bad Godesberg, 1972.
4. "The School System in the Federal Republic of Germany," *op. cit.*, p. 43.

RESULTS OF THE PROGRAM   245

5. For a thoughtful discussion of the problems of this type of evaluation, see Sharon Lee Mueller Norton, *The United States Department of State International Visitor Program: A Conceptual Framework for Evaluation.* Unpublished Doctoral dissertation. Fletcher School of Law and Diplomacy, Medford, Mass., 1977. See especially pp. 58–60, and Chapter V, "Summary of Findings of Past Evaluation Studies," pp. 83–149. See also, "Report of International Conference of Former Exchangees to the United States, June 15–19," 1953, Nuernberg, Germany, sponsored by HICOG, WNRC, RG 59, 64 A 200, Box 155; copy in CU/H.
6. "German Exchangees: A Study in Attitude Change," International Public Opinion Research, Inc., New York, 1953; copy in CU/H.
7. Robert T. Bower, Berta McKenzie, Burton Winograd, "An Analysis of Attitude Changes Among German Exchangees, Final Report," Bureau of Social Science Research, American University, Washington, D.C., for the Institute for Research in Human Behavior, Philadelphia, Aug. 1951; copy in CU/H.
8. "Study of Impressions and Disseminations by Information Specialists and Students from the Exchange of Persons Program," Report 224, prepared for the American Embassy, Bonn, by the Institut fuer Sozial-und Wirtschaftsforschung, Bad Godesberg, Dec. 1955. Copy in CU/H, hereinafter referred to as Report 224. See also, "Foreign Exchange Students Review their Stay in the United States," Bureau of Social Science Research, American University, Washington, D.C., Aug. 1953; copy in CU/H.
9. See "A Follow-up Study of German Teenager Exchangees," prepared by International Public Opinion Research, Inc., New York, 1954; copy in CU/H.
10. "Analysis of Programs, Attitudes and Reactions to the American Experience of 124 German Youth and Community Leaders," National Social Welfare Assembly, New York 1952; copy in CU/H.
11. Bower, McKenzie, Winograd, *op. cit.*, pp. 41–44, 49–52, 65; Report 224, *op. cit., passim.*
12. Report by Walter Gruen, student, Institute of Labor and Industrial Relations, 1953, WNRC, RG 59, 63 A 217, Box 313.
13. "Change in Attitudes of German Exchangees, A Preliminary Report on Thirty Leaders," Bureau of Social Science Research, American University, Washington, D.C., 1951; copy in CU/H.
14. "German Exchangees: A Study in Attitude Change," *op. cit.*, pp. vi, 55–58.
15. Letter to the author of Oct. 8, 1975, copy in CU/H.
16. Now renamed "Congressional Research Service."
17. Dr. Karl Lohmann, *Der deutsche Bundestag* (Frankfurt/Main und Bonn: Athenaeum Verlag, 1907), pp. 17, 127–8.
18. Semi-annual report on the International Educational Exchange Program for the Federal Republic of Germany and West Berlin for the period Jan. 1 to June 30, 1955; copy in CU/H.
19. HICOG, Office of Public Affairs Report, 1953, WNRC, RG 59, 64 A 200, Box 155.
20. Letter to the author of Dec. 12, 1975; copy in CU/H.
21. *Ibid.*
22. *Ibid.* Further examples are cited in Alina M. Lindegren's study "Germany Revisited—Education in the Federal Republic," U.S. Department of Health, Education and Welfare, Bulletin 12, 1957, reprinted 1960. While Ms. Lindegren noted in 1955 that, for the most part, the old pattern prevailed with schools reverting to pre-Nazi traditions, she recognized

significant changes, some of which, she suggests, might have been attributable to both the work of American experts and German exchangees, although, with the possible exception of the new emphasis on social studies in school curricula, she does not bring her conclusions down to specifics.
23. HICOG, Office of Public Affairs Report, 1953, *op. cit.*
24. Report on Effectiveness of Exchanges, HICOG, Office of Public Affairs, 1953, quoting Oskar Bezold, Managing Editor of *Westdeutsche Allgemeine*; copy in CU/H.
25. "A Cooperative Action Team in Action—An Observer's Report on 90 Days with the Team from Freiburg, Germany," and "Cooperative Action Teams—A Study of Effectiveness." Both studies prepared by International Public Opinion Research, Inc., New York, 1953, 1954; copies in CU/H. See also Jeanne Watson and Ronald Lippitt, "Cross-Culture Learning—A Study Among a Group of German Leaders," *News Bulletin*, Institute of International Education, XXX (June 1955), pp. 2–5, 19. This article summarizes the authors' findings contained in their book *Learning Across Cultures—A Study of Germans Visiting America* (Ann Arbor: University of Michigan, 1955), concerning 29 German visitors sponsored by the University of Michigan from 1949 to 1951.
26. For further detail see Bower, McKenzie, Winograd, *op. cit.*, pp. 118–119.
27. *Ibid.*, pp. 115–117.
28. Watson and Lippitt, "Cross-Cultural Learning," *op. cit.*, p. 3, arrived at a far less positive picture. It was their conclusion that "there was little change in the ideas and values which the visitors felt were evidence of German superiority." Examples quoted by the author were "ambivalence about authority, hostility toward peers, and preferences for external rather than intrinsic measures of success and failure. . . [also] ambivalence about interpersonal relationships."
29. *A German Appraisal of the Fulbright Program* (Frankfurt am Main: Divo-Institut, 1961). Copy in CU/H.
30. Bower, McKenzie, Winograd, *op. cit.*, pp. 33–86.
31. As Watson and Lippitt point out correctly, oftentimes these negative judgments involved a conflict of American values and practices with values which the Germans considered of utmost importance. "Cross-cultural Learning," (*op. cit.*, p. 4). The conflict emerged most sharply in the case of university students. See pp. 226–231.
32. Report 224, *op. cit.*
33. *A German Appraisal of the Fulbright Program*, *op. cit.*, pp. 115–166.
34. Bower, McKenzie, Winograd, *op. cit.*, p. 66.
35. "German Exchangees: A Study in Attitude Change," *op. cit.*, pp. v, 9ff.
36. Watson and Lippitt, *op. cit.*, p. 4.
37. Report by Hermann Muenster, student of agricultural economics, NARS, RG 59, 63 A 217, Box 303.
38. Watson and Lippitt, *op. cit.*, p. 5.
39. Bower, McKenzie, Winograd, *op. cit.*, p. 70.
40. *A German Appraisal of the Fulbright Program*, *op. cit.*, pp. 126, 134.
41. "A Cooperative Action Team in Action," *op. cit.*, pp. 125–130.
42. "A Follow-up Study of German Teenager Exchangees," *op. cit.*
43. *A German Appraisal of the Fulbright Program*, *op. cit.*, pp. 97–99, Appendix 17.
44. "German Exchangees: A Study in Attitude Change," *op. cit.*, pp. v, 17–19, 21.
45. Report by Karl Weigand, WNRC, RG 59, 64 A 200, Box 155.

RESULTS OF THE PROGRAM 247

46. See Walter Mischel, *Studies in German-American Post-War Problems: German Exchange Students at Ohio State University*, Department of Psychology, University of Colorado, Nov. 1957; copy in CU/H.
47. Report of Guenter Friedrichs, member of German student team observing student government at Minnesota, WNRC, RG 59, 63 A 217, Box 303.
48. Report of Ilse Abshagen, *ibid*.
49. *Ibid*.
50. Report by Fritz Encke, *ibid*.
51. Report by Guenter Friedrichs and Eva Giersberg, *ibid*.
52. *Ibid*.
53. Report from the University of Colorado, WNRC, RG 59, 64 A 200, Box 155.
54. Similar reactions were reported by other universities. Harvard, commenting on its experience with the student group assigned to it in 1952–53, found that a majority hoped to apply certain attitudes and institutions of the American campus to conditions at home, such as the informality of administrative practices and the powers exercised by the student electorate. Harvard, Final Report, June 1953, WNRC, RG 59, A 217, Box 303.
55. Reports by Assistant to Dean of Students and German students who were not team members, WNRC, RG 59, 63 A 217, Box 303.
56. Report of German team at Antioch College, 1953–54, NARS, RG 59, 63 A 200, Box 155.
57. Report by American Fulbright Professor Fritz Epstein, of the Library of Congress, visiting lecturer at Bonn University in 1954. Epstein concluded that the differences between American and German institutions being what they were, only expert counseling on the spot would enable the American student truly to benefit from German academic opportunities. He proposed that faculty members of German universities who were well-acquainted with American academic life should be asked to act as "counselors" or "advisers" to American students and thus facilitate their contact with the German teachers in their special fields. Files of USEC/G, Bonn.
58. Report by Alfred Toborg, Free University, 1959. Files of USEC/G, Bonn.
59. Report by Richard E. Kear, Frankfurt University, 1954, *ibid*., copy in CU/H.
60. Letter of Gerd Matthecka, student at Georgia Teacher's College, WNRC, RG 59, 64 A 200, Box 155.
61. Study by National Social Welfare Council on German Youth and Community Leaders, 1951, copy in CU/H.
62. Report 224, *op. cit.*
63. Bower, McKenzie, Winograd, *op. cit.*, p .47.
64. Letter from Willy Birkelbach, WNRC, 293 2/5.
65. Full citation under note 10, above.
66. Bower, McKenzie, Winograd, *op. cit.*, p. 51.
67. *Ibid*., p. 57.
68. "German Exchangees: A Study in Attitude Change," *op. cit.*, p. 34. A minority, though, still maintained that U.S. foreign policy was dictated by self-serving motivations, such as ridding the American economy of surplus commodities (24 percent) or establishing American domination over the rest of the world (16 percent). A comparison of their attitude with that of so-called "eligibles" (see above) shows no marked differences, an indication that exchangees did not so much reflect the impact of their

69. *Ibid.*, p. 42.
70. Bower, McKenzie, Winograd, *op. cit.*, pp. 99–104.
71. "An Evaluation of the Exchange Program in West Germany," prepared by the HICOG Evaluation Staff in conjunction with DIVO (Frankfurt am Main: Divo-Institut, 1954); copy in CU/H.
72. *Ibid.*
73. HICOG staff report, 1954, WNRC, RG 59, 64 A 200, Box 154.
74. IES staff memorandum by Francis J. Colligan, covering report cited in above note 73.
75. "West German Receptivity and Reactions to the Exchange of Persons Program," study conducted by HICOG, Sept. 1952, WNRC, RG 59, 64 A 200, Box 155. The study was limited to 1,200 persons above the age of 18. The total would have been substantially larger if it had included teenagers below that age group.
76. "A Study of the Extent and Nature of Exchangees' Contacts with the German Population," Report 221, Nov. 22, 1955, prepared by the Research Staff, Office of Public Affairs, American Embassy, Bonn, WNRC, RG 59, 62 A 200, Box 178; copy in files of Embassy, Bonn.
77. "An Evaluation of the Exchange Program in West Germany," *op. cit., passim.*
78. "Study of the Extent and Nature of Exchangees' Contacts with the German Population," *op. cit., passim.*
79. "Cooperative Action Teams—A Study of Effectiveness," *op. cit., passim.*
80. Instructions to University of Illinois, 1953, WNRC, RG 59, 63 A 217, Box 313.
81. Annual Report of USEC/G, Program Year 1954; copy in CU/H.
82. Annual Report of USEC/G, Program Year 1955; copy in CU/H.
83. Letter from Liesel Wolfslast, WNRC, RG 59, 64 A 200, Box 155.
84. Annual Report of USEC/G, Program Year 1954, *op. cit.*
85. *A German Appraisal of the Fulbright Program, op. cit.*, pp. 167–184.
86. *Ibid.*
87. The prevalence of personal over professional factors has been noted in a more recent study undertaken by Case Western University at Cleveland, Ohio. This study of a sample of German social workers who had spent some time in the United States under the auspices of the "Council of International Programs for Youth Leaders and Social Workers, Inc." (CIP) revealed that a majority of the participants considered their exchange experience to have had a greater social and cultural than a professional impact. Only some of the professionally more advanced participants showed a greater appreciation of newly acquired methods and skills. International orientation and better understanding of American life were mentioned most frequently as net gains of their stay in the United States. Career changes or advancement were mentioned in a few instances. So were pioneering projects to introduce new problem solving approaches. "Summary Evaluation" of study enclosed with letter to author from Thomas P. Holland, Associate Dean, Case Western Reserve University, Mar. 16, 1976, copy in CU/H.
88. HICOG–OPA-Ex Report, July 1954, WNRC, RG 59, 64 A 200.
89. HICOG Report, Vol. IV, May 1953, O/FADRC, 58 D 372, Box 3000; Report 224, *op. cit.*; oral interview with CIP Secretary General Dr.

Henry B. Ollendorff, Feb. 26, 1976, tape in oral history file CU/H; *CIP Directory, 1956–1973 Participants* (Cleveland: Council of International Programs for Youth Leaders and Social Workers, Inc., 1974).

90. Airgram from Amembassy Bonn to Department of State, June 18, 1974, files of American Embassy Bonn and Department of State. List of "Returned Exchange Program Grantees (International Visitors Program and Fulbright Program) Who Hold Important Positions in the German Federal Government and Political Parties." American Embassy, Bonn, files U.S. Information Service, Field Message Continuation Sheet.
91. Henry J. Kellermann, "Germany—Today and Tomorrow," Department of State *Bulletin*, XXVI (May 26, 1952), pp. 807–813; *ibid.*, XXVI (June 2, 1952), pp. 851–857.
92. Report by HICOG–PAO, Apr. 1953. WNRC, RG 59, 64 A 200.
93. *Ibid.*
94. *Ibid.*
95. Bower, McKenzie, Winograd, *op. cit.*, pp. 5–8.
96. *Ibid.*, p. 6.
97. *Ibid.*
98. "A Study of the Extent and Nature of Exchangees' Contacts with the German Population," *op. cit., passim.*
99. *Ibid.*
100. House Hearings, Dept. of State Appropriation Bill for 1956, 84th Cong., 1st sess. (Washington, D.C.: U.S. Government Printing Office, 1955), pp. 250, 251, 252, 253.

Epilogue

Epilogue

In the history of educational, cultural, and intellectual relations between the United States and other nations of the world, few events have been more dramatic or more significant than the educational and cultural program between the United States and Germany in the immediate post-World War II decade. During that period, more than 12,000 Germans and 2,000 Americans participated in what was the largest educational and cultural exchange program with another country that has ever been undertaken by the U.S. Government.

The present educational and cultural exchanges carried out between the two countries that are funded by the U.S. Government are modest compared with their earlier, immediate postwar dimensions. In 1966, the American Ambassador to Germany, George C. McGhee, wrote to Charles Frankel, Assistant Secretary for Educational and Cultural Affairs in the Department: "Our international visitor program has declined to a level which no longer bears meaningful relation to the number of actual and potential leaders in this country . . . For the first time in the postwar era new leaders are assuming office in Germany on national and state levels . . . German-American relations are entering a new phase. We should in fact be increasing rather than decreasing the size of our exchange program in order to make certain that knowledge of America and American viewpoints remain important ingredients in the experience of the coming generation of German leaders." [1]

Beginning in 1956 the program was funded from a single annual Congressional appropriation to support exchange programs with over 100 countries throughout the world. The number of exchanges between the two countries was gradually reduced to the level of exchanges with other major countries. By 1975 the annual number of participants had shrunk to a fraction (463) of the peak total in 1952 (3,415).

But the program has grown in other ways. In contrast to the earlier years, a large part of the funding is now from German sources. One of the most conclusive evidences of German official recognition

253

of the cultural factor in consolidating bilateral relations between the Federal Republic and the United States has been the increasing share of financial responsibility assumed by Germany for exchanges under the binationally administered Fulbright program. In 1962 Germany agreed to underwrite 50 percent of the budget. By 1975 it carried two-thirds ($1,699,000) of the total expenditure ($2,555,000). In various other related exchange activities, the financial contribution of the German government to the furtherance of closer cultural relations between the two countries now surpasses that of our own government.

Efforts on both the American and German sides to improve and refine the program continue. The problems that exist in the exchange program are the subject of continuing dialogue between the two governments, and both are in full agreement in their cooperative approach in evaluating them. One of these problems yet to be solved, for example, is the establishment of equivalence of academic curricula, examinations and degrees.[2] Another is that of greater participation of critical and social groups which represent significant trends in the national life of both countries. Still another is that of promoting the cooperation of scholars in fields of long-range international interest that constitute the paramount challenges of today's interdependent world, and which, because of their universality, reflect significant concerns in the national life of both countries.

Aside from the immediate postwar "educational reorientation" aspects of the late forties and early fifties, the basic objectives of the program remain unchanged: to enable each country to present an adequate image of its cultural achievements and to foster fruitful exchanges in the cause of mutual understanding. Mutual understanding is a complex, long-term task. Although relations between the two countries, to be sure, are excellent, stereotypes linger on on both sides of the Atlantic. A persistent effort is required to correct misconceptions and image distortions. Former Chancellor Willi Brandt probably thought along these terms when he said: "We shall have to devote time and effort to each other. We must get to know each other better, still more we must learn to live with each other. More young Europeans must have the opportunity of exploring the social landscape of America, of discovering America's outlook on life, of becoming familiar with its history, and the process must be reciprocal. In this we cannot put our faith in governments alone."[3] The HICOG program laid the foundation for this kind of approach. It has lost none of its validity.

Among the more recent expressions of German appreciation of American efforts to build up this relationship have been "The German Marshall Fund of the United States" for which the Federal

Republic provided 150 million Deutschmarks, starting in June 1972, and the "John J. McCloy Fund for German-American Exchanges," established in 1975.

The formation of the German Marshall Fund was announced by Chancellor Willi Brandt at a special convocation at Harvard University, on June 5, 1972. In his remarks on the occasion, the German Chancellor stated:

> "On the occasion of the 25th anniversary of the announcement of the European Recovery Program by Secretary of State George Marshall, we, my colleagues representing all parties of our Parliament, and I, wish to inform you of several measures taken by the Federal Republic of Germany with a view to closer understanding between partners on both sides of the Atlantic in the seventies and eighties . . .
>
> "The [German] Federal Government undertakes to provide the [German Marshall] Fund with 150 million Deutschmarks to be paid over the next fifteen years in installments of 10 million Deutschmarks due on the 5th of June of each year. All parties represented in the German Bundestag approved the Government appropriation bill for these funds . . .
>
> "Upon the suggestion of the Federal Government, the program of West European Studies of Harvard University will receive this year a non-recurring grant of three million Deutschmarks from the German Marshall Fund to establish a "German Marshall Memorial Endowment" for the promotion of European study projects . . .
>
> "The German Government has always attached special sigificance to exchanges with the United States in the field of science. This is also reflected in the consistent support it has given to the German-American Fulbright Program. So as to make it more effective the German Government has decided to increase its financial contribution substantially above the amount expected of it as a matching contribution—from the present two million to three and a half million Deutschmarks per year . . .
>
> "In order to improve co-operation in specialized fields between American and German research institutes, the German Government has adopted a sponsorship program for the exchange of highly qualified American and German scientists. The German Ministry of Education and Science will earmark five million Deutschmarks per year for this exchange program . . .
>
> "The Donors' Association for German Science, an institution established by German industrial and commercial firms, has undertaken to replenish by two and a half million Deutschmarks a year the amount made available by the Federal Government for the sponsorship program. These additional funds will be used for exchanges of scholars in the field of humanities . . ." [4]

The John J. McCloy Fund was conceived more directly as a gesture of reciprocation for the U.S. initiated and cosponsored exchange program. It was one of the many activities of the German

Government marking the Bicentennial of the American Revolution. On June 16, 1975 at a White House dinner announcing the establishment of the "John J. McCloy Fund for German-American Exchanges," Walter Scheel, President of the Federal Republic, himself a former participant in the U.S. Government's reorientation program with Germany, expressed the wish that this fund be recognized as a gesture of reciprocity and as a token of gratitude for the benefits he and his colleagues had derived from exchange visits. President Scheel said:

> "As the President of a parliamentary democracy who was himself for many years a member of the German Bundestag [Parliament], I wish on this occasion to convey another kind of thanks to the American people, the thanks of the German parliamentarians for the generous hospitality they have received in America . . . I myself was in the first group of members of the state parliament of North-Rhine Westphalia which visited your country in 1951. The friendly and generous reception we were given then so soon after the war had a profound effect on my views of America, I will not deny it. And all my colleagues at that time had the same experience." [5]

Today, the international cultural relations activities of the Federal Republic represent an important aspect of American and German foreign policy worldwide. Since the early seventies, German and American government officials have met annually to discuss ways to improve and extend cultural and educational relations between their countries.[6] These developments, and the extensive official and private educational and cultural linkages between individuals and institutions of the United States and the Federal Republic of Germany that exist today, grew out of the events recounted in the above pages.

Notes

EPILOGUE

1. Letter from Ambassador George C. McGhee to Charles Frankel, Assistant Secretary for Educational and Cultural Affairs, Dept. of State, Bonn, Dec. 15, 1966. Copy in CU/H.
2. See Ulrich Littmann (Executive Director, USEC/G) and Franz Eschbach, Working Papers Prepared at the Request of the German Federal Foreign Office, Bonn, Nov. 1974/Apr. 1975. Copy in USEC/G files, Bonn.
3. Speech at the Aspen Institute for Humanistic Studies, Aspen, Colorado, Sept. 28, 1970. Press release, German Information Center, New York, N.Y.

4. Speech by Chancellor Willi Brandt, Harvard University, June 5, 1972, Office of the German Marshall Fund of the United States, Washington, D.C., n.d., pp. 1, 10, 11. See also, "Five Year Report 1972–1977, The German Marshall Fund of the United States," 1977, published by same.
5. Toast by Herr Walter Scheel, President of the Federal Republic of Germany, White House dinner, June 16, 1975. German Information Center, New York, N.Y., 1975. For a description of the McCloy Fund, see "American Council on Germany," brochure issued by same, New York, n.d., and Press Release, Embassy of the Federal Republic of Germany, June 16, 1975.
6. "German/U.S. Cultural Talks," U.S. Department of State press release 191, Apr. 28, 1977.

Appendixes

APPENDIX I

Source: HICOG

GOAG – PUBLIC AFFAIRS
EXCHANGE OF PERSONS PROGRAM

CATEGORY	FY 1947	FY 1948	FY 1949	FY 1950	FY 1951	FY 1952	FY 1953	TOTAL
GERMAN-AMERICAN EXCHANGE								
<u>GERMANS TO U.S.</u>								
GERMAN LEADERS TO U.S.	8	18	542	1,288	987	1,186	861	4,890
GERMAN TRAINEES TO U.S.	—	—	87	242	536	382	359	1,606
GERMAN UNIVERSITY STUDENTS TO U.S.	—	214	240	448	401	220	183	1,706
GERMAN TEENAGERS TO U.S.	—	—	63	493	478	427	414	1,875
TOTAL TO U.S	8	232	932	2,471	2,402	2,215	1,817	10,077
<u>AMERICANS TO GERMANY</u>								
U.S. SPECIALISTS TO GERMANY	50	82	157	172	137	162	108	868
TOTAL U.S. – GERMANY	58	314	1,089	2,643	2,539	2,377	1,925	10,945
GERMAN – EUROPEAN EXCHANGE								
GERMAN LEADERS TO EUROPEAN COUNTRIES	21	14	—	—	681	1,309	—	2,025
EUROPEAN SPECIALISTS TO GERMANY	2	26	119	50	99	236	—	532
TOTAL GERMANY – EUROPE	23	40	119	50	780	1,545	—	2,557
GRAND TOTAL:	81	354	1,208	2,693	3,319	3,922	1,925	13,502

APPENDIX II(A)

Source: Germany 1947–1949, p. 180

US MILITARY GOVERNMENT IN GERMANY

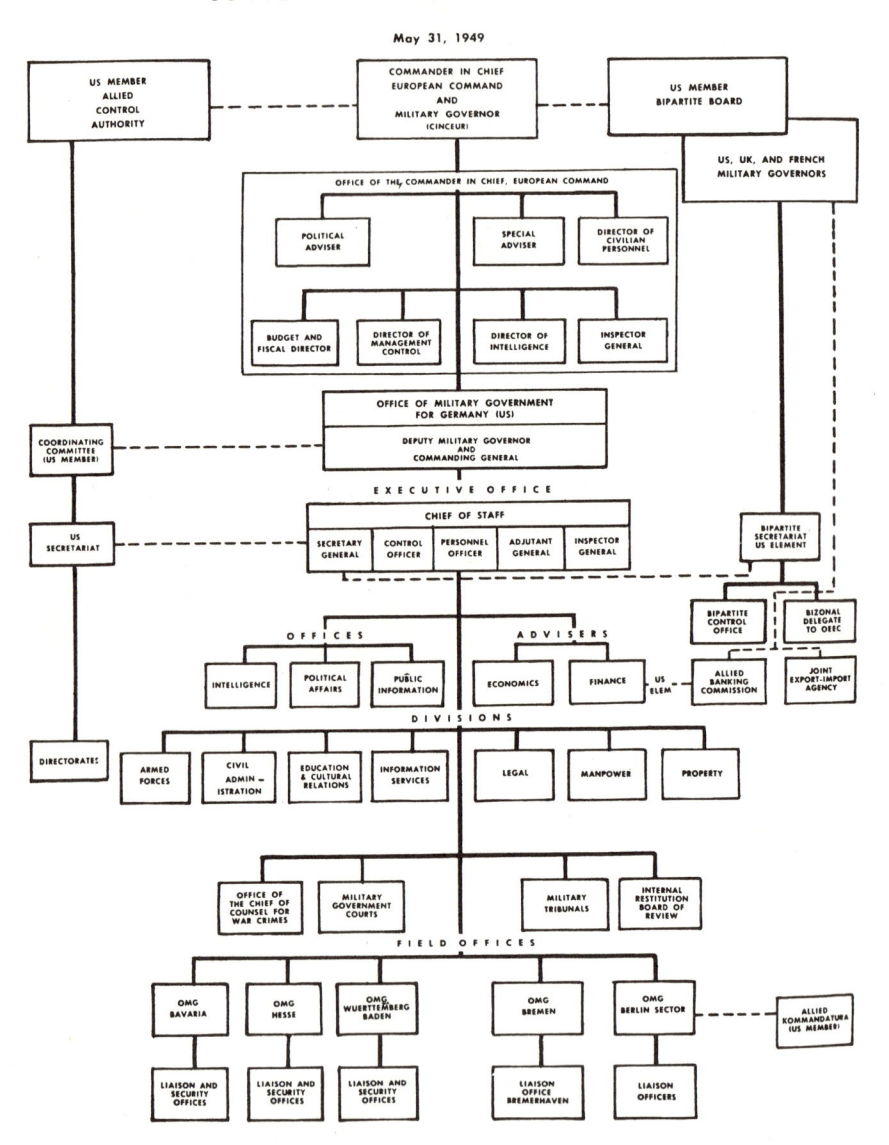

May 31, 1949

APPENDIX II(B)

Source: Germany 1947–1949, p. 183

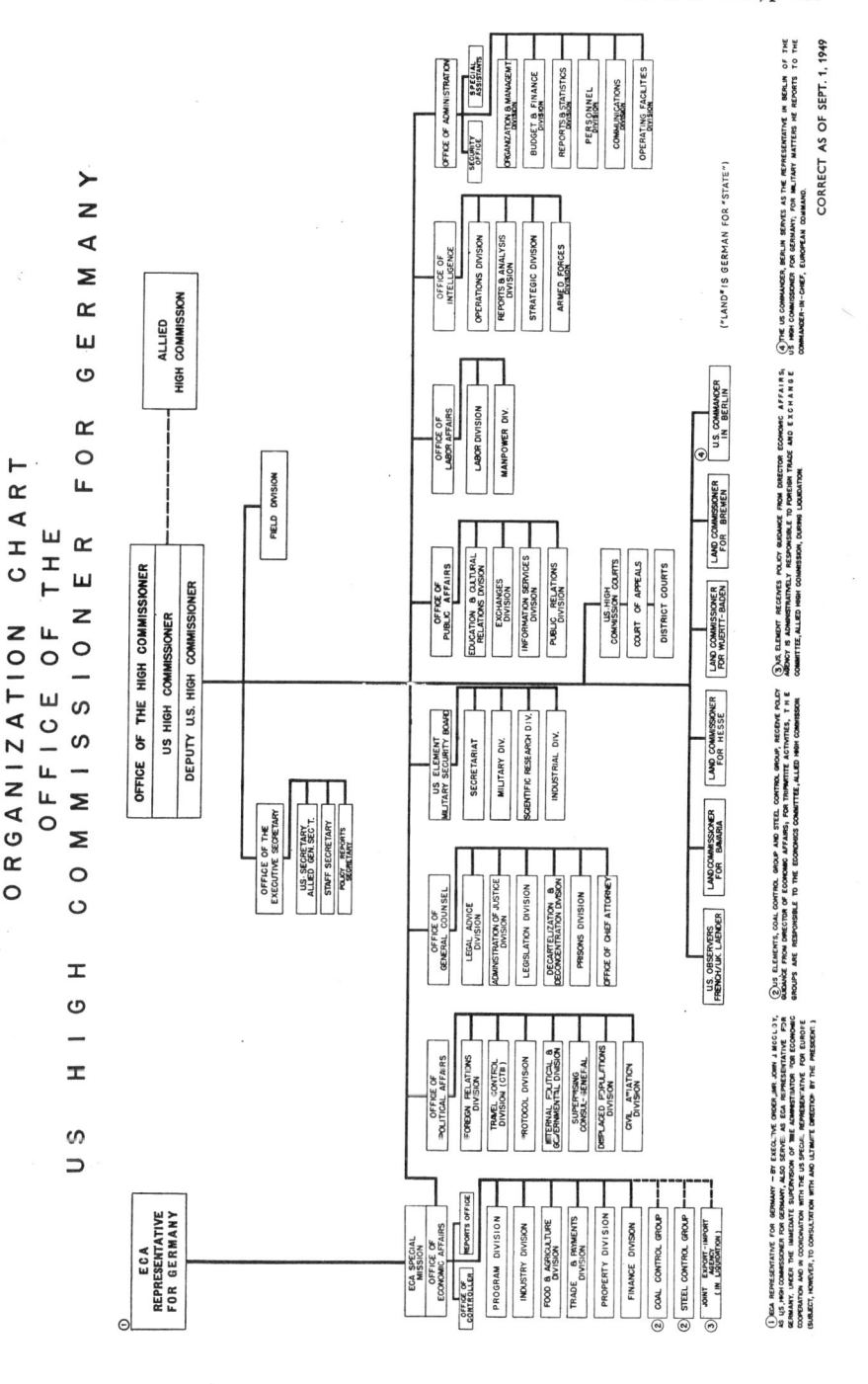

APPENDIX III

THE FOREIGN SERVICE OF THE UNITED STATES OF AMERICA
OFFICE OF PUBLIC AFFAIRS
EXCHANGE OF PERSONS DIVISION
US EMBASSY—Bonn, Germany

March 15, 1956

GERMAN EXCHANGE OF PERSONS PROGRAM (By Fiscal Years)

GERMAN-AMERICAN EXCHANGE
Germans to U.S.

Category	1947–48	1949	1950	1951	1952	1953	1954	1955	1956	Total
German Leaders	79	557	1,181	981	1,058	725	450	364	173	5,568
German Trainees		81	342	538	373	347	133	40		1,854
German Univ. Students	219	239	447	404	204	*178	*184	*185	*180	2,240
German Teenagers		65	495	485	429	414	226	169		2,283
Fulbright Lecturers, Scholars, and Teachers						*41	*48	*57	*52	*198
Total to US	298	942	2,465	2,408	2,064	1,705	1,041	815	405	12,143

APPENDIX III

Americans to Germany

US Specialists	132	157	172	137	109	73	30	12	10	832
US Lecturers, Scholars, and Teachers					26	*47	*58	*68	*55	*254
US Univ. Students						*192	*187	*192	*200	*771
Total to Germany	132	157	172	137	135	312	275	272	265	1,857
Total US–Germany	430	1,099	2,637	2,545	2,199	2,017	1,316	1,087	670	14,000

GERMAN-EUROPEAN EXCHANGE

German Leaders to European Countries	35	119	50	681	1,074					1,790
European Specialists to Germany	28			99	142					438
Total Germany–Europe	63	119	50	780	1,216					2,228
Grand total	493	1,218	2,687	3,325	3,415	2,017	1,316	1,087	670	**16,228

*Fulbright Program.
**70% men—30% women.

APPENDIX IV

Treaties and Other International Acts Series 2798

FEDERAL REPUBLIC OF GERMANY

Cultural Relations

Agreement effected by exchanges of notes;
Signed at Washington April 9, 1953;
Entered into force April 9, 1953.

The Secretary of State to the Chancellor of the Federal Republic of Germany

DEPARTMENT OF STATE
WASHINGTON
April 9, 1953

EXCELLENCY:

I have the honor to refer to conversations which have recently taken place between representatives of our two Governments concerning the cultural relations between the United States of America and the Federal Republic of Germany. I understand that it will be the intent of each Government:

1. To encourage the coming together of the peoples of the United States of America and the Federal Republic of Germany in cultural cooperation and to foster mutual understanding of the intellectual, artistic, scientific and social lives of the peoples of the two countries.

2. Recognizing that the understanding between its peoples will be promoted by better knowledge of the history, civilization, institutions, literature and other cultural accomplishments of the people of the other Government, to encourage the extension of such knowledge within its own territory.

3. To use its best efforts to extend to citizens of the other Government engaged in activities pursuant to this agreement such favorable treatment with respect to entry, travel, residence and exit as is consistent with its national laws.

4. To promote and facilitate the interchange between the United States of America and the Federal Republic of Germany of prominent citizens, specialists, professors, teachers, students and other youths, and qualified individuals from all walks of life.

5. As facilitating the interchange of persons referred to, to look with favor on establishment of scholarships, travel grants and other forms of assistance in the academic and cultural institutions within its territory. Each Government will also endeavor to make available to the other information requested by the other with regard to facilities, courses of instruction or other opportunities which may be of interest to nationals of the other Government.

6. To endeavor, whenever it appears desirable, to establish or to recommend to appropriate agencies the establishment of committees, composed of representatives of the two countries, to further the purpose of this agreement.

The responsibilities assumed by each Government under this agreement will be executed within the framework of domestic policy and legislation, procedures and practices defining internal jurisdiction of governmental and other agencies within their respective territories.

This understanding shall be applicable also in the territory of Berlin as soon as the Government of the Federal Republic of Germany makes a conforming declaration to the Government of the United States of America. [1]

I have the honor to propose that, if these understandings meet with the approval of the Government of the Federal Republic of Germany, the present note and your note concurring therein will be considered as confirming those understandings, effective on the date of your note.

Accept, Excellency, the renewed assurances of my highest consideration.

JOHN FOSTER DULLES
*Secretary of State of the
United States of America*

His Excellency
Dr. KONRAD ADENAUER,
*Chancellor of the
Federal Republic of Germany.*

The Chancellor of the Federal Republic of Germany to the Secretary of State

BUNDESREPUBLIK DEUTSCHLAND
DER BUNDESKANZLER

HERR STAATSSEKRETÄR,
Ich beehre mich, den Empfang der Note Eurer Exzellenz vom 9. April 1953 betreffend die kulturellen Beziehungen zwischen der Bun-

---

[1] Declaration made by note of Oct. 2, 1953, from the Chargé d'Affaires of the Federal Republic of Germany to the Secretary of State of the United States of America.

desrepublik Deutschland und den Vereinigten Staaten von Amerika zu bestätigen. Danach haben beide Regierungen die Absicht:

1. dahin zu wirken, dass das Volk der Bundesrepublik Deutschland und das Volk der Vereinigten Staaten von Amerika durch kulturelle Zusammenarbeit einander näher kommen, sowie das gegenseitige Verständnis des geistigen, künstlerischen, wissenschaftlichen und sozialen Lebens der beiden Völker zu fördern,

2. in der Erkenntnis, dass die Verständigung zwischen beiden Völkern durch besseres Wissen um die Geschichte, die gesellschaftlichen Lebensformen, die Institutionen, die Literatur und die übrigen kulturellen Errungenschaften des anderen Volkes eine Förderung erfährt, in ihrem Lande die Verbreitung dieses Wissens zu ermutigen,

3. nach Kräften sich zu bemühen, den Staatsangehörigen der anderen Regierung, welche sich Tätigkeiten widmen, die in den Rahmen dieses Abkommens fallen, hinsichtlich Einreise, Reise, Aufenthalt und Ausreise Vergünstigungen zuteil werden zu lassen, soweit sie mit ihren Landesgesetzen zu vereinen sind,

4. zu fördern und zu erleichtern den Austausch von hervorragenden Stattsbürgern, Sachverständigen, Professoren, Lehrern, Studenten und anderen Jugendlichen, sowie von geeigneten Personen aus allen Lebensgebieten zwischen der Bundesrepublik Deutschland und den Vereinigten Staaten von Amerika,

5. zur Erleichterung des Personenaustausches die Schaffung von Stipendien, Reisebeihilfen und Unterstützungen anderer Art innerhalb der akademischen und kulturellen Institutionen ihres Landes zu begünstigen; ferner bestrebt zu sein, sich gegenseitig über Vergünstigungen, Lehrgänge oder andere Möglichkeiten dieser Art Auskunft zu geben, die für Staatsangehörige des anderen Volkes von Interesse sein können,

6. so oft es wünschenswert erscheint, bestrebt zu sein, Ausschüsse aus Vertretern beider Länder einzusetzen oder deren Einsetzung geeigneten Stellen zu empfehlen, um dem Zweck dieses Abkommens zu dienen.

Die von jeder Regierung gemäss diesem Abkommen übernommenen Verpflichtungen sind im Rahmen ihrer Politik und Gesetzgebung, sowie der Verfahren und Methoden auszuführen, welche die Zuständigkeiten und Befugnisse der staatlichen und anderen Organe innerhalb ihres Landes regeln.

Dieses Abkommen gilt auch für das Land Berlin, sobald die Regierung der Bundesrepublik Deutschland gegenüber der Regierung der Vereinigten Staaten von Amerika eine entsprechende Erklärung abgibt.

Ich beehre mich, dem in der Note Eurer Exzellenz gemachten Vorschlag zuzustimmen und Ihnen mitzuteilen, dass die darin niedergelegten Abmachungen die Billigung der Regierung der Bundesrepublik Deutschland finden. Ihre Note und diese Note werden demgemäss als Bestätigung dieser Abmachungen angesehen, die mit dem heutigen Tage wirksam werden.

Genehmigen Euer Exzellenz die erneute Versicherung meiner ganz ausgezeichneten Hochachtung.

WASHINGTON, *den 9. April 1953.*

ADENAUER

Seiner Exzellenz
    Herrn JOHN FOSTER DULLES
        Staatssekretär der
            Vereinigten Staaten von Amerika

Translation

FEDERAL REPUBLIC OF GERMANY
THE FEDERAL CHANCELLOR

Mr. SECRETARY OF STATE,

I have the honor to acknowledge the receipt of Your Excellency's note of April 9, 1953, concerning the cultural relations between the United States of America and the Federal Republic of Germany. I understand that it will be the intent of each government:

[For the English language text of the understandings, see *ante*, p. 266.]

I have the honor to concur in the proposal made in Your Excellency's note and to inform you that the understandings set forth therein meet with the approval of the Government of the Federal Republic of Germany. That note and the present note, accordingly, are considered as confirming those understandings, which become effective on this date.

Accept, Excellency, the assurances of my highest and most distinguished consideration.

WASHINGTON, *April 9, 1953.*

ADENAUER

His Excellency JOHN FOSTER DULLES,
    Secretary of State
        of the United States of America.

APPENDIX V

Treaties and Other International Acts Series 2553

FEDERAL REPUBLIC OF GERMANY
United States Educational Commission in the Federal Republic of Germany

Agreement signed at Bonn, July 18, 1952;
Entered into force July 18, 1952.

The Governments of the United States of America and the Federal Republic of Germany;

Desiring to promote further mutual understanding between the peoples of the United States of America and the Federal Republic of Germany by a wider exchange of knowledge and professional talents through educational contacts;

Considering that Section 32 (b) of the United States Surplus Property Act of 1944, [1] as amended by Public Law 584, Seventy-ninth Congress, [2] provides that the Secretary of State of the United States of America may enter into an agreement with any foreign government for the use of currencies or credits for currencies of such foreign government acquired as a result of surplus property disposals for certain educational activities; and

Considering that the Surplus Property Sales Agreements of January 23, 1948 between the German Bizonal Economic Council and the Government of the United States of America [3] provides that the United States Government may require the accelerated payment of any part of the unpaid purchase price in local currency for use by the United States Government; and

Considering that the Federal Republic of Germany shall succeed to the rights and obligations of the Bizonal Economic Administration,

---

[1] 58 Stat. 782.
[2] 60 Stat. 754.
[3] Not printed.

according to Article 133 of the Basic Law for the Federal Republic of Germany (the Bonn Constitution), proclaimed May 23, 1949.

Have agreed as follows:

Article 1

There shall be established a Commission to be known as the United States Educational Commission in the Federal Republic of Germany (hereinafter designated "the Commission"), which shall be recognized by the Government of the United States of America and the Federal Republic of Germany as an organization created and established to facilitate the administration of an educational program to be financed by funds made available to the Commission by the Government of the United States from funds obtained from the Federal Republic of Germany in accordance with the Surplus Property Sales Agreements of January 23, 1948 between the German Bizonal Economic Council and the Government of the United States of America and with the Basic Law for the Federal Republic of Germany, proclaimed May 23, 1949 (the Bonn Constitution).

Except as provided in Article 3 hereof the Commission shall be exempt from the domestic and local laws of the United States of America as they relate to the use and expenditure of currencies and credits for currencies for the purposes set forth in the present agreement. The funds and property shall be regarded in the Federal Republic of Germany as property of a foreign government.

The funds made available under the present agreement within the conditions and limitations hereinafter set forth, shall be used by the Commission or such other instrumentality as may be agreed upon by the Government of the United States of America and the Federal Republic of Germany for the purpose, as set forth in Section 32 (b) of the United States Surplus Property Act of 1944, as amended, of

(1) financing studies, research, instruction, and other educational activities of or for citizens of the United States of America in schools and institutions of higher learning located in the territory of the Federal Republic of Germany, or of the Germans having their permanent residence in the Federal Republic of Germany and/or the Western Sectors of Berlin in United States schools and institutions of higher learning located outside the continental United States, Hawaii, Alaska (including the Aleutian Islands), Puerto Rico, and the Virgin Islands, including payment for transportation, tuition, maintenance, and other expenses incident to scholastic activities; or

(2) furnishing transportation for Germans having their permanent residence in the Federal Republic of Germany and/or the Western Sectors of Berlin who desire to attend United States schools and institutions of higher learning in the continental United States, Hawaii, Alaska (including the Aleutian Islands), Puerto Rico, and the Virgin Islands and whose attendance will not deprive citizens of the United States of America of an opportunity to attend such schools and institutions.

Article 2

In furtherance of the aforementioned purposes, the Commission may, subject to the provisions of the present agreement, exercise all powers necessary to the carrying out of the purposes of this agreement including the following:

(1) Plan, adopt, and carry out programs, in accordance with the purposes of Section 32(b) of the United States Surplus Property Act of 1944, as amended, and the purposes of the present agreement.

(2) Recommend to the Board of Foreign Scholarships, provided for in the United States Surplus Property Act of 1944, as amended, students, professors, research scholars, teachers, resident in the Federal Republic of Germany, and institutions of the Federal Republic of Germany qualified to participate in the program in accordance with the aforesaid Act.

(3) Recommend to the aforesaid Board of Foreign Scholarships such qualifications for the selection of participants in the programs as it may deem necessary for achieving the purpose and objectives of this agreement.

(4) Authorize the Treasurer of the Commission or such other person as the Commission may designate to receive funds to be deposited in bank accounts in the name of the Treasurer of the Commission or such other person as may be designated. The appointment of the Treasurer or such designee shall be approved by the Secretary of State and he shall deposit funds received in a depository or depositories designated by the Secretary of State of the United States of America.

(5) Authorize the disbursement of funds and the making of grants and advances of funds for the authorized purposes of the present agreement.

(6) Provide for periodic audits of the accounts of the Treasurer of the Commission as directed by auditors selected by the Secretary of State of the United States of America.

(7) Engage an Executive Director or Officer, administrative and clerical staff and fix and pay the salaries and wages thereof out of funds made available under the agreement.

Article 3

All commitments, obligations, and expenditures authorized by the Commission shall be made pursuant to an annual budget to be approved by the Secretary of State of the United States of America pursuant to such regulations as he may prescribe.

Article 4

The Commission shall consist of ten members, five of whom shall be citizens of the United States of America and five of whom shall be Germans having their permanent residence in the Federal Republic of Germany and/or the Western Sectors of Berlin. In addition, the principal officer in charge of the Diplomatic Mission of the United

States of America to the Federal Republic of Germany (hereinafter designated "Chief of Mission") shall be Honorary Chairman of the Commission. He shall cast the deciding vote in the event of a tie vote by the Commission and shall appoint the Chairman of the Commission. The Chairman as a regular member of the Commission shall have the right to vote. The Chief of Mission shall have the power to appoint and remove the citizens of the United States of America on the Commission, at least two of whom shall be officers of the United States Foreign Service establishment in the Federal Republic of Germany. The members of the Federal Republic of Germany shall be appointed and may be removed by the Federal Republic of Germany.

The members shall serve from the time of their appointment until the following December 31 and shall be eligible for reappointment. Vacancies by reason of resignation, transfer of residence outside the Federal Republic of Germany, expiration of service or otherwise, shall be filled in accordance with the appointment procedure set forth in this article.

The members shall serve without compensation but the Commission is authorized to pay the necessary expenses of the members in attending the meetings of the Commission and in performing other official duties assigned by the Commission.

Article 5

The Commission shall adopt such by-laws and appoint such committees as it shall deem necessary for the conduct of the affairs of the Commission.

Article 6

Reports acceptable in form and content to the Secretary of State of the United States of America shall be made annually on the activities of the Commission to the Secretary of State of the United States of America and to the Federal Republic of Germany.

Article 7

The principal office of the Commission shall be in, or near, the capital city of the Federal Republic of Germany, but meetings of the Commission and any of its committees may be held in such other places as the Commission may from time to time determine, and the activities of any of the Commission's officers or staff may be carried on at such places as may be approved by the Commission.

Article 8

The Federal Republic of Germany shall, as and when requested by the Government of the United States of America for purposes of this agreement, make available as payments against the Dollar indebtedness of the Federal Republic of Germany under either of the Surplus Property Sales Agreements of January 23, 1948 between the German Bizonal Economic Council and the Government of the United States of America, for deposit in an account of the Treasurer of the United States of America in the Federal Republic of Germany from Dollar credits arising under the Surplus Property Sales Agreements of January 23, 1948 between the German Bizonal Economic Council and the Government of the United States, amounts of currency of the Federal Republic of Germany until an aggregate amount equivalent to $5,000,000 (United States currency) shall have been made available provided, however, that not more than the equivalent in currency of the Federal Republic of Germany of $1,000,000 (United States currency) shall be made available during any single calendar year. The equivalent in United States currency of amounts of currency of the Federal Republic of Germany which are thus paid by the Federal Republic of Germany shall be credited as of the date of payment against the Dollar indebtedness of the Federal Republic of Germany under the appropriate agreement referred to above.

The rate of exchange between currency of the Federal Republic of Germany and the United States currency to be used in determining the amount of currency of the Federal Republic of Germany to be so deposited shall be that rate most favorable to the United States which, on the date of payment of such currency, is available to any party engaging in official transactions with the Federal Republic of Germany; provided such rate is not unlawful and, if both countries have agreed par values with the International Monetary Fund, is not prohibited by the articles of agreement of the Fund. [1]

The Secretary of State of the United States of America will make available for expenditure as authorized by the Commission currency of the Federal Republic of Germany in such amounts as may be required for the purposes of this agreement but in no event in excess of the budgetary limitations established pursuant to Article 3 of the present agreement.

Article 9

The Governments of the United States of America and the Federal Republic of Germany shall make every effort to facilitate the exchange of persons programs authorized in this agreement and to resolve problems which may arise in the operations thereof.

Article 10

Wherever, in the present agreement, the term "Secretary of State of the United States of America" is used, it shall be understood to mean the Secretary of State of the United States of America or any officer or employee of the Government of the United States of America designated by him to act in his behalf.

Article 11

The present agreement may be amended by the exchange of diplomatic notes between the Governments of the United States of America and the Federal Republic of Germany. This agreement is applicable also in the territory of Berlin (West) as soon as the Government of the Federal Republic makes a conforming declaration to the Government of the United States of America.

---

[1] Treaties and Other International Acts Series 1501; 60 Stat. 1401.

Article 12

The present agreement shall come into force upon the date of signature.

IN WITNESS WHEREOF the undersigned being duly authorized thereto by their respective Governments, have signed the present agreement.

Done at Bonn in duplicate, in the English and German languages, this 18th day of July, 1952.

JOHN J MCCLOY	ADENAUER
FOR THE GOVERNMENT OF THE UNITED STATES OF AMERICA	FOR THE GOVERNMENT OF THE FEDERAL REPUBLIC OF GERMANY
[SEAL]	[SEAL]

APPENDIX VI

Source: Office of Public Affairs, HICOG

GERMAN EXCHANGE OF PERSONS PROGRAM 1947–1954

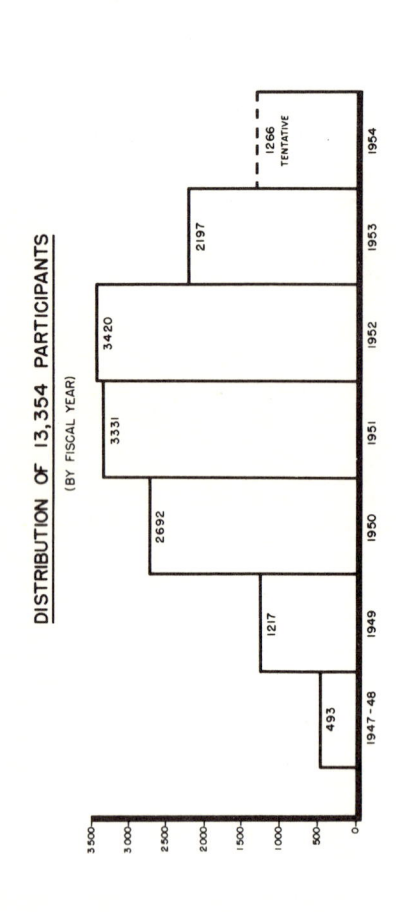

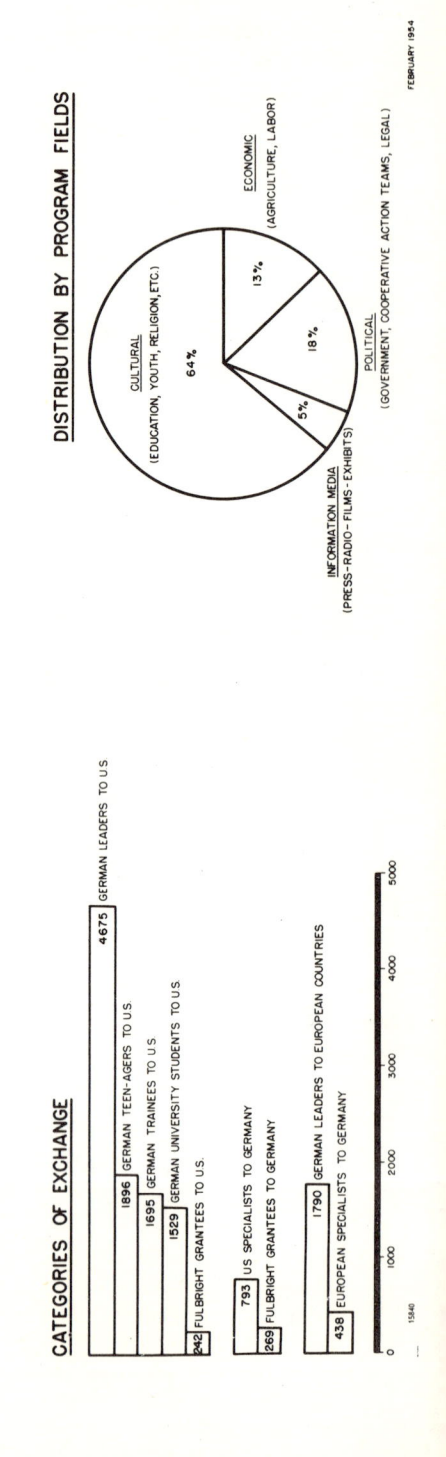

DISTRIBUTION OF 13,354 PARTICIPANTS
(BY FISCAL YEAR)

Fiscal Year	Participants
1947–48	493
1949	1217
1950	2692
1951	3331
1952	3420
1953	2197
1954	1266 (TENTATIVE)

CATEGORIES OF EXCHANGE

- 4675 GERMAN LEADERS TO US
- 1896 GERMAN TEEN-AGERS TO US
- 1695 GERMAN TRAINEES TO US
- 1529 GERMAN UNIVERSITY STUDENTS TO US
- 242 FULBRIGHT GRANTEES TO US
- 793 US SPECIALISTS TO GERMANY
- 269 FULBRIGHT GRANTEES TO GERMANY
- 1790 GERMAN LEADERS TO EUROPEAN COUNTRIES
- 438 EUROPEAN SPECIALISTS TO GERMANY

DISTRIBUTION BY PROGRAM FIELDS

- CULTURAL (EDUCATION, YOUTH, RELIGION, ETC.) — 64%
- ECONOMIC (AGRICULTURE, LABOR) — 13%
- POLITICAL (GOVERNMENT, COOPERATIVE ACTION TEAMS, LEGAL) — 18%
- INFORMATION MEDIA (PRESS–RADIO–FILMS–EXHIBITS) — 5%

FEBRUARY 1954

276

Acheson, Dean, 75, 158
Adenauer, Konrad, 76, 154, 160, 161, 171, 173, 233
Advisory Commission on Educational Exchange, 7–8, 9
Advisory Commission on Information, 7
Advisory Committee of the National Social Welfare Assembly, 120
Advisory Committee on Cultural and Educational Relations (*see also* Commission on the Occupied Areas), 66, 78
Albright, Raymond W., 193
Alexander, Thomas, 61
Allard, Lucile, 125
Allen, George V., 63, 87
Allied Control Council, 17, 18
  Directives and regulations, 21, 31, 55, 56, 57, 88, 219
American Houses, 230, 235
American Association of Colleges for Teacher Education, 68
American Association of University Women, 149
American Bar Association, 71
American Council of Learned Societies, 71, 177
American Council on Education (*see also* Commission on the Occupied Areas), 65, 66, 71, 137, 140, 143, 175
American Field Service, 122, 141, 168
American foreign policy:
  Defense policy, 233, 234
  GAI briefings, 87
  Germany, conceptions of, 236–237, 236, 238, 243, 244
American Friends Service Committee, 51, 65
American National Theater and Academy (ANTA), 126, 143
American Political Science Association, 71, 138

American professors, lecturers, and research scholars (Fulbright program), 179, 193–194, 264
  American history specialists, 181, 204
  Inter-Foundation Lectureship Program, 179, 194–195
  Lecturers defined, 194
  Numbers, 124, 177, 178
  Research and teaching subjects, 194
  Research scholars defined, 194
American racial discrimination, 127, 215, 223, 237
American specialists and experts:
  Art and music, 31, 45–46, 126–127, 143
  Civic leaders, 242
  Criticism of, 125
  Educators, 59, 65, 125, 126
  Fulbright program, 128
  HICOG program, 123–127, 135, 143, 147–148
  Numbers of, 44, 124, 261, 265
  OMGUS program, 24–32 *passim*, 43–46, 59, 65
  Selection and processing, 135, 143, 147–148
  Recommendations, influence, 43, 126
  Religious affairs, 126
  Specialist defined, 124
  Women specialists, 126
American students in Germany (*see also* Selection criteria), 242, 265
  Academic achievements, evaluation, 187
  Adjustment problems, 183–185, 230–231
  Definition, 131
  English language teaching, 193
  Fulbright program, 174, 177, 178, 183–185, 191–195, 204
  German students compared, 183, 232
  HICOG program, 143, 148
  International Holiday Courses, 47
  OMGUS program, 28, 34, 46–48, 65

American students in Germany—Con.
    Preferences in universities and subject matter, 192, 204
American studies, promotion, 179, 180–182
American teachers in Germany, 179, 181
    Adjustment problems, 183–184, 195
    Numbers of, 177, 178
Anderson, Judith, 126
Anderson, Mrs. Arthur, 125
Andresen, Mrs. Rachel, 141
Ann Arbor Council of Churches, 122, 141
Antioch College, 116, 229–230
Area Division for Occupied Areas (ADO), 63
Arpan, Floyd G., 141
Association for American Studies, 198
Association of American Law Schools, 71
Association of American Museums, 142
Austria:
    Exchange programs, 8, 10, 36, 65, 66, 93, 122, 138, 139
    Salzburg Seminar in American Studies, 68, 177

Backus, Howard P., 196
Baldwin, Roger, 124
Barrett, Edward W., 87
Barton, Betty, 130
Batson, Douglas N., 171
Bavaria, 40, 42, 220, 242
Beale, Howard K., 193
Beauchamp, George E., 139
Becker, Hellmut, 219
Belgian specialists, 49–50
Benton, William, 63
Berlin:
    American Memorial Library, 114, 216
    Free University of Berlin, 68, 146, 189, 190, 216
    Institute for Political Science, 125
    OMGUS exchanges, 40, 42
    School reform, 31
    Soviet blockade (1948), 80
    Western Sectors, applicability of Fulbright Act, 161, 174
Berlin Arts or Cultural Festivals (1951, 1952), 126, 143
Berlin Declaration (June 5, 1945), 17
Berlin Opera Company, 126

Bernstein, Leonard, 46
Biedenkopf, Kurt, 241
Bigelow, Karl W., 138
Black, Robert S., 196
Bologna Center (Italy), 177
Bonn Convention (1952), 76, 154, 173
Bonn University, 190
Boston Symphony Orchestra, 127
Brandt, Karl, 193
Brandt, Willi, 240, 254, 255 (quoted)
Branscomb, B. Harvie, 7–8
Brecht, Arnold, 124
Breitenbach, Edgar, 114
Bremen, 31, 40, 42
Bremerhaven, 220
Brethren Service Committee, 121, 122
Briarcliff College, 29
Bridges, Bernice, 120, 138, 139, 140
British Civil Service Commission and British Council, 163
Brown, Sterling, 125
Bryn Mawr College, 239
Bundy, Frederic O., 135, 196
Bungardt, Dr. Karl, 51
Bureau of European Affairs, 93, 166
Bureau of German Affairs (GER) (*see also* Office of German Affairs), 86, 87, 88, 89–90, 134, 135, 166
    Integration into Bureau of European Affairs, 166
Bureau of German Public Affairs, 148
Bureau of Public Affairs (State Department), functions, 87–88, 89
Bureau of the Budget, 60, 137
Burkhardt, Frederick, 88–89
Burns, Dr. Ralph A., 90, 143
Burton, Milton, 193
Byrnes, James F., 19
Byroade, Henry A., 87

Caldwell, Oliver J., 171
Campaign of Truth, 9, 158
Carnegie Endowment for International Peace, 65
Carnegie Institute of Technology, 116
Case Western University, 248
Catholic University of America, 125
Chamberlin, Dean, 197
Chapman, Everett G., 144, 197
Cherington, Charles R., 118
Cherrington, Ben M., 56
Civil Administration Division (OMGUS), 40, 49, 57, 59, 61, 62

INDEX

Civil Affairs Division (CAD) of the War (Army) Department, 47
  Personnel and Training Branch, 44, 63–64, 65
  Reorientation Branch, 38, 39, 41, 42, 44, 63–64
Clarke, Eric T., 31
Clausen, Dr. Theodor, 198
Clay, Gen. Lucius, 19–40 *passim*, 75, 76–77
  Newsprint restrictions, 26, 104
Cleveland International Program for Youth Leaders and Social Workers, Inc. (CIP), 139
Cold war, 6, 8, 83, 153, 156, 158–159, 233, 234, 235
Cole, Taylor, 124
Colligan, Francis J., 135, 172, 196
Cologne University, 189, 190
Columbia University, 65, 68, 104, 120, 121
  Law School, 239
Commission on the Occupied Areas (COA), 66–68, 78–79, 80, 137–138
Committee on Friendly Relations Among Foreign Students, 184
Community Education Branch (OMGUS), 56
Conant, Dr. James A., 166, 170, 197, 243–244 (quoted)
Conference Board of Associated Research Councils, 175
Conference of German University Presidents, 185
Constable, Dr. William, 45
Cook, Alice Hanson, 44–45
Cook, Donald B., 172
Cornell University, 121
Council of Europe, 156, 162
Council on Cooperation in Teacher Education, 71
Cox, Henry B., 197
Crespi, Leo, 93, 209
Cultural Agreement (1953), 159–162, 170–171, 266–269

Darmstadt Technical Academy, 47
Dean, Jonathan, 218*n*
DeLong, Vaughn, 134, 139
Denmark, exchange program, 49, 163
Department of Agriculture, 137
Department of Labor:
  Office of International Labor Affairs, 136–137, 138
  Women's Bureau, 107, 137, 149
Department of the Army (*see also* State-War-Navy Coordinating Committee), 38
Department of the Interior, 137
Department of State (*see also* State-War-Navy Coordinating Committee), 25
  Approval of candidates and projects, 38, 42, 44, 63, 146, 147, 188
  Bureau for Occupied Areas, 63
  Cultural relations policy, 3–10, 10–13, 95, 173, 174
  Division of Cultural Relations, 5–6
  Functions, 90, 133–136, 188, 196
  Grants-in-aid, 177
  Survey Mission (1948), 80
  Survey Mission, 1949 (Lehrbas Mission), 45, 80–83, 88, 115
Der Monat, 58
Detmold University, 190
DeYoung, Chris A., 125
Die Neue Zeitung, 58
Displaced persons and persecutees, travel to U.S., 26
Division of German and Austrian Information and Reorientation Affairs (*see also* Office of German Public Affairs), 150
Division of International Exchange of Persons (Department of State). *See under* Office of Educational Exchange
Donnelly, Walter W., 176, 197
Dorr, Harold, 125
Duke University, 193
Dulles, John Foster, 161, 170, 171
Dyke, Harold, 125
Easum, Chester V., 189, 197
ECA Technical Assistance Program, 150
Education and Cultural Relations Division (OMGUS), 33, 35, 40, 48, 49, 61, 62
  Cultural Affairs Branch, 41–43, 61, 62
  Education Branch, 48
Education and Cultural Relations Division (HICOG) (*see also* Exchange of Persons Branch), 89, 105, 108, 144
  Division of Cultural Affairs, 144, 166–167
  Group Activities Branch, 107

Education and Religious Affairs Branch (OMGUS), 24, 56, 61
Educational Interchange Council, 163
Educational reforms, 29–31, 33, 56–57, 59, 100–101, 210–211, 216–217, 219, 225–231
  Adult education, 21, 57, 107
  American-German education systems compared, 225–231
  Authority, 20–21, 22, 27, 31, 56–57, 76, 77–78, 100–101
  Child guidance, preschool education, and out-of-school treatment of children, 101, 181
  Civic education, 57, 111–112, 219
  COA recommendations, 78–79
  Comprehensive schools, development of, 211, 216, 219
  Curriculum changes, 179–180, 181, 216–217, 219, 246
  Education (Zook) Mission (1946), 23–25
  German Educational Council, 210
  Principles, 21–22, 23–24, 56, 77–80, 101, 210–211
  Resistance to, 21–22, 30–31, 78
  School libraries, organizational and administrational changes, 101, 219
  Two-track system, 21, 29–30, 59, 216, 217
  Women, status, 106
Eisenhower, Gen. Dwight D., 18, 56, 160–161, 170–171
Elliot, Mabel A., 193
Enters, Angna, 127
Episcopal Theological School, 193
Epstein, Fritz, 147
Erhard, Ludwig, 159, 241
Erlangen University, 148, 189
Espinosa, J. Manuel, 171
European Advisory Committee Directive, 12, 56
European Coal and Fuel Community, 156
European Coal and Steel Community, 162
European Command Headquarters, 45, 64
European Consultant Program, 49–50
European Defense Community, 156
European Exchange, 128
European Exchange Service, 128, 164

European Payments Union, 162
European Recovery Program, 83
European specialists (consultants) to Germany, 49–50
European unification, trend, 128, 235
Evangelical Church in Germany, Auxiliary Service, 164
Evarts, John, 31
Exchange of Persons Branch (Division) (HICOG), 89, 144
  Fulbright Commission liaison, 168, 198–199
  "Guiding Principles", 156–157, 211
  Land (State)/Exchange Branch, 144
  Organizational changes, 89–90, 165–167
  Political purposes, 5, 7–9, 11, 13, 37, 78, 108, 114, 157, 163, 243
  Revision from unilateralism to bilateralism, 153–168
  "Transition papers", 157–158
  World-wide program, 5–10
Experiment in International Living, The, 65, 126, 168, 185

Federal Security Agency, 137
Fehling, Dr. August, 197–198
Ferebee, Dr. Dorothy, 125
Fichter, Joseph H., 193
Fingerle, Dr. Anton, 219
Finland exchange program, 163
Food and Agriculture Division (OMGUS), 40, 49, 58, 60, 61, 62
  Land Office of Military Government, 48
Ford Foundation, 140
Foreign Service Institute, 147
François-Poncet, André, 76
Frank, Bruno, 31
Frankel, Charles, 253
Frankel, Hermann, 193
Frankfurt University, 148, 189
Free University of Berlin, 68, 148, 189, 190, 216
Freiburg University, 190
Fremont-Smith, Dr. Frank, 130
French exchange programs, 14, 141–142, 163, 191
  19th century, 5
Friedmann, Werner, 53
Fries, Charles C., 193
Fuess, Dr. Erwin, 198

INDEX

Fulbright, J. William, 173, 200–201 (quoted)
Fulbright Act (1946), 6–7, 9, 47, 156, 173, 174, 201
Fulbright-Hays Act (1961), 156, 201
Fulbright program, 24, 47, 143, 173–201, 264–265
   Administration in Germany, 165–166, 173, 174–175, 176, 195, 196–201, 223
   Administration in U.S. (*see also* Board of Foreign Scholarships, *infra*), 166, 175–177, 195–196
   American exchanges, numbers, 177
   American Program Unit, 198
   American studies in German universities, 179, 180–182
   Approach and emphasis, 179–180, 181
   Binational principle, 12, 173, 174, 176
   Board of Foreign Scholarships, 175, 179, 182, 188–204 *passim*
   Executive Agreement (1952), 168, 173–176, 201, 270–275
   Fulbright Commission (Binational Education Commission), 168, 173–189, *passim*, 197–201 *passim*
   Fulbright Scholarship Committees, 186–187, 199
   Funding in Germany, 168, 186, 201, 202, 253–256
   Funding in U.S., 7, 174, 175–177, 185, 197, 201–202
   German exchanges, number, 177–178
   German Youth Specialist Program, 179, 188–190, 202
   Inter-Foundation Lectureship Program, 179, 194–195
   Project approach, 177, 179, 182
   Reciprocity principle, 176, 177, 180
   Secretary of State, responsibility, 175, 177, 188, 196
   Special Projects, 179, 188–190
   Structure and scope, 177–178

General Federation of Women's Clubs, 149
Georgetown University, 193
Georgia Institute of Technology, 189
German Academic Exchange Service (DAAD), 164, 198, 199, 200
German-American cultural relations, 3–4, 8–9, 234–235, 241, 253–256
German Association of Universities, 200
German-British Exchange Office, 164
German Economic Council, 19
German Educational Reconstruction (GER), 163
German elite, 30–31, 96, 227, 228
German emigration, 240
German Employees Union, 103
German leaders and specialists to other European countries, 29, 34, 36, 48, 98, 128, 162–164, 173–174, 261, 265
German leaders and specialists to U.S., 36–41, 60, 68, 98–99, 129, 158–159, 178, 242
   Agricultural specialists, 99, 105, 137
   Community leaders, 107, 138, 140, 220
   Cooperative action teams, 112–114, 220, 225–226, 238
   Educators, 26, 59, 60, 68, 99, 100–101, 135, 225
   GAI briefing on U.S. foreign policy, 87
   Government officials and political leaders, 102–103, 138, 159, 167, 217–218, 240–241, 243–244
   Information media, 65, 99, 104–105, 137, 141, 220, 232
   Labor-management specialists, 57–58, 103–104, 137, 219
   Leaders, definition, 98–99, 130
   Legal affairs leaders and referendare, 99, 107–108, 138, 187–188, 203, 219
   Librarians, 102, 114, 142, 217
   Maternal and child care studies, 108–109
   Number of leaders, 100, 101, 103, 104, 107, 108, 109, 110, 112, 113, 114, 243, 261, 264
   Number of projects, 59–60, 99, 100
   Public health and welfare leaders, 99, 108–109, 137, 220
   Religious leaders, 26, 99, 109–110
   Results of visits. See Results of program
   Scientists, 26
   Social services specialists, 99, 114, 121, 140–141, 220, 232, 248

German Leaders—Con.
  Specialist defined, 129
  Visas and travel arrangements, 38–39, 113, 140
  Women leaders, 41, 99, 105–107, 137, 219
  Youth leaders, 99, 107, 110–112, 140, 141, 248
German press, 104, 105
German prisoners of war, 210n
German professors, lecturers, and research scholars, Fulbright program, 177, 183–185, 190, 198
German Research Society, 198, 199
German special study projects (Fulbright program), 177, 188
German students in America:
  Academic studies, 117, 118–119, 121–122, 190, 238–239
  Adjustment problems, 183–185, 214–215, 226–231
  American students compared, 184, 226–231
  Fulbright program, 185–190, 266
  HICOG program, 114–123
  Journalists, 120–121, 142, 189
  "Jungakademiker", 187, 199–200
  Land Student Exchange Committees, 42, 147
  Law students and referendare, 57, 119–120, 143
  Numbers, 43, 115, 122, 177, 261, 264
  OMGUS program, 24, 25, 26, 36, 41–43, 57, 60, 65
  Physicians, 188
  Project preferences, 189, 203–204
  Social workers, 121
  Student defined, 115
  Student government and nonacademic student activities, study of, 116–118, 220, 228, 229, 230
  Teenagers, 36, 43, 111, 122–123, 141, 142, 261, 264
  Theological students, 26
  Trade union leaders and potential managerial leaders, 121–122
  Trainee defined, 115–116, 119
  Trainee programs and projects, 36, 119–122
  Visits with American families, 119, 122–123
German students in Switzerland and Italy, 25

German Teacher Exchange Service, 198
German Trade Union League, 103
German universities:
  Bilateral relations with American counterparts, 68, 189–190, 192, 194
  19th century, 3
German Youth Specialist Program, 179, 188–190, 202
Germany (see also Occupation of Germany):
  Agreement on Basic principles, (1951), 154
  Basic Law (1949), 75–76
  Bonn Convention (1952), 76, 154, 173
  Bundestag, 101–102, 105, 106, 217, 218, 240, 241, 242, 256
  Democratic defense system, 218
  Emerging democratic leadership, 79, 85, 119, 120, 153, 156, 158–159, 181, 220
  Integration with Western Europe, 83, 154, 155, 156, 162, 173, 234, 235
  Organized religion, restoration, 56, 109–110
  Postwar recovery, 12, 19, 20, 57, 76, 140–141, 153, 178–179, 181, 216, 243
  Sovereignty, transition to, 75–76, 153–166 passim, 173, 233
Gerold, Karl, 53
Gerstenmaier, Eugen, 242
Giessen University, 190
Goerdeler, Benigna, 29
Goettingen University, 189, 190
Governmental Affairs Institute, 112, 138–139
Government and Relief in Occupied Areas (GARIOA), 81
Grace, Dr. Alonzo, 35, 50, 56, 77
Graulich, William, 197
Grigsby, S. Earl, 125
Grimm, Harold, 193

Hall-Johnson Choir, 126
Hallowell, John H., 193
Hallstein, Dr. Walter, 170, 176, 197, 210
Hamburg University, 190
Hamburg, school reform, 31

INDEX

Hamm-Bruecher, Hildegard, 118
Hartke, Rev. Gilbert V., 125
Hartshorne, Edward Y., Jr., 61
Harvard-Salzburg International Seminar, 68, 177
Harvard University, 116, 118, 189, 239, 247
Hastler, Arthur D., 193
Hatcher, Hazel, 125
Hayes, John N., 172
Hays, Maj. Gen. George P., 60
Heidelberg University, 47, 148, 190, 192
Heimpel, Dr. Hermann, 198
Herring, Pendleton, 125
Herz, John A., 193
Hesse, 40, 42
Hickey, Margaret, 125
HICOG (Office of the High Commissioner for Germany), educational and cultural exchange program, 4, 11, 43, 68, 95-128, 144-149
  Administration, 88-89, 133-149, 166-167
  Approval of American specialists projects, 124
  Authority, 78, 133, 144, 155-156
  Criteria and terms of reference, 83-85, 95-98, 145-146, 236
  Definition, 97
  German participation, 77, 82, 84, 85, 100, 133, 145, 155
  Information Services Division, 89, 144, 235
  Number of persons, 10, 95, 163
  Office of the Chief, 145
  Office of Economic Affairs, 100, 144
  Office of Labor Affairs, 100, 104, 144
  Office of Legal Affairs, 100
  Office of Political Affairs, 100, 144
  Organization, general, 76-77, 80, 81, 208
  Organization in Germany, 88-89, 144-149, 166-167
  Organization in U.S., 86-88, 133-143, 167-168
  Policy Paper (1951), 82, 155-159, 160
  Policy purpose, vii, 79-80, 82-83, 85, 95, 97, 106, 110-111, 116-117
  Political Affairs Committee, 76
  Private sponsorship, 65, 115, 122-123, 126, 142-143, 148
  Program changes, 81-90 *passim*, 144-146
  Project approach, 98, 99-100, 164-165
  Religious Affairs Branch, 56, 109
  Stratification, 82, 83-85, 96
Hilldring, Gen. John H., 63
Hille, Einar, 193
Holland, Kenneth, 196
Holm, Celeste, 126
Housing and Home Finance Agency, 137
Hovde, Frederick, 195
Huebinger, Dr. Egon, 198
Hull, Cordell, 6
Hulten, Charles M., 135
Hundhammer, Dr. Alois, 242

Indiana University, 117, 189, 193, 229
  School of Journalism, 141
Information and Educational Exchange Act of 1948. *See* Smith-Mundt Act
Institute for Research in Human Relations, survey, 221
Institute of International Education (IIE), 115, 118-119, 239
  Administration of student exchange program, 41-42, 63, 65, 134, 142, 175, 184-185, 204
Institute of Public Affairs, 164
Institute of Social Research (Frankfurt), 164
Inter-American Cultural Relations, Promotion, of, Convention (1936), 5, 9
International Assembly of Women, convention (1946), 40
International Bar Association, 71
International Council for Youth Self-Help, 128, 164
International Educational Exchange Service (IES), 86, 166, 171, 172, 175
International Federation of Agricultural Producers, 71
International Holiday Courses, 47
International Information Administration (IIA), 166
International Information and Educational Exchange Program (USIE), 87, 88, 133, 135

International Information Service (IIS), 166
International Student Service, 184–185
International Union of Local Authorities, 48
Inter-Nationes, 198
Irvin, Col. Leon P., 63

Jaeger, Richard, Vice President of Bundestag (quoted), 218
Janowitz, Morris, 193
Japan, exchange programs, 8, 14, 66, 68
Johns Hopkins University, 177
Johnson, Walter, 196
Johnson, Williard, 125
Johnstone, William C., Jr., 88, 135, 172
Josiah Macy Jr. Foundation, 130
Juilliard String Quartet, 126

Karlsruhe University, 190
Kiel University, 189
Kiesinger, Kurt Georg, 159, 241
Kirkpatrick, Ralph, 46
Kiwanis Club of Georgia, 122
Klemperer, Otto, 46
Kluncker, Heinz, 241
Kogon, Eugen, 53
Kolb, Dr. Walter, 198
Kraus, Prof. Herta, 43
Krekeler, Heinz, 160
Kress, Freiherr von, 219
Kronstein, Heinrich, 193
Kwiat, Joseph, 193

LaFarge, Rev. John E., 125
Latin American exchanges, 5–6, 9–10, 28
League of Women Voters, 41, 149, 219
Leary, Dr. Bernice, 43
Lehrbas, Lloyd, 81
Leverich, Henry P., 63
Library of Congress, 101, 142, 217
Linch, Sam H., 90, 177, 197
Loderer, Eugen, 241
Loewenstein, Karl, 125
Loyola University (New Orleans), 193
Lund, John, 196
Lyon, Cecil B., 166

MacLeisch, Archibald, 20, 22
Maffett, Dr. Minnie, 125

Maier, Franz Karl, 53
Mainz University, 190
Marburg University, 47, 148, 203
Marshall Plan, 12, 20, 153, 234
Max Planck Institute for Educational Research, 198, 219
McCardle, Carl W., 172
McCloy, John J., 76, 82, 173
  John J. McCloy Fund, 84, 255–256
McGee, Richard A., 125
McGhee, George C. (quoted), 253
McMahon, Col. Bernard B., 63
McManus, Msgr. William E., 138, 139
McRae, Col. Robert B., 63
Mead, Dr. John, 198
Mennonite Central Committee, 51
Meridian House, 140
Mettger, H. Philip, 138
Meyers, Franz, 219
Michigan Council of Churches, 141
Michigan State University, 103
Mills College, 193
Ministries of Culture (Germany), 199, 200
Mommer, Dr. Karl, 53
Monteux, Pierre, 128
Moody, George T., 196
Mueller, Dr. Gerhard, 52
Muenster University, 190
Munch, Charles, 128
Munich, 220
  International Youth Conferences (1948), 47
Munich University, 47, 148, 182, 190, 192, 242
Murphy, Robert D., 87
Musgrave, Richard A., 193

National Academy of Science, 140, 143
National Catholic Welfare Conference, 51, 125
National Conference of Christians and Jews, 71, 122
National Council of Catholic Women, 149
National Council of Jewish Women, 149
National Education Association, 65, 71
National Federation of Business and Professional Women's Clubs, 149
National 4–H Club Foundation, 122
National Grange, 122
National Research Council, 71, 175

INDEX 285

National Social Welfare Assembly, 71, 120, 140, 213–214, 233
National Women's Trade Union League of America, 149
Nazism (National Socialism), 17, 18, 20, 22, 23, 29, 33–34, 37, 39, 43, 108, 109, 120, 121, 180, 214
Neighborhood Settlement Association of Cleveland, Ohio, 188
Nelson, Ivan, 172
Netherlands, exchange programs, 49, 163
Neumann, Franz, 125
Neumann, Sigmund, 44, 125, 193
New York City Ballet, 127
New York School of Social Work (Columbia University), 120
Nicholson, Ralph, 88
Niemoeller, Pastor Martin, 40
Noce, General, 53
North Atlantic Treaty Organization (NATO), 154
Northwestern University, 120
  School of Journalism, 141
Norway, exchanges, 49

Oberlin College, 65
Occupation of Germany (*see also* Allied Control Council), 4, 17–22, 233
Occupation Statute (April 8, 1949), 77, 233
  Replacement by contractual arrangements, 153–154, 159–162
  Revision, 76, 78, 154
Office of Education, 137, 175
Office of Educational Exchange (OEX), 7, 88, 135, 150, 166, 172
  Division of Institutes and Libraries (ILI), 135
  Division of International Exchange of Persons (IEP), 39, 63, 88, 133–134, 136, 147, 166, 171, 196
  Fulbright Program Brand, 196
Office of German Affairs (*see also* Bureau of German Affairs (GER)), 87, 166
Office of German and Austrian Public Affairs (GAI), 87–88, 93, 134–135, 166
Office of German Public Affairs (GAI), 87, 135–136, 147

Division of Cultural and Social Affairs, 134, 135
Office of International Information, 6–7
Office of Public Affairs (HICOG), 10–11, 81, 88–89, 99, 100, 133, 144, 146, 167, 199
Office of Public Relations (HICOG), 144
Office of the Coordinator of Inter-American Affairs, 6
Office of the Cultural Adviser, Headquarters, European Command, 64
Office of the High Commissioner for Germany. *See* HICOG exchange program
Office of War Information, 6
Ohio State University, 189, 193
Oklahoma, 126
Ollendorff, Dr. Henry B., 141, 188
Olsen, Edward G., 125
OMGUS (U.S. Office of Military Government) reorientation program (*see also* Educational reform), 4–54 *passim*, 262
  Administration, 41–46, 55–68
  Authority, derivation, 55, 76
  Budget, 59, 62
  Communication media activities, 6, 33, 235
  Criticisms, 26, 30, 45, 60, 78, 114–115
  Education mission recommendations, 23–25, 26
  Eligibility of exchangees, 26, 27, 28, 36
  Funding (*see also* Volunteer projects, *infra*), 7, 8, 24–48 *passim*
  German role, 13, 20–21, 27, 28, 55–56, 58, 62–63
  Information Control Division, 45, 46
  Information Services Division, 58, 60, 61, 62
  Interchange of Persons Office, 61
  Inter-Divisional Reorientation Committee (IRC), 49, 58, 62, 81
  Legal Division, 40, 57, 61, 62
  Manpower Division, 49, 57–58, 61, 62
  Number of persons, 10, 29, 34, 40
  Number of projects, 40, 59–60
  Operational responsibility in Army, 66

OMGUS—Con.
  Policy, formulation, vii, 5–6, 8, 19–22, 33, 35, 63
  Procedures, standard operating, 36, 42–43, 49
  Project approach, 40, 58–60
  Religious Affairs Branch, 56, 61
  Technical and logistic support, stateside, 63–64
  Transfer of operation to HICOG, 12, 25, 66, 75–90, 143, 153
  Volunteer projects (sponsored by private institutions and organizations), 8, 22–45 passim, 55, 64–68
  Wells Mission, 32–36
Orientation program and centers, 67, 135, 136, 139–140, 142–143, 159, 184–185
  Washington International Center, 139, 140
Ormandy, Eugene, 128
O'Sullivan, Benjamin, 63
Owen, Ralph Dornfield, 193

Paganini Quartet, 128
Pendle Hill College, 65
Pennsylvania College for Women, 193
Pennsylvania State University, 126
Permanent Conference of Ministers of Culture, 198
Pfeiffer, Heinrich N., 198
Phillips, Dr. Burr, 43
Pollock, James, 125
Porgy and Bess, 127
Potsdam Conference (1945), 17
Princeton University, 193
Propaganda:
  Communist, 180
  Nazi, 5, 180, 214
  U.S. anti-Nazi, 6, 127
  U.S. counter-communist and Soviet, 9, 83, 127, 158
Public Affairs Office (HICOG). *See* Office of Public Affairs
Public Affairs Overseas Program Staff (POS), 63
Public Affairs Program (HICOG), 84, 95
  Budget, 84, 95–96, 162
  McCloy Fund, 84, 255–256
  Policy Paper (1951), 155–159, 160
  Reorganization, 86–90

Purdue University, 195

Read, James Morgan, 89, 101, 217
Rees, John R., 130
Reorientation program (*see also* OMGUS *and* Public Affairs Program), 4–13 passim, 20–40 passim, 82–83, 90, 144, 155, 180, 211
  Budget, 81, 84
  Change of controls, 12, 76–77
  COA role, 67, 78
  Democratic principles, promotion of, 4, 8, 10, 11, 21–39 passim, 49, 56–57, 58, 79–84 passim, 96–129 passim, 140, 144, 155, 157, 158
  Exchange program, importance to, 4, 35, 56, 61, 75, 96–97, 112, 120, 182
  Extension to British and French Zones, 82, 84, 85–86, 96, 146, 147
  German self-reorientation, 76–77, 124
  HICOG role, 10–11, 12, 78–90 passim, 124
  Stratification, 82, 83–85, 96
  SWNCC directives, 20–46 passim
Reschke, Oscar W., 53
Results of program, viii, 4–5, 40, 209–244
  Acceptance of democratic values, 97–98, 180, 181, 190, 213–214, 216, 218–219, 221–222, 223, 224, 225, 226, 229, 232, 233, 234, 242, 243
  Age groups, differences, 213, 214, 221–222, 233
  American exchangees, 190–192, 195, 233
  American experts and specialists, effect, 44–45, 46, 211, 216
  American way of life, 104, 118, 121, 122, 136, 165, 180, 181, 183–185, 190, 222–225, 231–233, 236–237, 243
  Assessment, difficulties, 209, 211, 240
  Bundestag, German defense system legislation, 102, 218
  Bundestag, restructuring of Research Division, 102, 217–218
  Changes in status, 240–241
  Changes in views and attitudes of visitors, 211–212, 213, 215, 221–224, 225, 232, 234, 235, 237–238, 243

INDEX

Results of program—Con.
  Direct personal actions taken, 209, 211, 219, 221, 235
  Dissemination of information to fellow countrymen at home, 114, 211, 232, 236–238
  Educational reforms. See Educational reforms
  Emigration to U.S., 240
  Evaluation and opinion surveys, 209–210, 211, 212, 221–222, 223, 233–234, 236, 237, 238, 248
  Exchangees' opinion of Germany and German politics, 235, 236
  Fulbright grantees, 183–185, 223–224, 225, 226, 230–231, 239–240
  German prisoners of war, study of American life, 210n
  HICOG followup programs, 212–213, 236, 242–243
  "Kultur" and professional achievements, 231–233, 239–241
  Lack of results, 45, 105, 221, 224
  Law and law enforcement reforms, 219
  Long-range effects, 40–41, 212–213, 237, 239–240, 241
  Opinions voiced by participants, 209, 213, 223–224, 225, 229–231, 232, 235
  Personal benefits, 238–244
  Political, social, and educational reforms, 4–5, 57, 102–103, 119, 210, 211, 216–221, 224, 241, 243
  Remilitarization, 233–234
  Social and professional groups, 213–214, 232, 240
  Teenagers, 123, 213, 215, 222, 233, 240
  Understanding purpose of exchange programs, 242
  Unfavorable impressions and criticisms of America, 118, 212, 214–215, 222, 223, 226–231, 237
  University students, 118, 214–215, 223–231, 235, 238–239
  West Berliners, 215, 237, 243
Reuter, Ernst, 127
Rheinstein, Max, 125
RIAS (Radio in the American Sector of Berlin), 58
Richter, Eva, 219
Richter, Dr. Werner, 198

Riddleberger, James W., 87
Riley, Russell L., 166
Robertson, Sir Brian, 76
Rockefeller Foundation, 65, 66
Roeloffs, Karl, 198
Roland, Joseph M., 171, 196
Roosevelt, Franklin D., 6
Rotary International, 123
Russell, Howard H., 171, 176 (quoted), 201

St. Louis University, 120
Saltzman, Charles E., 63
Sargeant, Howland H., 63, 87
Scammon, Richard, 125
Scheel, Walter, 159, 240, 256
Schmidt, Helmut, 240
Schroeder, Gerhard, 159
Schuetz, Klaus, 118
Schumacher, Kurt, 233
Scott, Tom, 46
Selection criteria:
  Academic standards, 28, 186, 188, 189, 191
  Acceptability to host country, 194, 195
  Definite goals, 27, 187, 190
  Fulbright program, 168, 178, 185–200 passim
  German participation, 62–63, 82, 85, 96, 145, 146–147, 148–149, 168, 200
  HICOG, 96, 98, 129, 143, 145–149
  Ineligibility, reasons, 37, 167, 187
  Language requirements, 27, 28, 36, 37, 130, 147–148, 167–168, 186, 188, 191
  OMGUS, 27–48 passim
  Personality, character, and other intangibles, 36–37, 186–187, 191–192, 195
  Probable influence on return, 27, 28, 37, 84, 96, 97, 98, 111, 157, 158–159, 167, 187, 188, 191–192, 195
  Security clearances, 26, 27, 28, 37, 38, 41, 43, 44, 134
  Youth, emphasis on, 37, 111, 185–189
Selke, George A., 125, 197
Shapley, Lilian, 125
Shartel, Burke, 193
Sims, Albert D., 157
Skidmore College, 190

Smith-Mundt Act (January 1948), 6–7, 8, 10, 137, 156, 158, 188
Snyder, Harold E., 66
Social Science Research Council, 175
Society for American Studies, 203
Spaulding, E. Wilder, 197
Speier, Hans, 22, 51
Spragg, S. D. Shirley, 193
Stanford University, 190, 193
State, Department of. *See* Department of State
State-War-Navy Coordinating Committee (SWNCC):
  Overall responsibility for exchange policy, 63
  Policy Statement (269/5), 20–21, 22, 27
  Policy Statement (269/8), 27, 28, 31, 36, 41, 43, 46
  Policy Statement (269/11), 36, 48
Stoltenberg, Gerhard, 240–241
Stone, Shepard, 88, 89
Stoska, Polyna, 128
Strauss, Franz Josef, 159, 241
Strecker, Mrs., 40
Stuttgart Technical University, 189
Swarthmore College, 68
Sweden, exchange programs, 54, 163
Switzerland, exchange programs, 48, 49, 54, 163
Syracuse University, 117, 229–230

Taylor, John, 61
Temple University, 193
Trade unions, 57–58, 103–104, 137
Travers, Patricia, 46
Truman, Harry S, 158

Union Theological Seminary, 65
Unitarian Service Committee, 68
United Kingdom:
  Exchange program, 14, 163, 191
  German specialists (consultants), visits, 48, 49
United Nations Educational, Scientific, and Cultural Organization (UNESCO), 154
United States Educational Commission in the Federal Republic of Germany (USEC/G). *See* Fulbright program: Administration in Germany

United States Information Agency (USIA), 166
United States Information Service (USIS), 166, 230
United States Office of Military Government. *See* OMGUS
United States public opinion, 6, 11, 39. 77, 86
University of California (Berkeley), 189, 193
University of Chicago, 65, 121, 189, 193
University of Colorado, 189, 229–230
University of Florida, 117, 229–230
University of Georgia, 65
University of Illinois, 121, 193
University of Iowa, 142
University of Kentucky, 120
University of Michigan, 116, 189, 193, 229–230
  Survey Research Institute, 104
University of Minnesota, 117, 118, 189, 193
  German students' clash of standards, 227–229, 230
University of Missouri, 120
University of Montana, 126
University of North Carolina, 117, 189
University of Notre Dame, 65, 193
University of Oregon, 120
University of Pittsburgh, 142
University of Rochester, 193
University of Wisconsin, 104, 121, 193

Varnay, Astrid, 127, 128
Vetter, Kurt, 241
Voice of America, 88, 236, 243

War Department (*see also* State-War-Navy Coordinating Committee *and* United States Department of the Army), 4
  Joint Chiefs of Staff directives, 18, 19–20, 21, 56
Washington conference and declaration (1951), 154, 156
Washington State University, 65
Webb, James E., 79–80
Weimar Republic, 119, 121, 211, 216
Wells, Dr. Herman B, 32–36, 46, 64, 66, 77, 78, 79, 137
Wells, Roger, 125
Wells Mission, 32–36

INDEX

Werner, Dr. Bruno, 160
West German Conference of German University Presidents, 198, 199, 200
Western Reserve University, 120, 188, 193
Wik, Reynold M., 193
Wilder, Thornton, 46
Wilk, Maurice, 127
Wish, Harvey, 193
Women, role and status, 40, 57, 82, 106, 216, 219
Women's Affairs Section (OMGUS), 57
Women's Bureau. *See under* Department of Labor
Woodhouse, Mrs. Chase Going, 44

World Council of Churches, 51
World Federation for Mental Health, 130
World Health Organization, 48, 154
Wright, Quincy, 125
Wuerttenberg-Baden, 40, 42
Wuerzburg University, 148, 190

Yale University, 190
Young Women's Christian Association, 139, 149
Youth camp, Lorelei Rock, 171
Youth for Understanding, 141

Zook, George F., 23, 78, 79
Zucker, A. E., 61

U.S. GOVERNMENT PRINTING OFFICE : 1978—O-253-620